A Lutheran Vocation

Philip A. Nordquist and the Study of History at Pacific Lutheran University

A LUTHERAN VOCATION

PHILIP A. NORDQUIST AND THE STUDY OF HISTORY AT PACIFIC LUTHERAN UNIVERSITY

EDITED BY ROBERT P. ERICKSEN AND MICHAEL J. HALVORSON

Pacific Lutheran University Press, 2005

Copyright © 2005 by Pacific Lutheran University

Published by Pacific Lutheran University Press
Pacific Lutheran University
Tacoma, WA 98447-0003

ISBN 0-87362-970-1

Printed in the United States of America

1 2 3 4 5 6 7 8 9 0

CONTENTS

PREFACE

This volume honors Philip Akerson Nordquist, now retiring after 42 remarkable years as a member of the Pacific Lutheran University history department. This 42-year tenure is the longest in the history of the department, and it represents a record unlikely to be eclipsed. Years alone, however, do not account for the full measure of Philip Nordquist's contribution to the university, nor for the energy and enthusiasm devoted to the completion of this *Festschrift*. He has been a towering presence on campus. That has been true in a literal sense, of course. During the 25 years he shared in the department with Christopher Browning, they were sometimes known as the "Two Talls," or perhaps, to some disinclined to look up, as the "Too Talls." Each of them has a stature, both literal and figurative, which has left PLU a much different and a much better place.

Philip Nordquist played a very important role in faculty governance at PLU, helping to create a system of participation admired and envied by faculty at other institutions. He has also represented PLU to the broader community through a large number of speaking engagements on and off campus. Many of these lectures have been to students, faculty, and alumni affiliated with the university, but he has also spoken widely at meetings in the broader world of Lutheran higher education. In all of this work, Philip Nordquist has been guided by the best principles of the Reformation, Martin Luther's commitment to faith *and* reason, and his willingness to wrestle honestly and intensively with the most challenging issues facing church and society. Such principles can be seen in Phil's work as historian of this university, especially in his centennial volume, *Educating for Service: Pacific Lutheran University, 1890-1990*. Each of these roles has helped to make Philip Nordquist a unique presence on campus for more than four decades. He has described, modeled, and inspired in others the Lutheran ideal of vocation, and it is his vocation as a Lutheran scholar and teacher which is celebrated in the title of this volume.

Most students remember other things about Philip Nordquist. They remember his wit as well as his rigor. They remember the incredible role that he and Helen have played at PLU, from hosting innumerable events in their home to attending innumerable events on campus. Most of all, Phil's students remember his inspiration toward learning. They have known him as a knowledgeable, wise, and demanding teacher, who exhibited a passion for history and a willingness to apply the methods of historical inquiry to the most important questions facing young students, Lutheran and otherwise. This retirement year (2005) has produced a plethora of emails filled with praise for Phil's wisdom, his teaching style, and his influence on two generations of students. One person spoke of a lifelong addiction to history and an insatiable need to travel back and forth to Europe, a set of ailments not entirely unwelcome. The most common tribute from former students has been a variation on one theme: "He taught me to think."

In October, 2004, Phil's colleagues in the history department hosted a special seminar, a "Phil Fest," to which some 750 history graduates since 1963 received an invitation. Five of the contributors to this volume, Christopher Browning, Robert Ericksen, Michael Halvorson, Samuel Torvend, and Molly Loberg, presented papers at the October event to honor Phil, and Megan Benton served as MC for the day. Each paper dealt with some aspect of German history, one of Phil's major areas of interest. A large number of people attended, many from the campus community, but with alumni in attendance from as far south as California and as far east as New Jersey and Georgia. This

Festschrift, then, developed as an outgrowth of the "Phil Fest," and in response to the widespread enthusiasm for Philip Nordquist's career and his impact on history majors at PLU.

Each of the editors of this volume attended PLU and studied history under Phil's guidance and inspiration. Robert Ericksen arrived in the fall of 1963, the same semester in which the young Professor Nordquist first began teaching in the department. Bob remembers the ubiquitous smoking of pipes, but also the individual professors, whose sterling reputation as excellent, interesting teachers and fountains of wisdom attracted him to the history major. Walter Schnackenberg, Peter Ristuben, and, of course, the young Nordquist, all fit this mold. Both Schnackenberg and Nordquist also pointed Bob toward his career in German history. Michael Halvorson arrived in 1981 and remembers Phil's suggestion that careers in computer science and history could overlap and prove mutually beneficial (which turned out to be true for Michael). He also remembers numerous long and entertaining discussions of Tudor historiography in the early 1980s, and extended essays written on Lawrence Stone's *The Causes of the English Reformation* and J.J. Scarisbrick's *Henry VIII*. Michael would like to thank Phil for sharing his passion for Reformation studies with him, and also for encouraging Michael to investigate the rich resources available for studying later Lutheranism in Europe, North America, and Africa.

ORGANIZATION

This volume contains two parts. Part 1 is devoted to teaching history within the PLU history department, and includes a biographical sketch of Philip Nordquist (Chapter 1) and an essay penned by Professor Nordquist himself (Chapter 3), which describes important figures and teaching trends within the department. Phil's essay also includes a complete list of the 26 faculty members who have taught fulltime in the history department since its beginnings, and a list of the 36 PLU graduates who have completed Ph.D. degrees in history through 2004. Since Phil took his place on the faculty in 1963, 25

PLU alums have earned a Ph.D. in history, with several additional degrees on the cusp of completion. This record, in large part a tribute to Philip Nordquist, places PLU among the top small universities in the country. The list would be even longer were it to include advanced degrees in law, theology, and other disciplines. Readers of this volume, for example, will note the Ph.D. in German language and literature earned by one of our contributors, Gerald Fetz, and the J.D. earned by another, Christian Lucky.

A second reflection on the history of the PLU history department (Chapter 2) comes from Christopher Browning, who served in the department from 1974 to 1999. Philip Nordquist played an important role in attracting Chris to PLU, and Chris in turn established himself as the most significant scholar ever to have taught at the university. He and Phil together influenced a large number of the PLU history majors who have gone on to academic careers, as well as the majority of the contributors to this volume.

The balance of this *Festschrift* (Chapters 4-14) illustrates the variety of disciplines and the quality of scholarship represented by his tory majors who have chosen to pursue a scholarly path. Four of our contributors have taught or now teach as full-time or adjunct faculty at their *alma mater*. The others teach at universities across the United States, except for one attorney and two junior scholars just completing Ph.D. degrees. The essays in this volume, therefore, reflect significant diversity in subject matter and chronology, and range from the reading habits of medieval women and discussions of Lutheran theology and practice, to recent themes in German history and historical memory in Japan. Harking back to the Scandinavian roots of this university, the contributors offer their projects as a *Smorgasbord* of historical reflections designed to honor Professor Nordquist and to suggest that his scholarly influence continues to be relevant and inspiring.

Among those history majors who studied at PLU during the most recent decade, the 1990s, two have contributed chapters to this volume. Molly Loberg, class of 1998, is now completing a Ph.D. in German history at Princeton. Her dissertation, which deals with politics and popular culture in Weimar Germany, is actually rooted in a senior thesis she wrote at PLU. After spending time in Germany on a Fulbright grant, Molly was courted by several top universities and ended up at Princeton. Laura (Ritchie) Gifford graduated from PLU in 2000. She is now working on the overlap of religion and anti-Communism in the McCarthy era, doing much of her research in the archives of the Nixon Library. Her contribution to this volume describes the connection between Billy Graham, a Protestant, and Father John Cronin, a Catholic, to Richard Nixon, especially during his vice presidential years. Laura will soon finish her Ph.D. in American history at UCLA.

Four contributors to this volume studied at PLU during the 1980s. This includes one of the co-editors, Michael Halvorson, class of 1985, who completed a Ph.D. at the University of Washington in Reformation and early modern European history, and joins the PLU history department fulltime with Professor Nordquist's retirement. He writes here about the late-16th-century solidification of Lutheran identity in Germany, especially in relation to two other groups, Jesuits and Jews. Mary Elizabeth Ailes, class of 1989, completed a Ph.D. in European history at the University of Minnesota, and now teaches history at the University of Nebraska at Kearney. Her contribution describes Danish mercenary soldiers fighting for England in the late-17th century. Michael Lynn also represents the class of 1989. After completing a Ph.D. at the University of Wisconsin, he took a position in the history department at Agnes Scott College in Georgia. His contribution here describes the rage for lectures in popular science which swept Enlightenment France in the 18th century. Christian Lucky, a third representative of the class of 1989, first left PLU with the support of a Fulbright grant and soon experienced the unexpected excitement of the Fall of the Berlin Wall. This solidified his interest in central and eastern Europe, and he has since spent considerable time in the region of the former Warsaw Pact nations. He also completed a law degree at the University of Chicago and joined a law firm in New York City, a position he recently left in order to renew his interest in public policy. He now holds a position with the Open Society Institute–Soros Foundation, where he focuses on the recovery of stolen public assets and the reform of natural resource extraction industries. Christian's contribution here analyzes the comparison between the

looting of the Russian economy since 1989 and the economic spoliation which occurred in early America.

Megan Benton, class of 1976, is one of two representatives of the
1970s in this volume. She specializes in the history of the book, having completed a Ph.D. dissertation at University of California, Berkeley, which she then published with Yale University Press. Her contribution here illustrates the convergence of women's history and her
own interest in the history of the book with a description of "books
of hours," devotional writings which offer the historian important
insights into the religious practices and reading habits of late-medi-
eval peoples. Samuel Torvend, class of 1973, also completed his PLU
education in the decade that stretched from Vietnam to Watergate
to Jimmy Carter. He is now a member of the religion department at
PLU, having completed a Ph.D. at St. Louis University. His contribution to this volume shows that there are important, and often over-
looked, connections between Martin Luther's early writings on Holy
Communion and the Christian community's responsibility for social
welfare and the poor.

Finally, the decade of the 1960s produced three history graduates who have contributed to this volume. Gerald Fetz, class of 1966,
earned his Ph.D. at the University of Oregon in German language and
literature. He has taught for many years at the University of Montana,
where he is now Dean of the College of Arts and Sciences. Fetz is also
a major figure in the German Studies Association, an organization
that encompasses both literature and history in its purview. In this
volume, Jerry betrays his debt, perhaps, to Phil Nordquist and those
early years studying history at PLU. He describes and discusses some
very complex ideas about memory and history to be found in the writings of W.G. Sebald, a childhood survivor of the Holocaust. Robert
Ericksen, class of 1967, completed his Ph.D. at the London School of
Economics and Political Science, University of London, and then, in a
pattern he shares with Megan Benton, published his dissertation with
Yale University Press. Since 1999, Ericksen has been a member of the
history department at PLU, successor to Chris Browning, and thereby
successor also to Walter Schnackenberg (a double heritage he knows
enough to appreciate). His contribution here involves a description of

Christian leaders in postwar Germany. Robert shows their eagerness to leave behind the Nazi past, and argues that this eagerness included a willingness to minimize and distort the past in the process. Neil Waters is the final member of the class of 1967 represented in this volume. He completed a Ph.D. in Japanese history at the University of Hawaii and then published his dissertation with Harvard University Press. He now holds the Kawashima Professor of Japanese Studies chair at Middlebury College in Vermont. Neil's contribution here describes the place of peasant riots in the modernization of Japan. He also considers the differing views of Japanese and non-Japanese historians in assessing these riots.

Acknowledgments

Financial support to underwrite this project was made possible through generous contributions from Robert Gomulkiewicz and Andrea Lairson and Bruce and Jill Bjerke. Robert is a 1983 alumnus of PLU, and Bruce graduated in 1972. Both credit Phil Nordquist as being an influential teacher, mentor, and friend who played an important role in shaping their lives. The co-editors have also relied extensively upon the energy, enthusiasm, and goodwill of many friends of Phil in the creation of this volume. That includes, above all, the contributors, who worked efficiently and who delivered and proofed their work in a more timely fashion than is usually experienced in academic publishing. In addition, we want to thank PLU President Loren Anderson and his staff, including his assistant, Laura Polcyn, for their vital support of this project.

In terms of the book's production, the editors are grateful for the support and publishing expertise of Robyn Ricks, who designed the book cover and jacket, completed all interior layout and typesetting tasks, and helped Michael Halvorson to create the book's interior design. PLU student Laura Callen (class of 2005), a gifted English major with minors in Latin and PLU's innovative publishing and printing arts program, also served as the book's production editor, and provided valuable copy editing and proofreading support. Brenda Murray and

Peggy Jobe skillfully managed numerous logistical and administrative tasks related to the book project and the October, 2004, seminar for Professor Nordquist. Finally, Helen Nordquist provided valuable encouragement and technical support along the way, and forced Phil to accept the acknowledgment and praise and of his students and peers, which he might have preferred implied or spoken, rather than printed for all to see.

Robert P. Ericksen
Michael J. Halvorson
Tacoma, Washington
March, 2005

PART 1:

TEACHING HISTORY AT PACIFIC LUTHERAN UNIVERSITY

CHAPTER 1

PHILIP AKERSON NORDQUIST: A PROFILE

Philip Akerson Nordquist is the grandson of Swedish immigrants who homesteaded in South Dakota in the 1890s, and the son of parents who headed west ahead of drought and depression. A native Washingtonian, he was born in Ellensburg in 1934, educated in the public schools of Lake Stevens, and graduated from Pacific Lutheran College in 1956. While a student at PLC, he was active in student government, wrote for the *Mooring Mast*, and played football and basketball for Marv Harshman. He was twice all-conference in basketball and twice captain of championship teams; he is still one of the leading rebounders in PLU's basketball history, and is one of eighteen who scored more than 1,000 points during their careers (1,139). He received his M.A. and Ph.D. degrees in history from the University of Washington in 1960 and 1964, and wrote his dissertation, "The Ecology of Religious Denominational Preference in the United States: 1850," under the direction of Thomas J. Pressly. He was only the second PLC graduate to receive a Ph.D. in history. He began teaching at PLU in 1963.

At PLU, Nordquist has taught History of Civilization and early modern European history courses to nearly 5,000 students. He has been particularly intent on producing high levels of scholarship in the senior history seminars, which he helped re-insert into the curriculum in 1964-65. He was also one of the founders of the team-taught, interdisciplinary alternative core curriculum Integrated Studies Program, which was launched in the mid-1970s and is now known as The International Core. He has taught in that program for more than 25 years.

From nearly the beginning of his tenure at PLU, Philip Nordquist has been involved in a rich variety of efforts to understand Lutheran higher education and particularly what it meant to be a Lutheran university set in the context of the Pacific Northwest. Among the many opportunities to address those issues and formulate university responses was service on the Commission on Academic Excellence from 1971 to 1973, participation in workshops organized by the Division of College and University Service of the American Lutheran Church at Concordia College in 1974, Luther College in 1975, Luther-Northwestern Seminary in 1978, and California Lutheran University in 1979. He was a member of a faculty committee that drafted a new mission statement for PLU in 1993 and a member of the planning committee for the Evangelical Lutheran Church in America, which launched the Vocation of a Lutheran College Conferences that are still taking place every summer. He also worked on the two recent long-range plans at PLU: the quite successful *PLU 2000* (where he was an essayist and editor) and *PLU 2010* (where he was co-chair of the Identity and Constituency section).

In addition to those responsibilities, Nordquist has served as department chair, faculty athletic representative (1966-78), faculty representative to the Board of Regents (1974-77), chair of the faculty (1996-98) and acting provost for six months beginning in the summer of 1998. He has also won a number of student-organized teaching and service awards. In 1983, the Alumni Association gave him its Heritage Award and in 1993, its Distinguished Alumnus Award. He has written and lectured extensively about Luther, Lutheranism, and Lutheran higher education, and in 1990, Nordquist wrote the centennial history of PLU: *Educating for Service, Pacific Lutheran University 1890-1990*. In 1970-71, Nordquist was a visiting scholar at the University of Geneva's Reformation Institute, and in 1978-79, he studied at Cambridge University in England. During the remodel of Xavier

Hall in 2000-01, a PLU lecture hall was named in Phil's honor, the Philip A. Nordquist Lecture Hall, an electronic classroom and meeting facility which held the PLC library reading room from 1939 to 1967.

Philip Nordquist is married to the former Helen Jordanger ('57) and they have two sons, Christopher, a graduate of St. Olaf College, and Paul, a PLU graduate.

CHAPTER 2

PHILIP NORDQUIST AND MY ARRIVAL AT PACIFIC LUTHERAN UNIVERSITY

Christopher R. Browning

In the spring of 1974, I was completing my graduate studies at the University of Wisconsin-Madison and applying for a job in what had suddenly become a very ugly market for applicants. In the surreal 1960s, the vast expansion of the university system to accommodate the baby boomers had resulted in an unprecedented opportunity for aspiring academicians. Then, quite precipitously, the bottom dropped out of this market in 1970, catching many graduate students already in the pipeline of graduate studies who now had little prospect of gainful employment in the career for which they were being trained. One result was that academic employers, who had suddenly turned from beggars to choosers, could indulge in a certain arrogance previously denied them. Some of the letters I received in that season of job-hunting were no credit to our academic culture.

There was one remarkable exception in my experience that spring, however. Having applied for the position at Pacific Lutheran University held by the late Walter Schnackenberg, I received a long and detailed letter describing the institution. The knowledge and appreciation of the history of the university, as well as affection for it, were transparent. It noted with pride the number of recent history majors who had gone on to noted graduate schools such as the London School of Economics (Bob Ericksen in this case), as well as one who had recently been named PLU's first and only Rhodes Scholar. The letter assured me that academic freedom, intellectual vitality, and teaching creativity were alive and well at PLU, and that great strides were being made in its evolution from a somewhat parochial to more cosmopolitan liberal arts university, one in which tradition and excellence were seen as complementary rather than contradictory. It assured me that PLU was a place where a faculty member could flourish as both a teacher and scholar. The author of that letter, no surprise, was Phil Nordquist.

Thus, when I flew into Seattle for my interview and was stunned by the view of the Cascades and Puget Sound from the air, I was already desperately hoping that this was the school that would become my academic home. To my great fortune, I was offered the job. As I was neither Lutheran nor Norwegian, in the context of PLU in 1974 this was to some extent what we would now call a "diversity hire." But that context was rapidly changing. Phil's assurances about the direction in which PLU was evolving, due in no small part to his own contributions as a faculty leader, were valid. For instance, only five years later the University tenured a Jewish faculty member for the first time in the history of the institution. This was Morty Rozanski, who was simultaneously the first historian hired at PLU to specialize in non-western history. He was also the founder of PLU's initial Global Studies program. Developments such as that, along with the creation of PLU's Integrated Studies Program, meant that my first years at PLU were ones of tremendous excitement and change, years that were also enriched by a deepening friendship with my senior colleague. It must be remembered that a 10 year age gap, when people are 40 and 30, tenured and untenured respectively, is much more significant than when both are gray-haired older faculty. Such a situation is all too often a recipe for rivalry and resentment, not friendship and support. That our relationship followed the latter, not the former, path was fundamental in shaping my experience at PLU.

As an historian, I don't believe in sugar-coating the past, and I won't pretend that life in the History Department was one of constant fair weather. Like many departments, we experienced a period of internal stasis and acrimony complicated by several of us being totally on the outs with key administrators who did not share our phi-losophy of how the department should govern itself or our vision of how it should evolve. These years of acrimony seemed intractable and unending at the time, but eventually passed away. In retrospect, the unpleasantness of this period was not without compensation. Barred from any meaningful participation in department and divisional af-fairs, I could devote more time to my own scholarship. The admin-istration was more than happy to grant me leaves of absence, and in a ten year period I was off campus for 3½ years. This was a period of intense research that laid the basis for virtually all of my subsequent publications. It was also a period of increased bonding, for I shared my situation of internal exile with Phil, and nothing brings people closer together than mutual affliction. Stigmatized as the twin pillars of obstruction, Phil and I could at least find solace and reaffirmation with one another. Without Phil as my anchor and reference point, the constant assurance that I was not alone in "seeing the snufalupa-gus" (to those of you who did not raise children during the Sesame Street era, I apologize for the obscure reference), my experience at PLU would have been greatly diminished. His clear sense of historical perspective about PLU, as well as his faith in the future of the univer-sity and our department, were crucial sustenance for me during that trying decade.

The situation during my last decade at PLU changed dramati-cally once again. Ironically, just as the university plunged into dra-matic financial crisis, followed by lean years of fiscal discipline and gradual recovery, the civility and collegiality of life in the department improved immeasurably. When I had an offer that I could not refuse and left PLU for Chapel Hill in 1999, departure was not easy. My wife and I had developed a network of deep friendships that simply could not be replaced when starting anew elsewhere. None of these friendships, of course, was longer or deeper than our relationship with Phil and Helen. For me, Phil continues to personify what is best about this institution. His commitment to excellence and high standards, his conviction that PLU can and must strive to preserve its sense of tradition and identity but simultaneously never compromise on issues of quality, his belief in the transformative powers of education that he conveys to his students, his call to colleagues that they take responsibility for their own faculty self-governance, and his unwavering integrity have helped to shape this institution in fundamental ways. He may retire, but equal to any of the key figures he has written about in his history of the University, his impact on PLU and his students and colleagues will be enduring.

CHAPTER 3

A Brief History of the Pacific Lutheran University History Department

Philip A. Nordquist

Was du ererbt von deinen Vätern hast,
Erwirb es, um es zu besitzen

What you have as heritage,
Take now as task:
For thus you will make it your own!

Goethe, *Faust*

History has been a part of the Pacific Lutheran University curriculum from the beginning and it was taught in a rigorous fashion according to the earliest catalogs. The early College Preparatory requirements, for example, included the histories of Greece, Rome, the Middle Ages, England, the modern world, and the United States, as well as Latin, Greek, Norwegian and German. The 1904-05 catalog read:

> All our institutions and many of our modes of action and habits of thought have come down to us from former generations. No conscious progress, no truly worthy reform can therefore be achieved without a knowledge of the relations which the present bears to the past. For that reason a very prominent place has been given to the study of history in the curriculum of the school.

There were no "professional" historians early on, however; history was taught by people trained in other disciplines, primarily the classics and theology.

The first more-or-less full-time historians appeared in the early 1930s: Alvar Beck (1929-35) and Geo Reneau (1933-52). Reneau was the first woman to teach history at PLU. She was educated at the young and lively University of Chicago (B.Ph., 1909, M.Ph., 1910) and she had a law degree (1944) via the extension courses offered by LaSalle University. According to published reports, Reneau was demanding, prepared her lectures carefully, and was the resident intellectual on the faculty. She taught History of Civilization.

The history department was strengthened in the later 1930s with the coming of Elvin Akre (1937-70). Trained in the classics and music at Concordia College in Minnesota, he came as dean of men and band director, but was soon teaching American and Ancient history. He received an M.A. degree from the University of Washington in 1941. Thousands of PLU graduates took Pacific Northwest History from Elvin Akre. His 33 years of service is the second-longest departmental tour of duty.

After World War II the department was further strengthened by the teaching and scholarly contributions of Magnus Nodtvedt (1947-63). He brought master's degrees in political science (Columbia) and theology (Princeton) and a doctorate in history from the University of Chicago. He required long term papers, extensive memorization, and factual accuracy as many alumni will remember. A flock of pre-seminary students took church history and the Reformation from Magnus Nodtvedt.

He also revamped the history curriculum so that it would provide appropriate coverage and scholarly depth. There were soon courses in ancient, medieval, Renaissance, Reformation, Old Regime, French Revolution, and nineteenth- and twentieth-century European history; Russian, Asian, and Latin American history courses were listed, as well as several American history courses. To top it off were Leopold von Ranke-type research seminars in both American and European history. Some courses were taught on two- or three-year cycles and some not at all (like the seminars), but the revamping reflected Nodtvedt's scholarly ambitions for the department.

The senior research seminars returned in 1964 and are still features of the history curriculum; they were accompanied by a senior level oral examination over a required reading list. Its demands and rigor survived until the early 1970s, when the number of majors made the examination logistically impossible. The research seminar was the first at the university; "capstone" courses are now required in all majors.

The 1950s brought Walter Schnackenberg (1952-73) and Paul Vigness (1956-65) to the faculty. Schnackenberg, with a Ph.D. degree from Washington State University, was the most influential faculty member at PLU in the 1950s and 1960s; he fought with great vigor for the liberal arts, greater democracy in the governance of the university, and a more up-to-date philosophy of Lutheran higher education. His participation in the process that led to the Faculty Constitution is one manifestation of his activity, but his greatest contribution to the department and university was in his teaching and influence on students. In the intellectually flaccid 1950s, and in an institution still dominated by descending administrative authority that it was constantly emphasized should not be questioned, Schnackenberg advocated informed and critical intelligence. In a 1953 pamphlet commissioned by the Evangelical Lutheran Church entitled "To Whom the Future Belongs: The Preparation and Stimulation of Students for Graduate Study," he wrote "students should be treated in every area of their collegiate experience as though they possessed intelligence." Students were and it was infectious, and many soon had a vision of education and what it might accomplish that went far beyond the limitations most had brought from their working class homes. Schnackenberg also thought that PLU graduates should be able to compete with the very best graduates from the very best institutions in the country. That seemed quite remarkable in the 1950s, but it also began to happen. (For one example of this success, see Table B at the end of this chapter.)

With a Ph.D. degree from Stanford and the definitive English language study of Norway's neutrality in World War I under his belt, Paul Vigness had retired from teaching in the California public schools before coming to Parkland at age 62. He taught nine years at PLU, published a book about Norway during World War II, retired a second time, and then began teaching at Faith Evangelical Lutheran Seminary in Tacoma, where he logged 25 more years of teaching before he died of a stroke at the age of 96.

Nodtvedt, Schnackenberg, and Vigness all published books in the 1960s, helping to establish an appropriate scholarly norm for the newly hatched university (1960). The importance of their scholarly contributions cannot be gainsaid; rigorous scholarship, effective teaching, and service to the university could co-exist.

New waves of faculty came in the next four decades, including the late Peter Ristuben (1960-66, 1968-69), an enormously energetic teacher and participant in the life of the new university. He left at the end of the 1960s for the adventure of college administration, and was president of Bethany College in Kansas when he died at age 56. The author of this brief history came in 1963, served on a myriad of regular and *ad hoc* committees, received awards from the Alumni Association in 1983 (the Heritage Award) and 1993 (the Distinguished Alumnus Award), and wrote the centennial history of PLU in 1990: *Educating For Service: Pacific Lutheran University 1890-1990*. His 42 years of service is the longest in the department. Arthur Martinson (1966-99), another graduate influenced by the ferment and excitement of the 50s, came in 1966. He was interested in Pacific Northwest history and wrote about local history and Mt. Rainier National Park. His students studied their home towns.

Except for the rejuvenation of the seminars, the curriculum was not much altered in the 1950s and 1960s. That would change with the leadership of three notable additions to the faculty in the 1970s: David Johnson, Christopher Browning, and Mordechai Rosanski.

David Johnson was a graduate of Hamline University and his doctorate came from the University of Kansas. He brought sanity and balance into the volatility still left over from the 1960s, and his teaching of twentieth century American History included the most recent scholarship. In addition, his preparation in Latin American and Mexican history brought new courses into the departmental curriculum and books into the library. Johnson left after his first sabbatical and devoted most of the next 25 years to development work at the University of Minnesota Medical School.

Browning (1974-99) was an Oberlin graduate with a Ph.D. degree from the University of Wisconsin and a dissertation on the Final Solution published in 1978: *The Final Solution and the German Foreign Office*. He was told in graduate school that such a specialty would be a blind alley professionally. He disagreed, persevered, and when Holocaust studies took off like a rocket a few years later he was in the midst of the most important interpretive debates and discussions of the next 25 years. At PLU, Holocaust and German history courses were added and students were caught up in the need to understand the Holocaust as deeply as possible, both morally and intellectually.

Articles and books flowed from Browning's computer, most importantly, *Ordinary Men* (1992), which re-arranged thinking about the Holocaust in important ways. His international reputation was dramatically recognized by the invitation to give the Trevelyan Lectures—probably the most prestigious English language lectureship for historians—at Cambridge University in England during Lent term, 1999. The lectures had been given by only a handful of American historians, none from west of the Mississippi River and none from a professor at a small university. The lectures were published by Cambridge University Press in 2000. Browning left PLU in 1999, after 25 years, to accept the Frank Porter Graham chair in history at the University of North Carolina. He is undoubtedly the most widely known and most influential scholar in the history of PLU.

Mordechai Rosanski, a student of modern China, was a Canadian with a doctorate from the University of Pennsylvania. He burst on the scene with great energy and soon established an Asian studies emphasis within the department and fused together various university programs into the Global Studies major that still exists. In 1983, he left for university administration and was soon president of the University of Guelf in Canada; he is now president of Rider University in New Jersey.

The history department has done more than its fair share in the production of college and university administrators. Three have become presidents after apprenticeships as deans (Ristuben, Rozanski, and James Halseth) and two are deans (Jack Bermingham and Edwin Clausen). David Johnson is involved in development.

Philip A. Nordquist

Half-a-dozen faculty members came and went in the 1980s, suggesting institutional and departmental ferment, tension between private initiative and community concerns, and some of the entrepreneurship that marked the decade. After coming in 1986, E. Wayne Carp remained in place, however; a native of Queens, New York, with a doctorate in American history from the University of California-Berkeley, he proved to be a demanding teacher and a scholar of the first rank. His first book was a prize-winning study of how the continental army was supplied and the relationship of that supply activity to eighteenth-century American political culture. His next three books on adoption in America made him a national and much consulted expert. In January, 2005, the university announced that Carp would be the first holder of the Benson Family Chair in Business and Economic History. The Benson Family chair is the first endowed chair in the institution's history; being the first recipient is a signal honor.

The 1990s brought several lively and able additions to the department. The average age certainly dropped. Trained in many of the latest developments in historical research and with a variety of interests, new faculty brought strengths (and added new courses) in women's and gender history, the history of slavery, Afro-American history, the Viet Nam War, the Civil War, Latin America, and World history. The quality of teaching remained high.

During the last 75 years, excluding one-year sabbatical replacements, 19 men and six women have taught in the history department at PLU; 23 have had Ph.D. degrees. They have published more than 30 books, some to national and international acclaim. Included have been two histories of PLU and one of Hamline University. Six have moved into university administration. (For a listing of the full-time faculty, see Table A at the end of this chapter.)

The best measure of a PLU department's success, however, is the quality of its students and their concerns and successes. Here, the history department is competitive with the better departments at similarly sized institutions around the country.

Since 1950, nearly 200 history graduates have become pastors (several have been elected bishop); almost as many have gone into the public schools. More than 25 have become lawyers and almost 40

14

have completed history doctorates; that figure places PLU in the top 5 percent of almost 900 private, primarily undergraduate institutions in the United States. (For these individuals, see Table B.)

Among the graduates can be found PLU's first Rhodes Scholar (Bruce Bjerke, '72), and several other firsts for PLU graduates: first doctorate from Harvard (Lloyd Eastman, '53), first doctorate from a foreign university (Robert Ericksen, '67, University of London), first recipients of D. Phil. degrees from Oxford (James Aageson, '70 and Harry Maier, '81), first books published by Harvard or Yale University Presses (Eastman, Ericksen, Neil Waters, '67, Richard Slatta, '69, and Megan Benton, '76). There are university presidents (Jon Wefald, '59, Kansas State University), several deans, and the director of a university press (Fred Bohm, '67, Michigan State University Press).

The scholarship produced by graduates like Lloyd Eastman, Thomas Reeves, Isaria Kimambo, Robert Ericksen, Neil Waters, Richard Slatta, Dale Soden, and Megan Benton (to mention only a few) has been widely recognized and in some instances has been described as definitive. Three examples from three different specialties will illustrate the point. The late Lloyd Eastman, the first PLU graduate to receive a Ph.D. in history, worked with John K. Fairbank at Harvard and taught at Connecticut College, Ohio State University, and the University of Illinois. The author of four books and more than twenty articles, he was thought to be the world's foremost expert on Chiang Kai-Shek and the Kuomintang era when he came to PLU in 1986 to give the Schnackenberg Lecture. His books were published by Harvard, Stanford, and Illinois.

Isaria N. Kimambo ('62), a native of Tanzania, received his doctorate at Northwestern University and has spent his teaching career at the University of Dar es Salaam where he has had a significant impact on education throughout the university (he served as chief academic officer) and Tanzania, but also on the development of critical and appropriate historiography at the university. He has written numerous articles and written, edited or co-edited nine books on East African religion and Tanzanian history. He is presently in semi-retirement, but remains very intellectually active.

Richard Slatta is a 1969 graduate—the most prolific class in the production of professional historians in the history of the department—and took his Ph.D. at the University of Texas. He teaches at North Carolina State University. Slatta is an expert on cowboys, banditos, gauchos, and various frontiers in North and South America (his comparative studies have been particularly interesting and important). He is the author of two encyclopedias, four books and numerous articles. His books have been published by Yale, Oklahoma, and Nebraska University presses, ABC Clio, and the Greenwood Press.

The students encouraged and the standards established by Nodtvedt, Schnackenberg, and others in the aftermath of World War II, and in succeeding decades, have produced quite remarkable results. Martin Luther wrote that "Historians are the most useful people and the best teachers, and they cannot be sufficiently honored, praised, and thanked." If that was Luther's conclusion it must be so. Certainly the history department faculty members who produced the post World War II curriculum and established demanding standards should be appropriately remembered and thanked. And it also needs to be remembered that several members of the department have played a disproportionately large role in the development of the university since 1960. That influence can be seen at many turns (the growing importance of the liberal arts, the importance of graduate study, the faculty constitution and faculty governance, attempts to explain what it has meant to be a Lutheran university set in the context of the Pacific Northwest, the remembering and writing of the university's history, and much more).

The tradition of scholarship, service, and teaching that has characterized the history department needs to be handed on to succeeding generations of faculty and students. That's certainly what Goethe meant when he said make the tradition your own.

TABLE A: FULL-TIME HISTORY DEPARTMENT FACULTY, 1929-2005

Elvin Akre, B.A. Concordia College, 1928, M.A., University of Washington, 1941 (at PLU, 1937-70).

Alvar Beck, Graduate of PLC, 1927. B.A., University of Puget Sound, 1928, M.A., University of Washington, 1929 (at PLU, 1929-35).

Carlton Benson, B.A., Colorado College, 1983, M.A. Indiana University 1988, Ph.D., University of California-Berkeley, 1996 (at PLU, 1996-).

Jack Bermingham, B.A., M.A., California State University-Northridge, 1972, 1973, Ph.D., University of California Santa Barbara, 1979 (at PLU, 1983-96).

Christopher Browning, B.A., Oberlin College, 1967, M.A., Ph.D., University of Wisconsin-Madison, 1968, 1975 (at PLU, 1974-99).

E. Wayne Carp, B.A., M.A., Ph.D., University of California-Berkeley, 1972, 1973, 1981 (at PLU, 1986-).

Edwin Clausen, B.A., University of California-Riverside, 1970, M.A., Ph.D., University of California-Santa Barbara, 1972, 1979 (at PLU, 1983-95).

Robert Ericksen, B.A., Pacific Lutheran University, 1967, M.A., State University of New York-Stony Brook, 1969, Ph.D., London School of Economics and Political Science, 1980 (at PLU, 1999-).

Michel Frank, B.A., City College of New York, 1934, M.A., Ph.D. New York University, 1935, 1949 (at PLU, 1935-51).

James Halseth, B.A., Concordia College, 1962, M.A., Eastern New Mexico University, 1963, Ph.D., Texas Tech University, 1973 (at PLU, 1966-68, 1970-80).

Gina Hames, B.A., M.A., Eastern Washington University, 1986, 1989, M.A., Ph.D., Carnegie Mellon University, 1992, 1996 (at PLU, 1997-).

David Johnson, B.A., Hamline University, 1961, M.A., Stanford University, 1963, Ph.D., University of Kansas, 1972 (at PLU, 1970-78).

Beth Kraig, B.A., San Francisco State University, 1979, M.A., Western Washington University, 1981, M.A., University of Chicago, 1984, Ph.D., University of Washington, 1987 (at PLU, 1989-).

Douglas Lee, B.A., Lewis and Clark College, 1967, M.A., University of Michigan, 1969, Ph.D., University of California-Santa Barbara, 1979, J.D., Northwestern School of Law, 1988 (at PLU 1992-96).

Kathryn Malone, B.A., Yale University, 1976, Ph.D., University of Pennsylvania, 1981 (at PLU, 1981-86).

Chandra Manning, B.A., Mt. Holyoke College, 1993, M.Phil., University College, Galway, Ireland, 1995, Ph.D., Harvard University, 2002 (at PLU, 2003-).

Arthur Martinson, B.A., Pacific Lutheran University, 1957, M.A., Ph.D., Washington State University, 1961, 1966 (at PLU, 1966-99).

J. C. Mutchler, B.S., M.A., University of New Mexico, 1990, 1992, Ph.D., Yale University, 2002 (at PLU, 1999-2002).

Magnus Nodtvedt, B.A., St. Olaf College, 1917, M.A., Columbia University 1920, B.Th., Luther Theological Seminary, 1925, M.Th., Princeton Theological Seminary, 1928, Ph.D., University of Chicago, 1950 (at PLU 1947-63).

Philip Nordquist, B.A., Pacific Lutheran University, 1956, M.A., Ph.D., University of Washington, 1960, 1964 (at PLU, 1963-2005).

Susan Randall, B.A., College of Idaho, 1972, M.A., Ph.D., University of Utah, 1975, 1979 (at PLU, 1979-83).

Geo Reneau, Ph.B., Ph.M., University of Chicago, 1909, 1910, Ll.B., LaSalle University, 1944 (at PLU, 1933-52).

Peter Ristuben, B.A., Concordia College, 1955, M.A., South Dakota State University, 1956, Ph.D., University of Okalahoma, 1964 (at PLU, 1960-66, 1968-69).

Mordechai Rosanski, B.A., McGill University, 1968, Ph.D., University of Pennsylvania, 1974 (at PLU, 1975-82).

Walter Schnackenberg, B.A., St. Olaf College, 1939, M.A., Gonzaga University, 1947, Ph.D., Washington State University, 1950 (at PLU, 1942-44, 1952-73).

Paul Vigness, B.A. St. Olaf College, 1917, M.A., Ph.D., Stanford University, 1924, 1930 (at PLU, 1956-65).

Table B: PLU Graduates with Ph.D. Degrees in History

Class	Name	Institution
1953	Lloyd Eastman	Harvard University
1956	Philip Nordquist	University of Washington
1957	Roger Bjerk Arthur Martinson	Washington State University Washington State University
1958	Norman Forness Thomas Reeves	Pennsylvania State University University of California-Santa Barbara
1959	Jack Holl Jon Wefald	Cornell University University of Michigan
1960	Thomas McLaughlin	Washington State University
1962	Isaria Kimambo	Northwestern University
1963	Dale Benson	University of Maine
1965	James Collier Louis Truschel	University of Michigan Northwestern University
1967	Frederick Bohm Robert Ericksen Neil Waters	Washington State University University of London University of Hawaii
1969	Larry Cress Richard Huling Daniel Miller	University of Virginia State University of New York-Binghamton State University of New York-Binghamton

Class	Name	Institution
1969	James Ojala	State University of New York-Binghamton
	Richard Slatta	University of Texas
	Marvin Slind	Washington State University
1973	Dale Soden	University of Washington
	Samuel Torvend	St. Louis University
1976	Megan Benton	University of California-Berkeley
1977	Sara Clausen	Vanderbilt University
1978	Roy Hammerling	University of Notre Dame
1979	Carol Staswick	University of California-Berkeley
1981	Harry Maier	Oxford University
	Charles Schaefer	University of Chicago
1985	Lane Fenrich	Northwestern University
	Michael Halvorson	University of Washington
1986	Jeffrey Hay	University of California-San Diego
1989	Mary Elizabeth Ailes	University of Minnesota
	Michael Lynn	University of Wisconsin
1990	Eric Ching	University of California-Santa Barbara

PART 2:

ESSAYS IN HONOR OF PHILIP A. NORDQUIST

CHAPTER 4

READING BY HEART:
BOOKS OF HOURS AND WOMEN'S WAYS OF READING

Megan Benton

Even as an undergraduate history major at PLU, I was strictly an Americanist. My three forays into European history were stellar, but unable to sway me: I was lucky enough to take one course from Dr. Schnackenberg in his last year of teaching, one from Chris Browning in his first, and one from a visiting grad student named Bob Ericksen. But it wasn't until some twenty years later that I managed to land in Phil Nordquist's classroom, when he graciously welcomed me into his Reformation history class. This abbreviated essay is partly the fruit of those lectures and of our conversations afterward exploring, with my novice's relish, territory so far afield from my own.

Toward the middle of the thirteenth century near Oxford in England, a young laywoman known to us, speculatively, only as Susanna did something extraordinary. She made herself visible, literally, to her own eyes and to posterity. While the rest of her identity remains shrouded in the silence of contemporary accounts, we can still see her today, portrayed five times in a small illustrated manuscript that she hired local illuminator William de Brailes to make for her. Her hair, clothing, and absence from historical records tell us that she was unmarried and neither a noblewoman nor a religious. She likely enjoyed some privileges of wealth and literacy, but she was nonetheless a member of the medieval gentry who so often disappeared without notice. With this commissioned book, however, Susanna not only gained a rare personal copy of a treasured text but also preserved, in a real sense, the smaller—and larger—story of her own otherwise-forgotten existence.

The central text of her book was a simplified version of Catholic prayer sequences, and as such it was not an original composition. Developed within monastic communities where daily life centered in complex religious rituals, these prayers were to be read or recited in observance of the liturgical hours of the day.[1] What made this book new and different was that it was explicitly designed for a lay user, so that she too could sanctify her life by approximating the devotional practices of the religious. Using a book to achieve such sanctity carried deeper dimensions of experience as well; it cultivated a sense of reading that drew upon different literacy skills and took place under different conditions than those of the traditional clerical readership.[2] In doing so, this little book enabled its owner to recognize herself as a discrete, significant participant in the panorama of Western Christian history. A new way of perceiving God's story, and of formulating one's own, was made possible when, in around 1240, de Brailes made for Susanna the earliest known book of hours.

For many owners, the book of hours became both agent and emblem of one's self. By enabling a private, particular relationship with God, Christ, Mary, and the huge family of saints, it came to shape a sense of personal identity that could be expressed through, preserved in, and transmitted by the book itself. This was true regardless of gender, but this book-derived spiritual and personal experience was from the start particularly salient and enduring for women. In fact, although books of hours were owned by both men and women, they were the first books that women were freely allowed, even encouraged, to use and consider their own. This essay explores the extraordinary popularity of books of hours, the increasingly gendered nature of the devotional reading that they fostered, the complex ways in which medieval and early modern women used and understood their books of hours, and how those relationships have influenced the subsequent roles that books have played in women's lives.

From the fourteenth century well into the sixteenth, the book of hours was one of the most commonly produced books in Christendom. It was also one of the first "popular" books in that it was produced for a general lay market rather than a clerical one. Both before and especially after the advent of printing in the 1450s, a book of hours was for many the first and often only book an individual might own. It initiated much of the Christian lay population into the world of books, especially in France, England, the Low Countries, and, to a lesser extent, Germany, Spain, and Italy. Before printing, the high cost of manuscripts and the low levels of literacy meant that lay ownership of books was largely limited to the wealthiest levels of society. Even so, by the fifteenth century, steady demand for books of hours had prompted a highly efficient system of "mass" manuscript production that enabled "anyone who was anyone" to own one.[3]

With printing, the number of books of hours soared. It became a genuine bestseller from the 1490s through about 1540. By the 1490s, the genre had become a lucrative and prolific specialty of Parisian printers, who printed some 90 percent of an estimated 1,585 European editions produced before 1600. An estimate of an average edition size of five hundred copies suggests that more than 792,000 printed copies (in addition to the small but still-active production of manuscript copies) were distributed throughout northern Europe. Eamon Duffy identified at least 114 editions for use in England alone by the 1530s, which he calculates conservatively to have yielded some 57,000 copies. A single French printer, François Regnault, produced for export to England 74 editions of the book of hours, or *primer* as it was called in England, between 1526 and 1538.[4]

The proliferation of copies and reduction in prices made possible by printing made ownership even more broadly accessible in the sixteenth century, perhaps even coming "well within the range of the poorest readers," as Roger Chartier contends. In 1548, for example, a Parisian printer/bookseller's stock included 148,000 copies of books of hours. This was not as anomalous as one might think; twenty years earlier in Amiens a bookseller's inventory revealed that of a total of 101,860 books in stock, more than 98,000 were copies of printed books of hours. Their prices ranged from as little as one sou for an unbound copy to twenty livres or more, depending on the binding. Similarly market-savvy printers in England offered primers in "formats ranging from the sumptuous to the skimpy, and varying in price from pounds to a few pence."[5]

What made the book of hours so acutely popular? In general, it was attractive for two major reasons, which correspond roughly to the changing nature of lay piety. In the thirteenth and fourteenth centuries, books of hours were a prominent part (among the courtly classes who could afford them) of a lay religious life that was expressed primarily through overt public gestures or "good works." These typically included support for religious orders, construction of chapels, and so on. When openly carried to Mass, books of hours were impressive objects redolent with Christian iconographic significance. Copies made for royalty and nobles—those most typically preserved today were often lavished with superb examples of medieval illumination, decoration, and binding. Noblewomen treasured their books of hours among their finest possessions, often keeping the small books with their prized jewels and rosaries. Especially in the thirteenth and fourteenth centuries, to own one—often a colorful, illuminated manuscript copy—was to make visible to all one's wealth, social prominence, and exemplary Christian piety.

By the fifteenth century, particularly successful members of the emerging merchant and professional classes embraced books of hours in part as tokens of prosperity that could align them with the "better" classes, much as buying a luxury car or joining a country club might do today. Shrewd printers, recognizing this market of buyers anxious for books that would help signal affluence, often enhanced their mechanically made books with special features of manuscript books, such as hand-ruled text lines and rubricated initials and borders, which imparted traditional beauty and value. Like most early book printing, which retained manuscript conventions of page design and decoration, particular care was taken so that printed books of hours might closely resemble "real" manuscript copies. Beauty and prestige were clearly crucial features for many owners of books of hours.

Given the conspicuous artistry that was often bestowed on books of hours, modern observers might assume that they served primarily superficial, vain, or disingenuous purposes, especially since a good number of these books' owners, and especially female owners, could only barely, if at all, read the Latin text.[6] While surely some owners valued prestige over piety, many others understood their books of hours as much more than a valuable piece of property. As the emphasis in medieval lay piety gradually shifted from public gestures to private devotion of the sort developed among monastic contemplatives, books of hours increasingly functioned in less ostentatious ways. Settled in the quiet corners of home, chapel, or garden, many users found in their book of hours not only a potent and treasured object that signified God's presence but a personal, prayerlike relationship to the page, the words, and the visual voices there. A devotional manuscript belonging to Elizabeth Scrope in the early sixteenth century contains a rubric that makes this explicit: "We schulde rede and vse books . . . for formys of preysynge and preyynge to god, to oure lady, seynt marye, and to alle the seyntes; that we myghte haue . . . vnderstondynge of god."[7] As "understanding" and pious feeling rather than simply pious action grew more valued, the role of books of hours changed, or expanded. Hilary Carey describes this shift as one from anti-intellectualism to literacy; I believe it was also a shift toward practices and values increasingly associated with women.[8]

This meditative mode of piety seemed to resonate from the pages of a sacred book; most medieval readers deemed the act of reading itself an encounter with the holy. In *In the Vineyard of the Text*, Ivan Illich reflects upon the nature of reading as understood by the twelfth-century theologian Hugh of St. Victor. In Hugh's view, one read (whether by pronouncing the words or by hearing them pronounced by another) in order to enter, to be possessed by, the Word of the text, not to extract information from it or to "use" it for one's own purposes. For Hugh, reading was a profound state of mediation between this world and God, a way of seeking wisdom through contemplation. Reading thus understood cultivated a set of qualities that Hugh described as virtues: humility, immersion in a life of quiet "exile" from mundane pursuits of fortune and power, and the renouncement of "superfluities."[9]

This ethic of reading took on a more literal dimension of exile from profane realities through a growing preference for silent reading, a technique made more possible when scribes began regularly to leave spaces between words in written texts. As silent reading diminished the status of prayer as a public act of piety, its implications moved in two directions. On one hand, silence embodied the spiritual receptivity of the kind of reading that Hugh understood. On the other hand, silence rendered the encounter between text and reader more private, a unique and particular experience.

Just as reading itself was seen as a spiritual endeavor, the initial advantages of silent reading were seen in its religious merits. While earlier medieval tradition maintained that prayer had to be voiced in order to be effective, by 1300 more compelling arguments exalted silent prayer as the more pure, more direct communion with God. Silent or "mental" prayer came from the heart, while vocal prayer was a more bodily manifestation from the lips, and therefore was somewhat diluted by the intervening noise and distracting activity.[10] Silence became an attribute of piety, accompanied by new postures for prayer such as clasped or touching hands and bowed head, gestures of humble submission. Such postures were increasingly also archetypally feminine.

Silent reading could deepen the intimacy and sense of sacred communication between the reader/pray-er and the book. It could also radically alter that relationship; silence ensured privacy and autonomy in reading, which in turn laid the groundwork for independent thought and a new sense of purpose in reading. Illich describes the ensuing revolution as one from "monastic" reading to "scholastic" reading. In the latter sense, reading becomes an act of empowerment rather than deference, undertaken to gain or acquire rather than to receive a divine presence emanating from the book. At its heart, this shift is about power. Since the mid-twelfth century, the age of emerging universities and the first stirrings of humanism in Italy, reading has been both a means of gaining and exerting power as well as of perceiving wisdom. Literacy in Latin took on a new worldly importance.

This was most explicit in the educational ideology of Italian humanism in the fourteenth and fifteenth centuries. The literacy and learning that humanism fostered were "meant neither for pure contemplation or prayer nor for the urban community writ large. Its orientation was that of practical life in society, and as such it was intended for the men most likely to hold positions of leadership."[11] As this notion of books as tools for shaping scholarly, civic, and professional identity crystallized, the two ideas of reading—one rooted in the cloistered world of pious devotion, and the other instrumental in forming and directing secular society—became increasingly gendered. Barred from participating in the public arenas of law, business, academe, and the priesthood, if women were directed toward reading at all, it would be postured in silence, reverence, and solitude—precisely the features of reading prompted by the book of hours. This is the form of reading prescribed in the early thirteenth-century *Ancrene Riwle,* the "rule" or guide written for three English anchoresses, women who literally walled themselves into cells in order to live undistracted lives of devotion and contemplation. "Spiritual joy," they were counseled, "comes from reading. . . . Often, dear sisters, you ought to say fewer fixed prayers so that you may do more reading. Reading is good prayer."[12]

The *Riwle* emphasized silence as a gesture of humility and submissive modesty, an essential feature of feminine piety. Reading was to be an act of listening, with the heart more than the ears, not an occasion to formulate a response or commentary. The male author of the *Ancrene Riwle* specifically warned against reading as a form of scholarship or intellectual exercise, since even theological insight invites teaching and recognition from others. Such a "foolish" woman would merit only censure for excessive talking, like "cackling Eve." Truly pious women were to emulate Mary, whose silent obedience was venerated.[13]

This devotional context permeated virtually every medieval and early modern prescription concerning literacy for women, whether lay or religious. In 1443 Gregorio Correr, a Venetian patrician humanist and theologian, urged the young, educated Cecelia Gonzaga to retreat within her father's house, living there as if she were in a convent, in disciplined asceticism and piety: "Pray frequently; with diligent reading feed your soul." That reading was to be circumscribed, however: "I forbid utterly the reading of secular literature, particularly the works of the poets. . . a bride of Christ may read only sacred books and ecclesiastical writers. So you must put aside your beloved Virgil. . . . Take up instead the Psalter [and], instead of Cicero, the Gospel. . . . Even if secular literature causes no harm beyond this, it leads the mind away from divine reading."[14]

The humanist goals of public leadership and rhetorical eloquence—the tool of persuasion and power—were antithetical to the medieval and renaissance ideal of women, which exalted chastity as a symbol of *resistance* to the world rather than participation in it. "An eloquent woman is never chaste," asserted a common saying of the time. If a woman read in humble submission to the wisdom and authority of the book, specifically religious texts, her chastity could be strengthened, humanists believed. This relatively enlightened view (rejecting the meaner notion that education would only fuel a woman's natural evil) premised one of the first full-scale treatises to advocate female education—albeit within the strict limits of propriety and usefulness—Juan Luis Vives's *De Institutione Foeminae Christianae,* translated into English in 1529 as *The Instruction of a Christian Woman.* Vives contended that a woman might be led to "goodnes and wysdome" through judicious reading. Echoing Correr's moral and spiritual emphasis of a half-century before, Vives counseled that because a woman "hath no charge to se to but her honestie and chastyte," she must avoid secular and imaginative literature, concentrating instead on religious works.[15]

The "feminine" sphere of reading to enhance piety was both increasingly separated from and subordinated to the expanding secular and "masculine" sphere of reading to participate in government, law, trade, science, and scholarship. But even as most women bowed their heads in the book-centered piety taught to them, they were not quite the victims of authority that one might think. Both at the more sophisticated levels of literacy enjoyed by some women religious or those in patrician and economically prosperous classes, with access to some small range of books, and at the simpler levels of "reading" practiced by the far greater numbers of women whose hands held only a book of hours, women developed their own ways of reading, of using books. They adapted the sanctioned practices of devotional reading to purposes not intended and to needs not anticipated by those who produced and procured the books for them. Within the parameters of the restricted realm allotted them—the world of piety and devotion so clearly mapped by the books of hours and their progeny of prayer books—women were able to derive emotional and even intellectual sustenance. They did so in a range of ways that mixed visual and textual literacy, inquiry and contemplation, submission to their circumscribed conditions and subversion of them. Books of hours show us the world in which many women first formulated the act of reading; the means by which they did so show us how women derived from that experience a wealth of personal value.

Caroline Walker Bynum attributes to the deprivation of sacerdotal experience the widespread phenomenon of female mysticism in the twelfth and thirteenth century, a mysticism dominated by an obsession with the Eucharist, believed to be an occasion for the ecstasy of direct union with God. The Eucharist, however, was a sacrament dispensed and controlled by priests. I believe that in the following centuries the book of hours, for those women fortunate enough to own one, appealed at least in part for similar reasons. It offered a relatively unmediated form of communication with God, a means of achieving what Bynum calls the "controllable, repeatable, coercible" union with the Logos, Christ.[16] It is no coincidence, I think, that the earliest known record of the prayers voiced at the elevation of the host is in the *Ancrene Riwle,* and that those prayers subsequently became a popular component in books of hours. Even more than receiving the Eucharist, reading a book—as Hugh and the medieval world understood the act—enabled one to enter into a spiritual state of God's presence when, where, and as often as one liked. Such direct communication helped the devout understand God less in remote king- and judge-like terms and more in terms of compassion and care. The book of hours, specifically developed for the laity, thus met the growing desire among the devout to participate more directly and actively in their own religious life, at once satisfying their spiritual hungers and diminishing their dependence on priests.

In many ways, the relationships developed with this first expressly personal book invited a certain understanding of "reading," a term less synonymous with actual literacy in the late medieval and early modern worlds than it is today. This fluid notion of functional literacy in turn yielded the spiritual and deeply private functions that held a distinctive resonance for women. For them, as for Hugh, reading meant pious meditation and reflection. This involved a subtle and complex relationship to the page that drew upon languages of color and iconography, both of images and of the letterforms. The most abstract iconographic presence was the ecclesiastical Latin of the formal prayers. Although vernacular glosses and rubrics had been incorporated into books of hours from the start (de Brailes added marginal comments and instructions in French in Susanna's book), until the early sixteenth century the liturgical texts generally remained in Latin. The devout would be familiar with the texts through countless repetition during Mass, of course, but seldom able to read it with full, literal comprehension. Because medieval thought associated the mind as much with the heart as the brain, one could "read" Latin through emotional, intuitive perceptions as much as through cerebral critical ones, aided if possible by vernacular glosses.[17] Indeed, the veiled inscrutability of Latin only added mystery and power to the experience of meditation, even if one could not translate the exact words into a vernacular.

This was especially true for women, religious as well as lay, who were rarely taught more than rudimentary Latin. Women were a significant audience for and providers of, as patrons and sometimes translators, a small but essential body of supplementary devotional literature in the vernacular intended to enhance the religious experience. In the mid-fifteenth century a manuscript called *The Myroure of our Ladye* was composed, in English, to translate and explain the Latin hours and offices to the nuns at Syon Abbey so that they might participate with better understanding; it emphasized that deepest piety is achieved through study, or "denoute redying of holy Bokes." Much as the anchoresses two hundred years earlier had been, these women were reminded that the nature and purpose of reading was for them to be strictly religious, experienced through emotional rather than intellectual labor: "study is a grete and vyolente applyeng of the harte wyth a greate & a fervuent wyll." *The Myroure* was meant not to replace the Latin but to help the sisters (and the few laywomen wealthy enough to commission copies of it) "more deuoutly and knowyngly synge yt & rede yt and say yt."[18] Here heartfelt, prayer-like immersion in the text was instrumental to achieving the spiritual enrichment these early readers sought. This posture, already recognized as feminine in the middle ages, became an increasingly gendered as well as spiritualized aspect of the practice of reading.

It must be remembered, however, that a much larger percentage of fifteenth- and sixteenth-century women could not read even a vernacular language. Especially for them, illustration was an instrumental feature of a book of hours, not only for its iconographic value but for its didactic and interpretive role. Images guided one's spiritual "feeling" of the prayers and served as visual markers, helping users find their place in the sequences and locate prayers for particular purposes. The holiness of the prayers and other texts was underscored by a hierarchical system of decorative initials and borders and of small but numerous illustrations usually depicting familiar scenes from the New Testament or the history of the early church. As the colophon of one book of hours published in 1533 by the Parisian printer Kerver explained (in French), boasting of the number and quality of its woodcut illustrations, "the picture is the writing of the laity; it is in effect so that those who do not know their letters may read and understand the secret of things."[19]

Images also depicted postures or activities to be properly associated with piety, devotion, or religious understanding. Usually the central text of a book of hours was the series known as the Hours of the Virgin, prayers that exalted Mary's piety and that were accompanied by a fairly standardized series of images from her life. In the scene of the Annunciation, Mary was frequently shown reading a book as the angel Gabriel announces that she is to be the mother of God. At this supremely holy moment, Mary's reading formed an important part of the iconographic message. Through the act of reading Mary, the perfect model of woman, submits to the Word of God and devotes herself to its inviolate message. This image must have inspired women users, who were themselves welcoming the Word of God into their hearts through their act of pious contemplation of the images and texts on the pages of their own book.[20] This mirror effect was deliberately sought by both producers and purchasers of books of hours; it was common for wealthy owners to order custom copies that included depictions of themselves and their family members in the pictures— sometimes marginally, just outside the frame of the established scene, and sometimes directly incorporated as a more intimate witness to the event or moment shown on the page.[21] But even for the many others whose copies were not so pictorially personalized, their own devotional act of contemplating the book, just as they saw Mary doing, put them into the story itself—making their own spiritual experience part of God's story too.

This image and others made more graphic the deep, cultlike devotion toward the Virgin Mary in the Middle Ages. Many women no doubt felt a particular affinity with the Mother of God because they were so often more the providers than the recipients of a mother-like love. The popular *Obsecre te* prayer usually included in a book of hours encouraged the devout to turn to the Virgin Mary as the mother they perhaps no longer had. Among the upper classes it was not uncommon for young girls of only six or eight to leave home to join a husband they had never met, or to enter a convent. Susan Groag Bell sees books of hours as an extension of the medieval mother-child relationship because they were so often a mother's special gift to her daughter. Through a book of hours, which was likely to be the child's first, perhaps only, book, a distant mother could direct her daughter's spiritual growth and education, as well as provide a surrogate source of comfort and companionship.[22]

One of the most moving depictions of this intimate connection between a woman and her book is the painting of Mary of Burgundy praying with her book of hours that is included in the exquisite little book itself, produced around 1480. Mary sits in the lower left corner of the painting, her eyes resting upon the opened book. The central scene behind her shoulder is seen as if through the window of her thoughts: The Virgin and her child, sit throned in a cathedral and attended by angels and worshipful laypersons, including Mary herself. As Virginia Reinburg interprets the scene, "what we see is Mary's visualization of the act of prayer. Through prayer Mary imagines herself in the Madonna's presence. Mary of Burgundy's closeness to the Virgin grows out of absorbed contemplation. Her Book of Hours creates a physical and psychic space for solitude and contemplation. The Virgin becomes her mother, her friend, a confidante to whom she can disclose herself, her pain, her joy."[23]

It is this role of the book of hours as a "physical and psychic space for solitude and contemplation" that has shaped one of the most enduring features of women's subsequent relationships to books. Both before and after women acquired full textual literacy, the book represented a time and place of her own in a life otherwise usually dominated by service and obedience to others. Books of hours offered not only the peace of private retreat but also active encounter with sympathetic and loving companions—Christ, the Virgin Mary, the saints. The heavily worn state of many surviving copies testifies to their intensive use (illustrations are sometimes nearly worn away from repeated stroking, for example). Those few women who could write as well as read provide more articulate testimony to this use of one's book as a site for private spiritual and emotional experience. When Mary Bohun, countess of Derby, inherited her father's manuscript psalter she made it more primerlike by adding to it some personal prayers selected, she noted, to "inspire her heart with an intense sweetness."[24]

This intimate relationship with books developed through devotional reading practices long outlasted books of hours per se, and it came to characterize attitudes toward certain secular texts as well; the book and its text were regarded as friends and confidantes. A few brief examples suggest the nature of this legacy. Grace Sherrington, born about 1552, married the "gallant but unwilling" Anthony Mildmay and subsequently lived with his Puritan parents rather than share her husband's life at Court. She steadfastly defended her preference for "solitarinesse" sheltered within her in-laws' house, explaining that "God did put into my mynde many good delights, wherein I spent my time allmost continually."[25] When in 1613 her portrait was painted, not unlike Mary of Burgundy some 130 years before, Grace Mildmay held a small prayer book.

Grace Mildmay's contemporary Lady Margaret Hoby was one of the first woman diarists in England, and her entries reflect the same inward spiritual gaze enacted through the pages of books. Lady Hoby recorded the unchanging daily routine of her Puritan endeavor toward piety. She reads, writes (usually in the sense of copying out a sermon or devotional text), and keeps a diary in her constant regimen of prayer and self-examination. Her books are her private chapels, wherein she seeks refuge from doubt and evil as well as sustenance for her religious quest.

A third early English diarist, Lady Anne Clifford (born in 1590), enjoyed greater wealth and social prominence than did either Mildmay or Hoby, but she too savored her books as her most trusted and reliable friends, especially in times of conflict with her husband (she married twice, unhappily both times) and uncle, who had usurped her inheritance. Like Mildmay, she lived in her husbands' homes but derived through privacy a sense of independent selfhood. "I lived in those my Lordes great familyes as the River Rhone runnes through the Lake of Geneva, without mingling anie part of its streams with that Lake, for I gave myself wholly to Retyredness as much as I could, in both those great families, and made good books and vertuous thoughts my companions."[20] Taught to read as part of a diligent Christian education, Mildmay, Hoby, Clifford, and other women derived meaningful comfort from their books. Their reading was active and purposeful, even if those purposes rarely had public consequence. They read to sustain their own spiritual, emotional, and intellectual world more than to exert an impact in spheres beyond home and family.

This mode of reading, historically more often associated with feminine than masculine practices, has often been characterized as a passive "consumption" of texts. Yet from the earliest opportunities of lay book ownership, books have been used effectively to address personal needs and desires. Evidence of this reader-controlled particularity of the reading experience is especially clear in the personalized manuscript books of hours. Each book's content as well as illustration was unique, reflecting the interests and needs of its owner. The book made for Susanna, the earliest known such owner, included prayers (in French) to Saints Margaret, Catherine, and the others to whom she apparently turned for special help and intercession; Claire Donovan describes these extraliturgical prayers as opportunities for deeply personal devotional interludes. Even after print, sometimes regarded as the agent of a mass culture imposed upon an easily manipulated public, individual readers retained agency and discrimination in their uses of the book. Although printed books of hours were in obvious ways far more standardized than their manuscript predecessors, they too could be quite distinctive. Not only was there sometimes considerable variation among editions in illustration and content, providing choices, but individual owners often added prayers or meditations collected from other sources and appended them to their copy of the printed book. As Duffy writes, this practice of personalizing their books of hours reveals

> a wide spectrum of lay people using and supplementing the Latin devotions of the primers with familiarity and freedom. Their Books of Hours, in which they copied the details of births and deaths just as later generations would do in the family Bible, were very much their own, and the devout scrawls which embellish or disfigure so many of the surviving *Horae* are eloquent testimony to their centrality in the devotional lives of their owners. If their Latin contents were not always fully understood in a way readily accessible to twentieth-century perceptions, they were certainly appropriated and used meaningfully by their first possessors.[27]

The relative freedom that printers enjoyed in determining the contents of books of hours (unlike the missal and bible, whose contents and dissemination were rigorously controlled by church and state authorities) enabled them to respond to buyers' interests and preferences.

One far-reaching consequence of this was the increasing inclusion of images that appealed to sensual as well as spiritual feelings. Critics have remarked on the "imaginative" qualities in the art of books of hours, embracing broader ranges of what readers might contemplate during their private hours spent with the book.[28] Intended to be viewed in solitude and privacy, unlike the public images of church art, pictures in books of hours increasingly included art that inspired meditations sometimes more voyeuristic than pious. They ranged from gruesome and macabre scenes illustrating the Office of the Dead to titillating eroticism (one favorite scene depicted Bathsheba in her bath, usually with a peeking David in the background). L. M. J. Delaisse relates this imagery to the growing influence and popularity of epic and romantic poetry, the stirrings of a culture straining to incorporate humanistic impulses. He also notes that literary manuscripts frequently resembled books of hours, particularly in their decoration, suggesting a further link between devotional texts meant to inspire piety and works of imagination meant to be understood in the heart as much or more than in the intellect.[29] Both genres would be increasingly associated with women.

A far greater loss of authoritative control occurred simply through the presence of a written text in the lives of ordinary people. That the book of hours was known as the primer in England underscores its role in hastening the shift from a pre-literate, intuitive form of reading into textual literacy itself. English books had always been less dominated by Latin than those of continental countries; fewer than half of English incunabula were in Latin, in contrast to the 83 percent of Italian incunabula, for example.[30] As early as 1490, William Caxton first printed a popular devotional text known as the "Fifteen Oes," attributed to St. Bridgit and so-named because it consisted of fifteen prayers beginning with the salutary "O," and it quickly became a standard addition, in English, to the central Latin texts of primers. Caxton's market was primarily the prosperous merchants and urban professionals in England who had the resources and the motivations to own books—in English. Their wives and daughters, according to Lotte Hellinga, were no less a significant market for vernacular reading. Even so, a fully vernacular book of hours appeared relatively late in England; editions in French had been produced since the 1490s, and vernacular versions were common in Germany and the Netherlands. It was not until 1527 that the first primer with an English title was issued, and 1534 the first all-English primer appeared. The bilingual primers circulating in England in the 1530s may have maintained the orthodox content of the core of the book of hours, but they also cleared the path for what Eamon Duffy called the "Trojan horse" of the vernacular into the Catholic liturgy and into the daily lives of the devout.[31]

By introducing the printed vernacular and, more fundamentally, the practice and significance of reading into private, daily life, the book of hours paved the way for the breakthrough into true literacy achieved by many through the proliferation of Protestant vernacular texts in the sixteenth and seventeenth centuries. Yet many Protestants remained wary of the book of hours, regarding it as a lingering stronghold of papist "tomfoolery," as Luther called it. Dismayed at the great popularity of printed German versions of the books of hours, known as the *Hortulus animae* (Garden of the Spirit) or *Paradisus animae* (Paradise of the Soul), Luther countered in 1522 with his own vernacular personal prayer book. He fumed that books of hours "are puffed up with promises of indulgences and come out with decorations in red ink and pretty titles." He urged "everyone to break away from using the Bridget prayers and any others which are ornamented with indulgences or rewards" and to instead rely upon the "plain, ordinary" Lord's Prayer. In fact, Luther's *Personal Prayer Book* shrewdly resembled the Catholic books of hours it criticized (later editions were decorated in red ink) but its contents were recast in a purely biblical, evangelical context. Saints and the Virgin Mary were excluded or radically demoted. [32]

In both Catholic and Protestant societies women's reading was for the most part successfully channeled into the quiet, acceptable streams of piety. Of course not all women accepted lightly the constraints imposed by such strict devotional fare. Scholars have brought to light an impressive array of women who chafed under the oppressive restrictions of their day. This important recovery of the activities of literate women who resisted their conditions should not obscure, however, full considerations of those many more women who—like Susanna, Mary of Burgundy, and Margaret Hoby—read with Christian devotion, apparently acquiescing to the limited parameters of their lives. In fact, women's devotional reading might be compared to the critically problematic genre of romance reading today. Both genres are fundamentally conservative, modeling and affirming traditional patriarchal social roles and values. Both are seen to victimize the women who read them by providing a fantasy or otherworldly realm that distracts them from and disguises the failings of "real" life.

Women's religious reading, exemplified by their encounter with a book of hours, might be understood in terms similar to those that

Janice Radway proposes in her analysis of women's romance fiction reading in modern-day America. Despite what at first glance appears to be merely the "ritual consumption of patriarchal clichés dispensed by others," she contends that women readers of the romance genre in fact alter the mass-made books to suit their own purposes. Radway finds their use of the books less a passive and uncritical consumption of mass culture than "mildly subversive" uses of the book as a private place, a barrier against the demands of family and domestic responsibilities.[33] She sees such reading as a woman's means of addressing her own needs, interests, and desires. Radway's ethnographic research into the practices of romance reading confirms what historians of book culture increasingly assert, that throughout history readers have appropriated even such straightforward and seemingly formulaic texts as almanacs and saints' lives and books of hours to suit their own emotional, intellectual, and social conditions.

The relationships that medieval and early modern women developed with what was likely their first book, a book of hours or similar devotional prayer book, foreshadow the nature and purposes of much of women's subsequent reading. Its legacies include the qualities that Radway recognized at the core of contemporary romance reading: the book as companion and source of comfort and self-care; reading as a form of privacy and solitude; reading as a means of empathetic community with others; and reading as a way of achieving centrality in the story—whether of this world or of the next. Books of hours provided thousands of women not only the heightened spirituality they craved but also sanctuary and nurturance in the act of reading itself. It is with books of hours that I believe women first exercised the patterns of adaptation and appropriation that historians, literary critics, and others have detected in subsequent women's ways of reading.

ENDNOTES

1. The actual contents of books of hours varied considerably according to regional and local liturgical customs as well as individual owners' preferences, but the genre typically included the following, all in Latin: a calendar marking saints' days and religious festivals; the four gospel lessons extracted from the Mass service book (the missal); the Hours of the Virgin (Matins, Lauds, Prime, Terce, Sext, None, Vespers, and Compline); the somewhat shorter Hours of the Cross; the "Obsecro te" and "O intemerata" prayers to Mary; and the Penitential Psalms. Additional prayers, sometimes in vernacular languages, usually followed. For an introduction to the content of books of hours, see Roger S. Wieck, ed., *Time Sanctified: The Book of Hours in Medieval Art and Life* (New York: George Braziller, 1988); and Claire Donovan, *The de Brailes Hours: Shaping the Book of Hours in Thirteenth-Century Oxford* (Toronto: University of Toronto Press, 1991).

2. Claire Donovan describes this manuscript as a "perfect devotional manual for a laywoman" because of several features of its design and layout: its small size (7 by 6 inches), large script, plentiful illustrations (111), and emphasis on the Virgin Mary through its central cycle of prayers (ibid., 23).

3. Wieck, *Time Sanctified,* 29.

4. For statistics of books of hours production, see Henri-Jean Martin and Roger Chartier, eds., *Histoire de l'editione francaise* (Paris: Promodis, 1982); Eamon Duffy, *The Stripping of the Altars: Traditional Religion in England, c. 1400-c. 1580* (New Haven, Conn.: Yale University Press, 1992), 211-212; and Mary S. Erler, "*The Maner to Lyue Well* and the Coming of English in François Regnault's Primers of the 1520s and 1530s," *The Library,* 6th ser., 6 (1984): 232.

5. Roger Chartier, "Culture as Appropriation: Popular Cultural Uses in Early Modern France," in *Understanding Popular Culture: Europe from the Middle Ages to the Nineteenth Century,* ed. Steven L. Kaplan (Berlin, New York, and Amsterdam: Mounton, 1984), 239-40; R. A. Houston, *Literacy in Early Modern Europe: Culture and Education, 1500-1800* (London and New York: Longman, 1988), 188; Duffy, *Stripping of the Altars,* 209.

6. Calculations of medieval and early modern literacy are notoriously slippery: evidence is elusive, definitions are problematic (many were able to read but not write), and distinctions between skills in Latin and in vernacular languages are not always maintained. David Cressy, however,

estimates lay literacy in England in 1500, for example, at around 5 percent for men and 1 percent for women. The latter would have been primarily in vernacular languages. See David Cressy, *Literacy and the Social Order* (Cambridge: Cambridge University Press, 1980), 177.

7. Ann M. Hutchison, "Devotional Reading in the Monastery and in the Late Medieval Household," in *De Cella in Seculum: Religious and Secular Life and Devotion in Late Medieval England,* ed. Michael G. Sargent (Cambridge: D. S. Brewer, 1989), 224.

8. Hilary M. Carey, "Devout Literate Laypeople and the Pursuit of the Mixed Life in Later Medieval England," *Journal of Religious History* 14 (1987): 361-81.

9. Ivan Illich, *In the Vineyard of the Text: A Commentary to Hugh's Didascalicon* (Chicago: University of Chicago Press, 1993), 124, 15-6.

10. See Paul Saenger, "Books of Hours and the Reading Habits of the Later Middle Ages," in *The Culture of Print: Power and the Uses of Print in Early Modern Europe*, ed. Roger Chartier, trans. Lydia G. Cochrane (Cambridge: Polity Press, 1989).

11. Harvey J. Graff, *The Legacies of Literacy* (Bloomington: Indiana University Press, 1987), 80.

12. M. B. Salu, trans., *The Ancrene Riwle* (Exeter: University of Exeter Press, 1990), 127.

13. Ibid., 28-9.

14. Margaret L. King and Albert Rabil, Jr., eds., *Her Immaculate Hand: Selected Works By and About the Woman Humanists of Quattrocentro Italy* (Binghamton, N.Y.: Medieval and Renaissance Texts and Studies, 1983), 102-3.

15. Juan Luis Vives, *Instruction of a Christian Woman*, trans. Richard Hyrde, in *Distaves and Dames: Renaissance Treatises for and about Women,* ed. Diane Bornstein (Delmar, N.Y.: Scholar's Facsimiles and Reprints, 1974), Bii*r.*

16. Caroline Walker Bynum, *Jesus as Mother: Studies in the Spirituality of the High Middle Ages* (Berkeley: University of California Press, 1982), 135-6, 285.

17. Saenger, "Books of Hours," 145. See also Sandra Penketh, "Women and Books of Hours," in *Women and the Book: Assessing the Visual Evidence,* ed. Jane H. M. Taylor and Lesley Smith (Toronto: University of Toronto Press, 1996), 270.

18. J. H. Blunt, *The Myroure of oure Ladye,* Early English Text Society Series, no. 19 (London: Trubner, 1873), 64-5.

19. For an excellent discussion of pictures as the language of the illiterate, see Michael Camille, "Seeing and Reading: Some Visual Implications of Medieval Literacy and Illiteracy," *Art History* 8 (1985): 26-49.

20. There has been much attention paid to the significance of Mary portrayed as a reader while God, Christ, and male saints are often portrayed writing. Beginning in the fourteenth century Mary is often shown being taught to read (but not to write) by her mother, St. Ann, using a book of hours or similar prayer book as a text. This emphasis on Mary as a reader rather than a writer has led Susan Schibanoff to argue that this image helped to discourage the few learned female writers at the time. See "Botticelli's Madonna del Magnificat: Constructing the Woman Writer in Early Humanist Italy," *PMLA* 109, 2 (1994): 190-206.

21 Claire Donovan notes that in six of the eight earliest, thirteenth-century English books of hours, their laywomen owners are portrayed in the book (*de Brailes Hours,* 152).

22. Susan Groag Bell, "Medieval Women Book Owners: Arbiters of Lay Piety and Ambassadors of Culture," *Signs* 7, 4 (1982): 763.

23. Virginia Reinburg, "Prayer and the Book of Hours," in *Time Sanctified: The Book of Hours in Medieval Art and Life,* ed. Roger Wieck (New York: George Braziller, 1988), 44.

24. Jeremy Catto, "Religion and the English Nobility in the Later Fourteenth Century," in *History and Imagination: Essays in Honor of H. R. Trevor-Roper,* ed. Hugh Lloyd-Jones, Valerie Pearl, and Blair Worden (London: Duckworth, 1981), 49.

25. Dorothy M. Meads, ed., *Diary of Lady Margaret Hoby, 1599-1605* (London: Routledge, 1930), 52.

26. D. J. H. Clifford, ed., *The Diaries of Lady Anne Clifford* (Wolfeboro Falls, N.H.: Alan Sutton, 1991), 94.

27. Duffy, *Stripping of the Altars,* 225. See also Mary C. Erler, *Women, Reading, and Piety in Late Medieval England* (Cambridge: Cambridge University Press, 2002).

28. See Michael Camille, *Image on the Edge: The Margins of Medieval Art* (Cambridge, Mass.: Harvard University Press, 1992); and Martha Driver, "Pictures in Print: Late Fifteenth- and Early Sixteenth-Century English Religious Books for Lay Readers," in *De Cella in Seculum: Religious and*

Secular Life and Devotion in Late Medieval England, ed. Michael G.
Sargent (Cambridge: D. S. Brewer, 1989).

29. L.J.M. Delaisse, "The Importance of Books of Hours for the History
of the Medieval Book," in *Gatherings in Honor of Dorothy E. Miner,* ed.
Ursula E. McCracken, Lilian M.C. Randall, and Richard H. Randall, Jr.
(Baltimore: Walters Art Gallery, 1974), 224.

30. Rudolf Hirsch, *Printing, Selling, and Reading: 1450-1550* (Wiesbaden:
Otto Harrassowitz, 1974), 134.

31. Lotte Hellinga, "Importation of Books Printed on the Continent into
England and Scotland before c. 1520," in *Printing the Written Word: The
Social History of Books, circa 1450-1520,* ed. Sandra Hindman (Ithaca,
N.Y.: Cornell University Press, 1991), 219-20; Edwyn Birchenough, "The
Prymer in English," *The Library,* 4th ser. 18 (1938): 181; Duffy, *Stripping
of the Altars,* 222.

32. Luther's prayer book was first published in June 1522. Its popularity was
such that nine editions appeared that year, and a total of twenty-four
editions were published before 1531. Clearly intended for the common
reader, it was priced (with paper covers) at only twenty pfennig. See
Personal Prayer Book, ed and trans. Martin H. Bertram, in *Luther's Works,*
ed. Gustav K Wiencke (Philadelphia: Fortress, 1968): 43: 11, 12-3, 7.

33. Janice Radway, "Reading Is Not Eating: Mass Produced Literature
and the Theoretical, Methodological, and Political Consequences of a
Metaphor," *Book Research Quarterly* 2 (Fall 1986): 13-4. See also Radway's
Reading the Romance: Women, Patriarchy, and Popular Culture (Chapel
Hill: University of North Carolina Press, 1984).

Chapter 5

Luther's Early Thought on Social Welfare

Samuel Torvend

If there is any image that captured the imagination of the women and men who were caught up in that tumultuous and complex phenomenon called the reformations of the sixteenth century, one might have recourse to the image of a stream or spring of fresh, flowing water. While many reformers of the period speak of light breaking into a time of darkness or the dawn emerging from a seemingly endless night, their constant return to the image of a spring or font of clean, rushing water remained central. There should be no surprise in this. The reformers of church and society in northern Europe were deeply influenced by their humanist colleagues in the south who pointed to the classical inheritance of antiquity and said, in effect, let us turn to the sources—*ad fontes*; to the springs—and so embrace and establish in our time the Golden Age of our ancestors. When the northern reformers of Christianity looked to the past, however, their eyes did not fall first on the works of Aristotle and Plato, Cicero and Seneca, but the texts of the Jewish and Christian Scriptures and the writings of the Hellenistic and Roman bishops and teachers who were among the first commentators on the significance of Scripture.

CLEARING AWAY DEBRIS AROUND THE SPRING

Convinced that they lived in a religious system filled with corruption, these reformers, all of whom began their lives as baptized, Catholic Christians, were of one mind that the authentic springs of Christian teaching and spirituality had been successively clogged, polluted, and obscured by a tangle of almost impenetrable branches that had grown steadfastly since at least the twelfth and thirteenth centuries.[1] To engage in the process of reform, then, was to pull away the overgrown branches of papal control, to pick up and cast aside the rocks of churchly abuses, to uproot and burn the pernicious weed of late medieval teaching which obscured access to the spring of God's own freely flowing life.[2] To clear away what they believed was the accumulated bracken of the previous four hundreds, the reformers found in their reading of Scripture the clippers, the shovel, the hoe that would reveal what Luther called "the pure spring of the Gospel."

Indeed, the reformers' use of the literary metaphor of the free and flowing spring was often juxtaposed next to visual images of Luther and his colleagues working in vineyards.[3] In the center of one such image, Lucas Cranach the Younger has placed a large fountain spilling forth running water being channeled by little canals—dug by the reformers—throughout the vineyard so that all the vines might grow. In contrast to the verdant land of the reform, one can see in the same painting parched and ruined fields presided over by the pope, who watches as monks and friars cut down and burn the vines, a veritable wasting of the plantation. This artistic image of evangelical propaganda underscores the reformers' insistence that the water is to be shared; it is to flow freely though the landscape of what they knew as a Christian society.[4]

Peter Matheson, the Australian Reformation scholar, notes that "the Reformers did not dredge Scriptures for proof texts . . . Rather, when we read their sermons and pamphlets we find biblical personalities and images swimming up to the surface of their minds. An . . . eruption of the biblical imagination of the patriarchs, prophets, psalmists and apostles took place."[5] I would say it this way: the reformers became newly aware of the dangerous and invigorating memory of the Scriptures and allowed that memory to flow throughout the imaginative landscape of their culture. In particular, they recovered the "earthy humanity" of the Scriptures and the humanity of the earth-born Christ so that, for instance, a contemporary German ruler could see in the mirror of the Hebrew Bible not only the nobility of his office but also the tragic consequences of Israel's rulers who failed to govern with justice for the destitute or German peasants might recognize in the mirror of the New Testament the poor and hungry peasants favored by Jesus. Such acute reading of the biblical text, I would claim, allowed the reformers to recognize in their own age the poor and the hungry poor theologically as the recipients of Christ's welfare and socially as persons in need of the Christian community's welfare, its food and drink, its water and bread.

EARLY CONCERN FOR THE POOR

That theological claims always possess social implications was not lost on those who led the first wave of reform in 16th century Germany, namely Martin Luther, priest and professor of theology, and his colleague in the classics, Philip Melanchthon. Indeed, it would seem that Luther's initial foray into public life—his invitation to the university faculty to debate 95 contested points—can be read not only as theological document but also an ethical and economic one. For instance, in his 41st thesis,[6] he argues that the grave difficulty with the sale of indulgences is that they will lead people not only to think that they can somehow bribe the deity into giving them preferential treatment but also distract them from a truly good work. "Christians should be taught," he writes, "that [the person] who gives to the poor or lends to the needy does a better action than if he or she purchases indulgences" (Thesis 48). They should be taught, he adds, that the person who fails to help the poor, even though he or she may purchase an indulgence, gains nothing but the anger of God (Thesis 45). Indeed, when he speaks of the pope who has sanctioned the sales of indulgences and will use the profit gained in order to build a new St. Peter's, Luther levels a stinging indictment of religious leaders who line their pockets with the money of the poor: "Christians should be taught," he writes, "that, if the pope knew the [monetary] exactions of the indulgence [-sellers], he would rather [have] the church of St. Peter . . . burned down to ashes than be built with the skin, flesh, and bones of his sheep,"(Thesis 50) the poor. It would be a better work to sell off the church's material goods and repay the poor who have been "conjured" by religious entrepreneurs [i.e., the sellers of indulgences] (Thesis 51). The indictment is clear: church leaders welcome the patronage of the wealthy in their building projects but fail to direct them toward the poor who rightfully deserve their "investment," while the poor are duped into believing that they must give what little money they have to church agents in hopes of an other-worldly reward. They may need bread to survive, but they receive only a piece of paper.

Food for the Poor

Needless to say, Jews and Christians know something about bread, that is, about food. Both are meal keeping communities: the Sabbath meal, the Passover seder, and the Christian Eucharist construct meaning, albeit in different ways, yet all three meal practices suggest who gives food, how food is to be shared, and who needs food. As a scholar of the Hebrew Bible and as a priest who presided at the Mass, Luther himself knew something about the history, practice, and theology of food distribution as presented in the central texts of both Jews and Christians. It should come as little surprise, then, that his modest advocacy on behalf of the poor in 1517 would be expanded in 1519 in his treatise on the Eucharist and the brotherhoods,[7] an essay written not for clergy but for laypeople and dedicated to a laywoman, Margaret, Duchess of Brunswick, an essay, furthermore, that would eventually win him the condemnation of Pope Leo X six months after its publication.

In this seminal work, he began a criticism that would endure throughout his life, namely, that religion or faith is unhealthy when it serves only the interests of the individual or the group, when it is inner-directed rather than being outer-directed toward public life and what he quaintly but forcefully calls "the neighbor in need." At the time in which he wrote the essay, the city of Wittenberg boasted twenty lay religious fraternities—small in comparison to the 127 listed in Hamburg but nevertheless a sizable number relative to the population of the city. Tracing their origins to the German *Schutzgilden*, the religious fraternities of the late Middle Ages were founded to meet the spiritual and social needs of their members, both during life and at death. In this regard, a lay brotherhood also functioned as burial society, the members annually paying dues so that at death two services would be provided: a proper burial Mass and the recitation of a certain number of pre-paid Masses to ensure that the deceased was released more rapidly from the purgative state of the afterlife into union with God. Of course, those with "wealth" would benefit far more rapidly from their "investment" in this financial "service" than those who possessed more modest means. What remained, so Luther observed, were the poor who had no means to purchase temporal or spiritual favors. If they suffered in life, they would certainly suffer much longer in death.

I would suggest that what Luther offers in this essay is a question, one that asks how religious practice might inform public policy. His initial criticism of the fraternities is that they ostensibly collect funds from their members in order to assist their own in need. "The brotherhood," he writes, "is supposed to be a special convocation of good works; instead it has become a collection of money for beer."[8] Well, we might demure and ask, "What's a thirsty German to do?" Yet the records of the city of Wittenberg reveal enormous fines directed at the fraternities because of the damage caused to public and private property after weekly meetings that turned into drunken rampages through the city streets. This complaint is minor, however, in comparison to the other charges he brings against this remarkably popular institution of late medieval and early modern life. While Luther recognizes—with some hesitation—the good that can accrue to workers who are organized for the sake of promoting their particular craft, he offers sharp criticism of the inner-focused character of these associations: they can, in other words, only care for their own well being. "In the [brotherhoods]," he writes, "[people] learn to seek their own good, to love themselves, to be faithful only to one another, and to presume to stand higher before God than others."[9] Such groups, he suggests, are a case study in group selfishness, a lobbyist's dream come true, except in this case, the object of such concerted effort by the association is not focused on a legislator or ruler but—if one can imagine—the divine ruler and judge of the living and the dead.

Charitable Giving and Human Need

The problem with the brotherhoods as well as the monastic communities that served as late medieval centers of social welfare, he argues, is that while they might be a source of food for the hungry, they actually give their members the impression that the *act* of giving itself was more important than the person in need. "It was not the poor person who counted, "writes Louis Chatellier in his study of early modern charity, "but the act accomplished in the sight of God or for the good of the [institution of the] church."[10] Of course, this was the dynamic that drove Luther and his colleagues to utter distraction and invective: one did not need to please the deity; in fact, according to Luther, one could not please or appease the deity. Such appeasement is what children attempt to do in order to win the favor of their parents or avert their anger. But if one could not please the deity, one could do this: one could, he writes, "gather provisions and feed a tableful of poor people."[11] At first hearing, the suggestion sounds sweet, almost too sweet. But one instruction is worth noting: Luther calls for those who have adequate means to share food at table with those in need, that is, to share a meal with others as other human beings who can become knowable. The emphasis shifts, in this simple instruction, from the act of giving to the needs of the person, from food as commodity to be consumed to food as unexpected gift to be shared between people.[12]

Religious Practice as Model for Social Welfare

Thus, what we begin to discern in *The Blessed Sacrament* is a line of thought from which Luther will never depart as he responds in essays and letters to the questions raised by citizens or city councils that come to embrace what he calls "evangelical" reforms. Put simply, the meal practice of the Christian community—its Eucharist or Supper—becomes the model through which he develops his thought on social welfare. If, in the late medieval world in which he was raised, the primary focus of one's life was preparation for one's death in order to secure a favorable disposition from the deity for all eternity, Luther reverses the movement by arguing that the primary function of religion, for him Christianity, is to move one into this world that is filled with remarkable needs. The Mass—the central meal practice of Christianity—is thus deconstructed of an older meaning in order to be reconstructed. For Luther and his colleagues, it can no longer be viewed as a means through which one approaches a distant ruler or judge, as if participation in its actions would somehow secure a better outcome for the individual. Rather, it is the means through which food and drink are shared with humans in this world so that they might learn to share food and drink with the hungry poor of their own communities. Luther thus holds religious practice and social welfare together, the former as the model for the latter:

> When you have partaken of this sacrament [the Lord's Supper], you must in turn share the misfortunes of the fellowship. Here your heart must go out in love and learn that this is a sacrament of love. As love and support are given you, you in turn must render love and support to Christ in his needy ones. You must feel with sorrow all the unjust suffering of the innocent, with which the world is everywhere filled to overflowing. You must fight, work, pray, and—if you cannot do more —have heartfelt sympathy. [For] here the saying of Paul is fulfilled, "Bear one another's burdens, and so fulfill the law of Christ" [Gal. 6:2].[13]

Such a theological and ethical connection is rooted, for Luther, in the practice of the early Christian community. "In times past," he writes, " this [meal] was so properly used, and the people were taught to understand this fellowship so well, that they gathered food and material goods in the church, and there distributed among those who were in need." He continues: "We have a vestige of his practice in the little word 'collect' in the mass which means a general collection, just as a common fund is gathered to be given to the poor."[14]

Social Welfare Practice

Indeed, we know that once monastic communities closed or were suppressed in regions of Germany that accepted the "Lutheran reform," established centers of social welfare began to vanish. The responsibility for feeding the hungry, for supporting a network of public social initiatives, was accepted by or transferred to parish or town councils. In 1522, three years after the publication of his essay on the Eucharist and the brotherhoods, members of the city parish of Leisnig, near Leipzig, wrote Luther, asking him for advice on how they might organize their worship and establish a common chest from which they could serve a variety of social needs.[15] In his preface to their agreement on a common chest, he claims that the goods of the church are common property for all who are in need.[16] Such goods are not to be controlled by rulers, monks, or clerics but by the people and their representatives so that there might be an equitable distribution of food and drink, clothing, other provisions, and money to all who are in need. Such distribution is to take place at the end of the Sunday service so that the people might come to recognize that the practice of receiving food and drink (that is, bread and wine) in the Mass is to be extended to those who have material need. Support of the common chest is the responsibility of "every noble, townsman and peasant who shall according to his ability and means, remit in taxes for himself, his wife, and his children a certain sum of money to the chest each year."[17] There is to be no begging, Luther argues, because the people are to know all the poor as their neighbors and be able to discern who is in real need. Thus, within this civic context, individual need was to be clearly recognized and met.

Conclusion

In *New American Blues: A Journey Through Poverty to Democracy*, his book on the humanities, political life, and poverty in America, Earl Shorris claims that "Martin Luther may have reinvented [social] welfare but . . . [later] Protestant clergy never washed the feet of the poor."[18] Indeed, Luther himself wondered if such social welfare initiatives would ever take hold and actually work.[19] We do know, as Carter Lindberg makes clear, that "[he] was ever ready to serve the poor and oppressed who constantly presented themselves to him" throughout his life.[20] His correspondence, treatises, sermons, and programs manifest a person who, it seems, was deeply engaged in the social crises of his turbulent time, some of which, one could argue, he himself seemed to have created. And this, too: we have the evidence, a body of work, despite the charge of "conservative ethics" leveled by some commentators against him,[21] that Luther's contribution to an urban and communal social ethic might have been greater than previously imagined, a contribution still undiscovered. The tantalizing question remains, asked by the skeptical social historian in each of us: did it make any difference to those who held no social, economic, political, religious, or educational privilege? Were their feet actually washed, their thirst quenched, their hunger satisfied?

ENDNOTES

1. "The obvious decline of the late Renaissance church was the latest stage in a grad-
    ual process which had been going on since . . . the twelfth century [namely], the
    corruption of Christian doctrine and ethics. The distinctive ideas which thinkers
    such as Luther and Calvin held to [supported the claim] that Christian faith and
    practice had been obscured, if not totally perverted, through a series of develop-
    ments in the Middle Ages. According to these [reformers], it was time to reverse
    these changes, to undo the work of the Middle Ages, in order to return to a purer,
    fresher version of Christianity which beckoned to them across the centuries. The
    reformers echoed the cry of the humanists: 'back to the sources' (*ad fontes*), back
    to the Golden Age of the church, in order to reclaim its freshness, purity and vi-
    tality in the midst of a period of stagnation and corruption," in Alister McGrath,
    Reformation Thought (Oxford: Blackwell, 1999), 3-4.

2. "One must teach and believe: 'I must and will hear and seek no work, no worship
    of God, no spirituality, no holy life other than that of this [human] Christ, or that
    which he transmitted to the apostles, and the apostles, in turn, transmitted to the
    preachers. When I hear these, I hear Christ himself; and when I hear Christ, I hear
    the Father.' Thus all must be woven together and interrelated. And if the relation-
    ship is right, all must follow a straight line. It is like tracing and following a river
    or a brook to its source, the spring. I drink the water from the pipes. It comes from
    the brooklet; and this, in the end, flows from the spring. . . . Thus it all proceeds
    as God has arranged it: and *I constantly see and hear [Christ] through the pipes if I
    follow the brooklet which flows from Christ and leads to the spring,*" in *Sermons on
    the Gospel of St. John* in *Luther's Works* [hereafter *LW*] 24 (St. Louis: Concordia,
    1961) 70-1, emphasis mine. The Gospel of John was Luther's favorite, the only
    gospel that he commented on in its entirety. The symbol of the spring appears in
    this gospel. "Even without unraveling the meaning of Jesus' symbolic actions and
    metaphorical speech, something basic about God is revealed through Jesus' min-
    istry in John's Gospel. His words and deeds are consistently intended to benefit
    his audience. He does not, for instance, curse his enemies or work 'punishment
    miracles' that bring affliction upon others . . . if John presents Jesus as the one who
    has come to reveal what God is like, then the first things Jesus reveals is that God
    loves the world and desires to bless and to save rather than to punish or condemn
    (John 3:16-7). The metaphors and miracles all point to this, summoning positive
    images of light and life, seeing and healing, God is not here likened to a raging
    fire that threatens to destroy the undeserving (Deut. 4:24). *All the images chosen
    are inviting: running water (4:10-5), an open door (10-9), bread (6:32-5) and wine
    (2:1-11), birth (3:3-5) and resurrection (11:23-5).* In fact, the Johannine writings
    present God as one who is not to be feared (compare Matt. 10:28), as one whose
    'perfect love casts out fear' (1 John 4:18)," in Mark Powell, *Fortress Introduction
    to the Gospels* (Minneapolis: Fortress, 1998), 132.

3. See, for example, Lucas Cranach the Younger's *The Vineyard of the Lord* (1569), located in St. Mary's Church, Wittenberg.

4. Luther uses the image of the church-as-vineyard to describe the "gushing forth of the Gospel" creating new growth and life while Pope Leo X described Luther as a "wild boar" wrecking havoc in "the Lord's vineyard." The text from John reads: "I am the true vine, and my Father is the vinegrower. He removes every branch in me that bears no fruit. Every branch that bears fruit he prunes to make it bear more fruit. You have already been cleansed by the word that I have spoken to you. Abide in me as I abide in you. Just as the branch cannot bear fruit by itself unless it abides in the vine, neither can you unless you abide in me. I am the vine, you are the branches. Those who abide in me and I in them bear much fruit, because apart from me you can do nothing. Whoever does not abide in me is thrown away like a branch and withers; such branches are gathered, thrown into the fire, and burned. If you abide in me, and my words abide in you, ask for whatever you wish, and it will be done for you. My Father is glorified by this, that you bear much fruit and become my disciples" (15:1-8).

5. Peter Matheson, *The Imaginative World of the Reformation* (Minneapolis: Fortress, 2001), 42.

6. *LW* 31: 25-33.

7. "The Blessed Sacrament of the Holy and True Body of Christ, and the Brotherhoods," in *LW* 35:49-73.

8. *LW* 35:68.

9. *LW* 35:70.

10. Louis Chatellier, *The Europe of the Devout: The Catholic Reformation and the Formation of a New Society* (Cambridge: Cambridge University Press, 1989), 133.

11. *LW* 35:68.

12. Martha Stortz, "Practicing What It Means: Welfare Reform and the Lord's Supper," *Currents in Theology and Mission* 26:1 (February 1999): 30.

13. *LW* 35:54.

14. *LW* 35:57.

15. "Ordinance for a Common Chest, Preface to the Fraternal Agreement on the Common Chest of the Entire Assembly at Leisnig, 1523," in *LW* 45:161-194.

16. *LW* 45:173.

17. *LW* 45:192.

18. Earl Shorris, *New American Blues: A Journey Through Poverty to Democracy* (New York: W.W. Norton, 1997), 205.

19. *LW* 45:167.

20. Carter Lindberg, *Beyond Charity: Reformation Initiatives for the Poor* (Minneapolis: Fortress, 1993), 119.

21. For instance, Ernst Troeltsch, *The Social Teaching of the Christian Churches*, trans. Olive Wyon (New York: The Macmillan Company, 1931), and Reinhold Niebuhr, *The Nature and Destiny of Man* (New York: C. Scribner's Sons, 1943). Carter Lindberg offers his critique of Troeltsch and Niebuhr in "Reformation initiatives for social welfare: Luther's influence at Leisnig," *Annual of the Society of Christian Ethics* (1987): 79-99.

CHAPTER 6

LUTHERANS, JESUITS, AND JEWS: CONFESSIONAL CONFLICT IN LATE REFORMATION HILDESHEIM

Michael J. Halvorson

On June 16, 1593, Heinrich Heshusius entered the city of Hildesheim in North Germany to enroll as the town's Lutheran superintendent. Heshusius had been nominated by Martin Luther's successors in Wittenberg, formally called by the town council of Hildesheim, and was to receive a regular salary from the Hildesheim municipal government and the cathedral church of St. Andreas, which had enjoyed continuous Lutheran worship since the Schmalkald Wars 50 years earlier.[1] As a superintendent, Heinrich Heshusius would be the town's major spiritual leader and ecclesiastical administrator, responsible for managing the city's Lutheran pastors, preaching and celebrating the sacraments, and exercising church discipline throughout the region, so that the community might be protected against vice and immorality, and especially the inroads of confessional rivals such as Roman Catholics, Calvinists, and Anabaptists.

Heshusius arrived with a particular brand of enthusiasm for his work. Over the previous decade he had been schooled in the methods of biblical criticism and taught the current subtleties of Lutheran dogma, he had implemented mission strategies for expanding the Lutheran church, and he had sharpened his rhetorical and polemical skills through public disputations and debates.[2] Heshusius had served as a professor of philosophy at the University of Helmstedt, he had

59

worked as a church superintendent in the city of Tonne in Thuringia, and he was near the completion of a doctorate in theology from the University of Rostock. In addition, Heinrich Heshusius was the son of the well-known Lutheran theologian Tilemann Heshusius, who had spent much of his career involved in bitter struggles not only with Roman Catholics, Anabaptists, and Calvinists, but also fellow Lutherans. Most recently, Tilemann had been arguing with the architects of the 1577 Formula of Concord, who sought to unite German Lutherans under a comprehensive statement of faith and doctrine.[3] Indeed, considering the father's long theological legacy, the first thing that Mayor Joachim Brandis asked Heinrich Heshusius when he arrived in 1593 was whether he agreed with his father's criticisms of the Formula of Concord and, in particular, his father's novel teachings about the nature of Christ?[4] Most importantly, could Heinrich join the council and the residents of Hildesheim in accepting the unmodified Formula as the definitive statement of what Lutherans believed and confessed?

When Heinrich consented and promised to defend the Formula with his words, deeds, and life, both men were undoubtedly relieved.[5] A close working relationship between the mayor and the town's superintendent would be crucial for clarifying Lutheran doctrine, establishing order in the region, and enforcing social discipline. Not only would Heinrich Heshusius turn out to be a different theologian than his father, but the 1590s would turn out to be a different era in the development of Lutheran belief and practice. Replacing the freewheeling debates about the legacy of Luther in the middle decades of the 16th century, and especially the tendency among some Lutheran theologians to make concessions to Reformed princes and traditions, the Lutheran pastors of the late 16th and early 17th centuries increasingly emphasized strict Lutheran orthodoxy and conformity in the face of religious and political rivals.

Confessional orthodoxy was paramount in Hildesheim because, as mayor Brandis further explained, the town had recently been rocked by a series of religious disputes. On March 8, 1592, a group of Lutheran pastors had formally petitioned the town council to track the activities of Jesuit priests in the area. According to the pastors, the Jesuits were dangerous newcomers who were criticizing Lutheran dogma, expanding their missionary efforts, and threatening the moral fabric of the city.[6] The current crisis had long been anticipated, because Hildesheim was situated within a Roman Catholic bishopric ruled by a prince-bishop who enjoyed both ecclesiastical and secular authority. Although the 1555 Peace of Augsburg granted the city of Hildesheim a certain measure of spiritual autonomy, including the ability to choose its own religion, the current prince-bishop, Ernst II of Bavaria (r. 1573-1612), was not content with his minority position.[7] After all, Hildesheim had long been the seat of the local bishop, and it remained an important destination for Catholic pilgrims seeking spiritual renewal and healing. The Catholic cathedral in Hildesheim had been founded in the 9th century by Charlemagne's son, Louis the Pious, and the cathedral held the relics of Bishop Bernward (r. 993-1022), which it continues to possess to this day. As a result, Ernst II saw Hildesheim as an important nexus of Catholic tradition and vitality, and he coordinated his effort to support Hildesheim Jesuits with the Catholic dukes of Wittelsbach, who were engaged in Counter Reformation activities throughout the Holy Roman Empire.[8]

What made matters more startling for the mayor and the Lutheran pastors was that Ernst II had also been encouraging Jews to settle in Hildesheim, and this initiative seemed like another prong in the prince-bishop's attack. Specifically, Ernst II had elevated a talented Jewish financier named Nathan Schay in his court, and the bishop had rewarded Nathan's service by allowing the Schay family and several other Jews permission to relocate and settle in Hildesheim.[9] Although this pro-Jewish policy might have seemed sensible enough to Ernst II, it was controversial in North Germany, because since the 15th century Jews had been systematically forced out of much of Western Europe.[10] In the territories surrounding Hildesheim, edicts that reinforced the expulsions had been issued in 1543 (Braunschweig), 1546 (Braunschweig-Wolfenbüttel), 1553 (Braunschweig-Lüneburg), and 1590 (Braunschweig-Wolfenbüttel). Hildesheim had thus emerged as one of the only areas within Northern Germany that Jews were allowed to resettle legally. The rest of the Holy Roman Empire continued its historic persecution of Hebrews because they feared the dangerous moral influence of Jews who resisted the Christian Gospel, refused to integrate into Christian society, engaged in usurious business practices, and committed alleged crimes such as ritual murder and host desecration.[11]

Despite a few appeals to Jewish communities in the early Reformation period, the Protestant Reformation as a whole had done little to change preconceived notions about Jewish culture and identity.[12] The Hildesheim town council thus feared inroads from three areas as Heshusius arrived to take up his post as Lutheran Superintendent: they feared Counter Reformation Jesuits bent on reversing the Lutheran Reformation, they feared Ernst II, a powerful prince-bishop who hoped to erode the town's religious and political freedoms, and they feared the new influx of Jews, who appeared as old rivals under the new protection of Roman Catholic administrators.

In this essay, I will describe the confessional conflict that arose among Lutherans, Jesuits, and Jews in late Reformation Hildesheim, and I will suggest that through this episode we learn something deeper about the process of confessionalization in Reformation Germany and the complicated dynamics of Christian-Jewish relations during the same period.[13] During the late Reformation, Jews were often negatively associated with Roman Catholics, Calvinists, and Anabaptists by Lutherans, because each group offered an alternative to Lutheran doctrine that seemed threatening, obsolete, stiff-necked, or deluded. As confessional conflicts among Lutherans, Calvinists, and Catholics took on greater fury before the outbreak of the Thirty Years' War (1618-48), Jews were used increasingly as foils by both Protestants and Catholics in their political and ideological struggles. Heinrich Heshusius is an important example of this development, because during his term as Lutheran superintendent he argued for both the expulsion of Jews and Jesuits from Hildesheim, and also the conversion of local Jews through Lutheran baptism if the Jews were willing to accept core Christian doctrines and make a public statement of faith. By preaching vehemently against the Jews, but also publishing sympathetic accounts of Jews when they did convert, Heshusius left an ambivalent legacy toward Jews and Jesuits that would prove influential in future confessional disputes.

HILDESHEIM'S POLICIES AGAINST JESUITS AND JEWS

In September, 1593, three months after Heshusius's arrival in Hildesheim, the town council met to discuss the formation of a small Jesuit school near the Roman Catholic cathedral, which served as a gathering place for the small number of remaining Catholics in Hildesheim. The situation was distressing, and the men decided that they would formally protest the formation of the school in letters to Rudolf II, the Holy Roman Emperor in Prague, and also to Ernst II, who had recently been appointed Archbishop of Cologne and had relocated his court there.[14]

The council and the superintendent also renewed their criticism of the Jews in Hildesheim by condemning a new synagogue that had been built near the edge of town, arguing that the irreverent ceremonies held there publicly slandered God. The accusation that synagogue worship slandered God, and in particular Christ and the Trinity, was not a new criticism. Numerous medieval and contemporary Christian authors had imagined that through their public and private worship the Jews denied the divinity of Jesus and routinely called him a bastard [*Hurkind*], saying that Mary begat Jesus in adultery with Joseph, a simple carpenter [*Zimmerman*]. In a 1595 sermon that recalled many of these standard accusations against the Jews, Superintendent Heshusius reported in no uncertain terms that Jews routinely called Jesus' mother Mary a whore [*Hure*] and a "manure heap" [*Misthauffen*], and that in their synagogue worship Jews cursed [*fluchen*] Jesus three times daily in terrible ways, concluding their prayers with the invective that Jesus' name be erased from human memory.[15]

The accuracy of Heshusius's claims against the Jews is of course highly suspect; but in the anti-Semitic atmosphere of the 1590s, the town council was enraged by them and responded by severely condemning local synagogue worship as blasphemous, recalling the 1457 edict that originally expelled the Jews from Hildesheim.[16] In the council's opinion, the 1457 expulsion made Jewish worship illegal, even if Ernst II had the technical right to allow Jews to resettle in a town in over which he had administrative authority. The council concluded that the synagogue should be dissolved, and that the original 13 Jewish families could only remain in Hildesheim if they paid an annual "protection tax" to the city treasury. In addition, no other Jews would be allowed residence in the city after these Jews had relocated or died.

The Baptism of Michael Duelke

Like many Lutheran superintendents before him, Heinrich Heshusius argued that the only legitimate way for Jews to be fully accepted into Christian society was through the sacrament of baptism. Although few Jews actually converted to Christianity during the Reformation period, both Protestants and Catholics continued to promote Jewish conversion through sermons, public disputations, and financial incentives, and when Jewish baptisms did occur they were often highly publicized.[17] It is highly relevant, therefore, that on August 12, 1595, a nineteen year old Jewish man named Michael Duelke approached Superintendent Heshusius to renounce his Jewish faith, request baptism according to the Lutheran rite, and take up residence in the city.[18]

Realizing the spiritual significance of this request, but also the general climate of distrust and the possibility of fraud, Heshusius began a careful correspondence with Lutheran theologians in Wittenberg, Braunschweig-Wolfenbüttel, and Hessen-Kassel, asking his colleagues if they had also baptized Jews recently and under what conditions. In addition, he initiated a series of longer meetings with Michael Duelke that began catechetical instruction in the Christian faith, explored the young man's family history, and introduced the Jew to the town's civic and spiritual leaders. Heshusius wrote in a report of the proceedings, published the next year in Leipzig, that Duelke had received some basic instruction in Christianity from a brother in Breslau, and that another Hildesheim pastor, Bartholomei Volfarri, had recently baptized a young Jew with apparent success.[19] However, Heshusius also believed the contemporary German adage that warned "When the mouse can eat the cat, then the Jew will become a good Christian."[20] In other words, Jews might ask for baptism, or receive it, but true converts were rare. Michael Duelke was suspect not only because he was a Jew, but also because he was a newcomer to the city. He was only distantly connected to the dozen or so Jewish families that still resided in Hildesheim, and relations between Jews and Christians had never been worse.

Since Duelke was asking to be baptized at the same time that the town council was planning a move against both Jews and Jesuits, the matter was especially sensitive. Although the council theoretically supported the idea that a young Jew could convert to Lutheranism, only a meticulous process would insure a legitimate conversion. Accordingly, the preparation for baptism took about five weeks, and it involved a series of meetings between Duelke, Heshusius, members of the council, Lutheran pastors in the area, and finally, the influential Braunschweig Superintendent Polycarp Leyser, who had arranged for Heshusius's appointment in 1593 and traveled to Hildesheim now for a special visit. As Heshusius continued to focus on catechetical instruction, he worked from an innovative booklet that he had published the previous year in Leipzig, which featured alternating pages of the Psalms and Luther's Small Catechism.[21] During the questioning, Duelke appears to have articulated a clear understanding of Lutheran teaching and Christian doctrine, and he answered questions about his family background with poignant honesty, reminding Heshusius that due to recent expulsions, most of his family had either died or moved East to Poland.

The city's interest in the Jew's baptism was so great that the council decided the baptismal service should be held outside in the town's market square, and a special platform was erected that contained a pulpit and a portable baptismal font.[22] The city seemed simultaneously enraged at the town's Jews but also fascinated that one might renounce his people and tradition, becoming a Christian. But then came a new development. Word arrived from Georg Schönfeldt, the Lutheran Superintendent in Kassel, that Michael Duelke had sought baptism in that town as well. Worse, Duelke had been accused of theft in Kassel, and was now wanted for investigation of the charges.[23] The claims were unfortunate, for at about the same time Duelke had been caught stealing money from a local student in Hildesheim, and Duelke had confessed to both charges of theft, as well as lying to cover up his past in Kassel. Michael was jailed at the town hall while the town council discussed his case. After a brief discussion and encouragement from the new mayor, Henni Arneken, the council agreed to make an example of the Jew, and for his assorted crimes Michael Duelke was sentenced to death by hanging. However, he would still be allowed Christian baptism first if he wished, since the state of his mortal soul was also important and Superintendent Heshusius continued to believe in the young man's earnestness.

On September 19, 1595, Michael Duelke was baptized in front of a large crowd in the Hildesheim town square, according to the Lutheran rite, and given the name Jacob. The congregation sang Luther's baptismal hymn, "Christ Our Lord to Jordan Came," and Heshusius preached a baptismal sermon which vigorously attacked traditional Jewish stubbornness but also reminded the congregation that they should act positively toward Jews like Jacob if they confessed and called on the Lord.[24] Duelke was questioned publicly in front of the crowd about his Christian faith, and he was able to describe the subtleties of Christian doctrine as Superintendent Heshusius had helped him to do. An assistant pastor baptized Duelke in the portable font on the scaffolding, and the crowd cheered. Shortly afterwards, however, the convert was led from the baptismal platform to the gallows outside of town. Jacob Duelke prayed with Heshusius, who accompanied him there, and the Jew was then hung by the neck until he died early the next morning.[25] Joachim Brandis' diary for the day indicates that the crowd thoroughly enjoyed this "entertainment," having no trouble seeing the irony of the situation.[26]

Nathan Schay, *Blutschande*, and the Case for Expulsion

The tense situation between Lutherans, Jesuits, and Jews continued to simmer in the Autumn of 1595, while in the background the town council, the prince-bishop, and the Emperor each argued that they alone enjoyed ultimate political jurisdiction over the city. Far from being unique, Hildesheim was experiencing many of the same political and religious dislocations that other German towns and principalities were feeling during the Reformation, when numerous urban governments struggled for autonomy and authority with powerful territorial lords, bishops, and princes.[27]

Yet a month after the disappointing execution of Jacob Duelke, Heinrich Heshusius learned something that, for him, finally offered the moral and legal grounds for moving systematically against all the Jews in Hildesheim. In October, 1595, he discovered an impropriety involving Nathan Schay that seemed an affront to both Jewish and Christian tradition, and this realization prompted him to demand the removal of all Jews from the city. Six months earlier, Schay's wife had died, and he had remarried his dead wife's sister without the permission of the town council. A similar second marriage had apparently happened four years earlier, when a Jew named Marx had also married his dead wife's sister—again, without the permission of the council or the ecclesiastical superintendent. Both marriages were judged by Heshusius to be scandalous cases of *Blutschande* (incest), since both men had selected their sister-in-laws as their second wives, and, like Roman Catholics, 16th century Lutherans continued to be concerned about maintaining an appropriate degree of separation between families and family members when marrying.

The fact that Jewish tradition in the early modern period seemed to allow such a marriage made no difference to Heshusius, and he cited Leviticus 18:18 as further proof: "You shall not take a woman as a rival to her sister, uncovering her nakedness while her sister is alive." Although a close reading of this Levitical "Holiness Code" seems to make the matter at least ambiguous—if the original married sister is *no longer alive*, the prohibition against sexual relations appears not to apply—Heshusius argued that the basic thrust of the scripture was clear: to contemplate marriage within the family, and especially with a sister-in-law, broke long-standing marriage taboos and regulations in Christian society. The fact that these basic guidelines had been ignored twice, combined with all the other problems that the Jews had created in Hildesheim, brought an obvious conclusion—the Jews were morally corrupt and should be removed from the city immediately.[28] The obstinate Hebrews now threatened one of the crucial bedrocks of community life—marriage.

Waiting no longer, Heshusius took to his pulpit at St. Andreas Church and preached several sermons that denounced the Jews and their sinful behavior, mixing his current criticism with formulaic diatribes that had been used for centuries to smear the Jews. He said that the Jews had harmed the community by committing incest, that Jews continued to charge excessive interest, and that in all of these crimes they showed their allegiance to the devil.[29] Going further, Heshusius specifically tied the Jews to the Jesuits in Hildesheim, suggesting that both groups were heretics who harmed the community by their very presence.[30]

Although Mayor Arneken did not personally support the biblical basis for Heshusius's criticism, and actually wrote to the theological faculty at Wittenberg for further advice on Leviticus 18:18, he nonetheless agreed that the time to expel the troublesome Jews had arrived.[31] Despite the prince-bishop's support of Nathan Schay and his family, the town council met in their chambers and drafted a harshly worded expulsion notice dated October 14, 1595.[32] The male members of the Jewish community were to leave *that same day*, and the women and children were to follow *within three days*. As during previous expulsions, the authorities expected the Jews to move gradually toward Poland, Lithuania, and the lesser populated areas of Eastern Europe, which had been a haven for Jews since the original expulsions in the 15th century. Heshusius supported the formal edict with a pastoral letter of support, and the document was signed by the town's eleven Lutheran pastors. As the expulsion notice directed, the Jews were forcibly expelled from Hildesheim that very week, and by the end of October none remained in the city. Although most attempted to live a short distance away with family members, Nathan Schay remained defiant and traveled directly to the court of Ernst II in Cologne to lodge a formal, written protest.

In December, 1595, the town council continued on the offensive, this time criticizing the Hildesheim Jesuit school again, calling it a dangerous and subversive institution.[33] The Jesuits were now residing in a place called *Kleinen Tuimhose* near St. Martin's Church, which had been authorized by Ernst II, and they were trying to make inroads in the evangelical community by offering Roman Catholic Mass and encouraging the veneration of the saints. The mayor and Superintendent Heshusius formally wrote Ernst II and Emperor Rudolf II to remove the Jesuits, but by late January, 1596, word came back from the Emperor mandating that the Lutheran clergy, council, and guilds tolerate the Jesuits and allow them to co-exist under the terms of the 1555 Peace of Augsburg.[34]

In February, Heshusius, Brandis, Arneken, and other leaders composed a second letter articulating more general concerns about Jesuits in the area.[35] The Lutherans called the Jesuits "Esauiter," a derogatory reference to Jacob's rebellious older brother Esau in Genesis Chapter 25, and argued that the Counter Reformation evangelists were the enemies of Christ and the Truth. The Jesuits relied mistakenly on works for their salvation, and did not teach the importance of faith in the Christian life.[36] Worse yet, the rabble-rousers preached incessantly, spreading their foul doctrines in the fragile community that had already been damaged by controversy. Although Heshusius was not technically able to exercise church discipline over those associated with the historic Roman Catholic cathedral, he insisted that they stop their harmful evangelizing. Throughout Germany similar confessional conflicts raged that pitted Lutherans, Jesuits, and Calvinists against each other, and they would grow in intensity as the Thirty Years' War approached.[37] In Hildesheim, the Lutheran-dominated government closed ranks and sought the upper hand against their rivals.

JESUITS AND JEWS REINSTATED

The fascinating conclusion to this episode is that neither expulsion strategy worked for very long in Hildesheim. Beginning in 1596, and continuing for several years, the council's decisions to block or remove rival Jewish and Jesuit groups were overturned one by one. In both cases, the persecuted minorities appealed to higher authorities that were politically more powerful, and the archbishop and Emperor used imperial law and judicial privilege to insist that both Jesuits and Jews be allowed to remain in Hildesheim. In a series of courteous but firm directives, Emperor Rudolf II insisted that the Jesuit school and limited Roman Catholic worship be allowed to continue on the basis of the Peace of Augsburg. The town council risked an imperial edict if they persisted in persecuting Roman Catholics who enjoyed an historic foothold within the bishopric.

The Jewish case was more complicated, because the Wittenberg theologians had indeed argued that Marx and Schay violated ecclesiastical and imperial law by marrying a close family member.[38] However, in August 1596, the Emperor claimed that *he* was the final arbiter of Jewish policy in the Holy Roman Empire, and that the Jews must be readmitted to Hildesheim as long as they were willing to pay an annual protection free (*Schutzgeld*) to the city council. The council still refused to readmit the Jews, and the case dragged on for five years until 1601, when 11 of the original 13 Jewish families were allowed readmission for a protection fee of 1200 Gulden paid in advance to the Hildesheim city treasury.[39] Among this number were Nathan Schay and his controversial wife, plus several additional family members. The Jews were allowed to reside in the same part of town that they had inhabited earlier, although the council insisted that any previous debts the citizens might have owed the Jews must now be forgiven.[40] In addition, no new synagogues or schools were to be built, and new families would not be permitted to settle in the town. The Emperor had once again emerged as the protector of the Jews, and his political will was simply more authoritative than that of the town council.

Heinrich Heshusius was not alive to see the final agreement between the city council, the Jewish community, and the Emperor. In 1597, Heshusius died in a disastrous epidemic of the bubonic plague that killed 4,247 people in the town (about ⅓ of the population), including his wife, Gesa, and the couple's four children.[41] Heshusius was 41 years old, and he undoubtedly died feeling his personal struggle for orthodoxy had produced mixed results, as it had for his father a generation earlier. Heshusius's will survives today in the Hildesheim city archive, as do several of his polemical and pastoral writings.[42] Unlike the first generation or two of Lutheran reformers, who saw their primary mission as preaching Luther's message of justification by grace through faith and gradually reforming worship and the sacraments along evangelical lines, Heshusius saw his primary task as systematizing and defending a mature Lutheran tradition that had powerful ecclesiastical and secular rivals. Lutheranism was not yet secure in the Holy Roman Empire, and while some princes and territorial governments supported Luther's teachings and the Augsburg Confession, many did not. Accordingly, Heshusius's characteristic intolerance, zealousness, and polemical fervor offer important insights into the complex and inadequately understood age of orthodoxy that emerged in the decades after the Formula of Concord, and which gave religion and politics in the 17th century its unique temperament. Heshusius was a complex figure who moved back and forth among the boundaries of institutional loyalty, confessional politics, traditional anti-Semitism, and a deeply held Lutheran piety.

A much more noble character in this particular struggle may have been Nathan Schay, the esteemed Jewish financier who protected his kinsmen and continued working after his return to Hildesheim as an advisor to Elector Ernst II. Indeed, Schay fits the profile of an emerging class of upwardly mobile "court Jews" (*Hofjuden*) who took advantage of improving economic conditions in Germany in the late 16th and early 17th centuries, especially in the courts of powerful men such as Ernst II and the Holy Roman Emperor. Nathan Schay was successful because he had financial savvy and the ability to seek redress through the law and through the more informal networks of patronage and court politics. His case seems to support the recent historiographic conclusions of J. Friedrich Battenberg and Jonathan Israel that life may have been better for Jews in the ecclesiastical territories of early modern Germany than in the secular territories.[43]

This study also indicates that relations between Christians and Jews in the early modern period must be seen in the context of relations among Christian confessional groups, such as Lutherans, Catholics, and Calvinists. For the Lutherans of this divided city, the only acceptable Jews were those who abandoned their faith and became Christians, just as the only acceptable Catholics were those who converted to Lutheranism and were integrated into the evangelical community. The toleration of other creeds, of other understandings of Christ and Christian truth, was something quite rare for most Lutherans of the late 16th century, as it was for most Catholics, Calvinists, and Anabaptists. Religious plurality endangered not only individual salvation but also the satisfying and very medieval vision of a godly community united through shared principles, beliefs, and institutions.

ENDNOTES

1. Important documents relating to political conditions within Hildesheim and the work of Heinrich Heshusius can be found in Emil Sehling, *Die evangelischen Kirchenordnungen des 16. Jahrhunderts*, vol. 7/2 (Tübingen: J.C.B Mohr, 1980), 792-828; Joachim Barward Lauenstein, *Hildesheimische Kirchen und Reformations Historie...*, Theil 2 (Hildesheim, 1735); M. Buhlers, ed., *Joachim Brandis' der Jüngeren Diarium* (Hildesheim: Gebr. Gerstenberg, 1902); Peter Aufgebauer, *Die Geschichte der Juden in der Stadt Hildesheim* (Hildesheim: Bernward Verlag, 1984). Archival materials are located in Stadtarchivs Hildesheim (Am Steine 7, Hildesheim), abbreviated below as Sta. Hild.

2. For examples of his training as a theologian and skills as a disputant, see Tilemann Heshusius and Heinrich Heshusius, *Propositiones de Lege Divina* (Henricopoli [Wolfenbuettel], 1578); Johann Olearius and Heinrich Heshusius, *Disputatio de infantum baptismo contra anabaptistarum errores* (Helmstedt, 1580); Tilemann Heshusius and Heinrich Heshusius, *Propositiones de Deo: De quibus, Deo iuvante et Spiritum largiente* (Helmstedt, 1580).

3. For the historic context of the Formula of Concord and the most authoritative translation, see Robert Kolb and Timothy J. Wengert, eds., *The Book of Concord: The Confessions of the Evangelical Lutheran Church* (Minneapolis, MN: Fortress Press, 2000), 481-660.

4. For Tilemann Heshusius's theology and his influence as a controversialist, see Thilo Krüger, *Die Christologie Tilemann Heshusens (1527-1588)*, (Göttingen: Vandenhoeck & Ruprecht, 2004).

5. Buhlers, *Joachim Brandis' der Jüngeren Diarium*, 335.

6. Rotraud Ries, *Jüdisches Leben in Niedersachsen im 15. und 16. Jahrhundert* (Hannover: Hahnsche Buchhandlung, 1994), 302.

7. Aufgebauer, *Geschichte der Juden in Hildesheim*, 89, 93.

8. Jonathan Israel, *European Jewry in the Age of Mercantilism, 1550-1750*, 3rd ed. (London: Vallentine Mitchell & Co., 1998), 34-5.

9. Aufgebauer, *Geschichte der Juden in Hildesheim*, 88-105.

10. Jews were expelled from Vienna in 1421, Cologne in 1424, Augsburg in 1439, Bavaria in 1450, and Hildesheim in 1457. In Spain, Ferdinand and Isabella expelled all the Jews who would not convert to Christianity in 1492, and in Portugal, Italy, Germany, and the Netherlands, the pattern of forced resettlement was similar. As conditions deteriorated, the Jews moved eastward to the frontier communities of Poland, Lithuania, and the Ottoman Empire. See Israel, *European Jewry in the Age of Mercantilism*, 5; Ries, *Jüdisches Leben in Niedersachsen*, 56.

11. On Christian prejudice and the representation of Jews in early modern Germany, see R. Po-chia Hsia, "The Usurious Jews: Economic Structure and Religious Representations in an Anti-Semitic Discourse," and Miri Rubin, "Imagining the Jew: The Late Medieval Eucharistic Discourse," in R. Po-chia Hsia and Hartmut Lehmann, eds., *In and Out of the Ghetto: Jewish-Gentile Relations in Late Medieval and Early Modern Germany* (Cambridge: Cambridge University Press, 1995); R. Po-chia Hsia, *The Myth of Ritual Murder: Jews and Magic in Reformation Germany* (New Haven, Conn., 1988); Ora Limor and Israel Jacob Yuval, "Skepticism and Conversion: Jews, Christians, and Doubters in *Sefer ha-Nizzahon*," in Allison P. Coudert and Jeffrey S. Shoulson, eds., *Hebraica Veritas? Christian Hebraists and the Study of Judaism in Early Modern Europe* (Philadelphia: University of Pennsylvania Press, 2004), 159-80; Dean Phillip Bell, *Sacred Communities, Jewish and Christian Identities in Fifteenth-Century Germany* (Leiden: Brill Academic Publishers, 2001); Kenneth R. Stow, *Alienated Minority* (Cambridge: Harvard University Press, 1992); Gavin I. Langmuir, *Toward a Definition of Antisemitism* (Berkeley: University of California Press, 1990).

12. Heiko A. Oberman, *The Roots of Anti-Semitism in the Age of Renaissance and Reformation*, trans. James I. Porter (Philadelphia: Fortress Press, 1984); Scott Hendrix, "Toleration of the Jews in the German Reformation," *Archive for Reformation History* 81 (1990): 189-245.

13. For a review of the concept of "confessionalization" in early modern Germany, see Joel F. Harrington and Helmut Walser Smith, "Confessionalization, Community, and State Building in Germany, 1555-1870," *Journal of Modern History* 69 (1997): 77-101; Hans J. Hillerbrand, "Was there a Reformation in the Sixteenth Century?" *Church History* 72 (2003): 525-52; John M. Headley, Hans J. Hillerbrand, and Anthony J. Papalas, *Confessionalization in Europe, 1555-1700. Essays in Honor and Memory of Bodo Nischan* (Hants, England: Ashgate Publishing Company, 2004); Michael Halvorson, "Baptismal Ritual and Court Culture during the Late Reformation," *Lutheran Quarterly* 18 (2004), 406-34.

14. Although Ernst II became the Archbishop of Cologne and resided in the imperial city with his court, he continued to have ecclesiastical authority over the Bishopric of Hildesheim, ruling as Administrator. However, his physical distance from Hildesheim seems to have emboldened Heshusius and the city council.

15. Henricum Heshusium, *Bericht von einem Juden / so die Tauffe zu erst betrieglich gesuchet / und doch durch Gottes Bericht wunderbarlich zu erkentnis seiner Sünden kommen / Die Tauffe erlanget / und in warem Glauben und bekentnis des Herrn Christi bestendig verharret ist / bis an sein Ende* (Leibzig: Abraham Lamberg, 1596), 41.

16. For an analysis of this edict, see Aufgebauer, *Geschichte der Juden in Hildesheim*, 70.

17. For a sample of conversion reports from late Reformation Germany, see Martin Friedrich, *Zwischen Abwehr und Bekehrung, Die Stellung der deutschen evangelischen Theologie zum Judentum im 17. Jahrhundert* (J. C. B. Mohr, Tübingen, 1988).

18. Heshusium, *Bericht von einem Juden,* 5-17; Buhlers, *Joachim Brandis' der Jüngeren Diarium*, 372-3.

19. Heshusium, *Bericht von einem Juden*, 6-7; 45-6.

20. "Wenn die Kaze die Mauß frist / so wird ein Jüde ein rechter Christ." Heshusium, *Bericht von einem Juden*, 46-7.

21. Heinrich Heshusius, *Einfeltige kurtze Anleitung, wie man die Psalmen Davids nach der Lehre des heiligen Catechismi lesen...* (Leipzig, 1594).

22. Buhlers, *Joachim Brandis' der Jüngeren Diarium*, 372-3; Heshusius, *Bericht von einem Juden,* 39.

23. Heshusius, *Bericht von einem Juden*, 17-9.

24. Ibid., 39-49.

25. Heshusius portrays the new convert heroically, and does not mention his execution or physical suffering. When asked if the Jew wanted a drink, Heshusius records Duelke as saying: "Ich wil nicht trincken / ich wil jezt balt mit meinem Herrn Jesu Christo trincken / im ewigen Leben." ("I will not drink; I will drink very soon with my Lord Jesus Christ in eternal life.") Ibid., 68.

26. Buhlers, *Joachim Brandis' der Jüngeren Diarium*, 373.

27. For a discussion of this general pattern, see Berndt Hamm, "The Urban Reformation in the Holy Roman Empire," trans. Thomas A. Brady, Jr., in *Handbook of European History, 1400-1600*, vol. 2, edited by T. Brady, H. Oberman, and J. Tracy (Leiden, The Netherlands: E. J. Brill, 1995), 193-227.

28. The letters written by Heshusius and the town council about this matter are collected in a large packet in Stadtarchivs Hildesheim. See Sta. Hild. Best. 100/91, Nr. 109.

29. Ibid., fol. 171-4.

30. Aufgebauer, *Geschichte der Juden in Hildesheim*, 93.

31. When Daniel Hoffman replied on behalf of the Wittenberg theologians in 1596, he advised the council that it was indeed wrong for Schay to marry his dead wife's sister. See Sta. Hild. Best. 100/89, Nr. 11. For a printed copy of the letter and a discussion of the legal and theological debate that continued into the 18th century, see Friedrich Ernst Kettners, *Gründliche Untersuchung....Ob jemand seines verstorbenen weibes leibliche schwester... heyrathen darff?* (Quedlinburg, 1707).

32. Sta. Hild. Best. 100/91, Nr. 109.

33. Buhlers, *Joachim Brandis' der Jüngeren Diarium*, 380-2; Aufgebauer, *Geschichte der Juden in Hildesheim*, 93.

34. Sta. Hild. Best. 100/91, Nr. 109.

35. Buhlers, *Joachim Brandis' der Jüngeren Diarium*, 384.

36. Ibid. For the complete correspondence on the Jesuits and their replies, see Sta. Hild. Best. 100/91, Nr. 109.

37. For a summary of the imperial cities in Reformation Germany and their approach to the problems of confessional conflict and toleration during the late Reformation, see R. Po-chia Hsia, *Social Discipline in the Reformation, Central Europe 1550-1750* (London: Routledge, 1989), 73-88. Note especially the case of Strasbourg, where in 1598 the Lutheran citizens called themselves "good Christians," as opposed to "Jews, sectarians, papists, and Calvinists." The Strasbourg Jesuits were persecuted consistently until the 1681 annexation of Strasbourg into Catholic France; ibid., 74-5.

38. Kettners, *Gründliche Untersuchung....Ob jemand seines verstorbenen weibes leibliche schwester... heyrathen darff?*, 25-30.

39. Sta Hild. Best. 1, Nr. 431.

40. Sta Hild. Best. 50/154, Bd. 2, fol. 162-3; Aufgebauer, *Geschichte der Juden in Hildesheim*, 97-101.

41. Details relating to the 1597 plague and the death of the Heshusius family can be found in Buhlers, *Joachim Brandis' der Jüngeren Diarium*, 417-9.

42. For Heshusius's will, see Sta Hild. Best. 100/160, Nr. 233.

43. J. Friedrich Battenberg, "Jews in Ecclesiastical Territories of the Holy Roman Empire," in Hsia and Lehmann, eds., *In and Out of the Ghetto*, 272.

CHAPTER 7

DEFENSE AND DIPLOMACY: DANISH MERCENARIES IN ENGLISH SERVICE 1689-1698

Mary Elizabeth Ailes

In 1689, James II, who had recently lost command of the English kingdom during the Glorious Revolution, sailed to Ireland to rally the Irish behind his attempt to reclaim his English crown. In response, the newly crowned king of England, William III, sent a military force to Ireland to secure his control of the region. This was not, however, the only military threat to William's political position. As the contemporaneous ruler of the United Provinces of the Netherlands, William was also concerned with the growing military threat of Louis XIV of France's expansionist foreign policy.[1] To strengthen his diplomatic and military situations both in the Netherlands and in the British Isles, William sought to conclude alliances with states outside of France's sphere of influence. In particular, William's diplomats tried to create ties to the Scandinavian kingdoms of Denmark and Sweden because of their strategic positions in northern Europe and their influence over the Baltic trade in grain and naval supplies. Throughout the ensuing Nine Years' War (1688-97) that William III and his allies fought against France, Denmark and Sweden remained neutral.[2] During the war's initial stages, however, the Danish king Christian V allowed William III to hire regiments from the Danish army to support his military campaigns in Ireland and the Netherlands. Granting permission to a foreign ruler to hire Danish regiments marked a reversal in seventeenth-century Danish military policy. Previously, Danish monarchs maintained the army at the strongest levels possible and supplemented the native forces with mercenaries hired from the Holy Roman Empire and the British Isles.[3] By the 1680s, however, the Danish king confronted the problem of how to maintain the army during an era of peace in a kingdom with limited resources. The agreement signed between William III and Christian V regarding the hiring of Danish regiments, thus marked a new approach to military finance in the Danish kingdom and represented Christian V's attempt to exert diplomatic influence in European affairs despite his kingdom's limited resources and declining political fortunes. The purpose of this article is to discuss Denmark's place in William III's diplomatic and military plans during the Nine Years' War, the benefits to the Danish crown of hiring out a portion of its army, and the fate of the Danish soldiers in William's service.

Danish Foreign Policy

At the beginning of the seventeenth century, Denmark enjoyed the position of being the dominant political power in the Baltic region. Over the next one hundred years, however, the political fortunes of the Danish crown declined precipitously as it unsuccessfully fought wars against its neighbors Sweden and the Holy Roman Empire.[4] The military losses in these conflicts led to the Danish crown being forced to transfer control of the Norwegian provinces of Halland, Böhusland, Jämtland, Härjedalen, the province of Skåne, and the Baltic islands of Ösel and Gotland to the Swedish crown. By 1660, the Danish crown had to share control of the Sound, the only navigable entrance to the Baltic, with Sweden, which severely reduced the Danish government's ability to influence northern European politics and economics.[5] During the 1670s, the Danes tried to recover their former territories on the Sound's eastern shore through an invasion of the Swedish kingdom's southern regions. Once again, the Swedish army defeated the Danes, but because of diplomatic maneuvers on the part of Sweden's ally, France, the Swedes were not able to capitalize on their victory.[6] As a result of a century of warfare between the two Scandinavian kingdoms, the balance of power shifted in favor of Sweden. Through military victories, the Swedish crown established an empire that included modern day Sweden, Finland, Estonia, Latvia, and scattered territories within the Holy Roman Empire along the Baltic's southern shore.

As the political position of Denmark declined, its rulers formed alliances with states outside of the Baltic in order to seek revenge upon the Swedes and to increase their ability to exert influence within the greater sphere of European affairs. In particular, the Danes turned to the United Provinces of the Netherlands for aid and support. Throughout the seventeenth century, the United Provinces was constantly interested in Scandinavian affairs. It sought to maintain a balance of power between Denmark and Sweden, to insure constant access to the area's markets in ship building supplies and grain. For the Dutch, who during this century created a vast trading empire in Europe and Asia, maintaining good relations with the Scandinavian powers was essential as the Baltic trade was viewed as "the mother trade" upon which the United Province's economic wealth rested.[7] Particularly during the middle decades of the seventeenth century, the Dutch republic maintained particularly close ties to the Danish kingdom as a means to counterbalance the growing influence of the Swedish empire in the Baltic region.[8]

By the 1680s, however, ties between Denmark and the United Provinces were breaking down. In the first years of the decade, the Swedish kingdom and the Dutch Republic developed closer diplomatic ties as each held grievances against the expansive foreign policy of Louis XIV. For the Dutch, the French policies threatened a renewed invasion of the United Provinces as Louis sought to enlarge and secure his kingdom's borders. For the Swedes, fear that Louis' foreign policy could drag the Swedish kingdom into a renewal of the warfare of the 1670s, which it could ill afford, caused many members of the Swedish royal council to favor an alliance with the Dutch to counterbalance French expansion into the Holy Roman Empire.[9] Diplomatic ties between the two states were strengthened through a series of treaties signed throughout the 1680s, which granted Dutch merchants favored status in the Baltic and promised the United Provinces the use of 6000 Swedish troops for its potential campaigns against France.[10]

In comparison, Danish foreign policy throughout the 1680s focused upon recovering the provinces on the eastern side of the Sound, which had been lost to Sweden in 1658, and in claiming sovereignty over the territory of the duke of Holstein-Gottorp, who was a Swedish ally. While seeking retribution against Sweden for the loss of Danish territories was always foremost in the minds of the Danish councilors, the issue of the Danish king's rights to the lands in the regions of Schleswig and Holstein dominated Danish foreign relations during this period. The relative authority that the duke and the king possessed in the region rested upon a series of agreements created during the sixteenth century. In some cases, each ruler exercised complete authority over particular areas in the region. In other cases, the rulers held power jointly. The political basis of this arrangement was so convoluted and contradictory that conflicts were bound to arise over sovereignty within the region.[11] Hence, to protect their political rights against the encroachment of Danish royal power, the dukes of Holstein-Gottorp maintained close diplomatic ties with the Swedish kingdom throughout the seventeenth century. This arrangement benefited the Swedish kings because Schleswig-Holstein presented a convenient location for launching attacks on southern Denmark and it strengthened the Swedish crown's influence within the Holy Roman Empire.[12]

To strengthen his military position against the Swedish crown and the Duke of Holstein-Gottorp and to reassert Danish royal authority in the region, Christian V signed a treaty with France in 1682. According to the treaty, the French crown was to supply Christian V with a subsidy of 200,000 *riksdaler* annually for eight years to enable the Danish king to outfit an army to attack Swedish territories in northern Germany. The planned invasion was not, however, successful because Louis XIV was unwilling to lend the necessary support as he feared a conflict in the Baltic between Denmark and Sweden would lead to more widespread political instability in northern Europe.[13] In 1684, Christian V decided to assert his authority in the region through a military occupation of the duke's territories in Schleswig.

Because they feared a Baltic war would disrupt trade in the area, the rulers of England and the United Provinces persuaded the Danish king to submit to their arbitration. The outcome of these negotiations was the Treaty of Altona (1689), which allowed the duke to reclaim his territories and reestablished the status quo in the duchies.[14]

During the negotiations surrounding the Treaty of Altona, the Danish king began to turn away from his French allies and seek closer diplomatic relations with England and the United Provinces. Throughout the 1680s, it had become clear to Christian V and his councilors that Louis XIV was not particularly concerned with Danish affairs in Northern Germany and was unwilling to grant the support necessary to launch a full scale attack against the duke and his Swedish allies. As a result, Christian V's diplomats sought to renew ties with the Maritime Powers, now under the leadership of William III, hoping that England and the United Provinces would supply the aid that Louis XIV had been unwilling to grant. Stronger diplomatic relations with the Maritime Powers also held the potential of loosening these states' ties to the Swedish kingdom, which continued to be the main barrier to Danish expansion in the Baltic region.[15]

For William III, meanwhile, weakening Christian V's dependency upon French subsidies was important because in a war against France, the Danish kingdom could be a dangerous enemy. With its territorial claims in the northern regions of the Holy Roman Empire, the Danish king could launch an attack upon the Empire, thus diverting attention away from the campaigns against Louis XIV. Additionally, the Danish kingdom controlled the lucrative Norwegian timber trade, which the English and Dutch navies could not afford to lose. Finally, Norwegian ports might provide shelter to French navy vessels, which could be used to harass English and Dutch shipping in the North Seas.[16]

Negotiations to develop closer ties between Denmark and the Maritime Powers began in 1688, but ultimately an alliance was not signed. While William III wanted to break Danish ties with France, he feared that a formal alliance with Denmark might drive the Swedish government to consider closer diplomatic relations with Louis XIV given the traditional antagonism between the Danish and Swedish kingdoms. Additionally, William could not afford to pay the subsidies the Danish ruler demanded as a condition for concluding the alliance. At the same time, the Danish kingdom could not afford to fight a full scale war or maintain its army without foreign monetary aid. Instead, Christian V proposed allowing William III to hire regiments of the Danish army for use in the British Isles or the Netherlands. Such an arrangement would benefit both sides as William would receive supplemental troops to aid in his military campaigns and Christian V could express his friendship to the Maritime Powers without having to commit his kingdom to entering the war.[17]

BENEFITS OF HIRING OUT THE TROOPS

During the summer of 1689, negotiations regarding the troops commenced in Copenhagen with the English diplomat, Robert Molesworth, overseeing the talks. A treaty was signed by Christian V in August, 1689, and by William III in September, 1689, guaranteeing that the English king would hire 6000 foot soldiers and 1000 cavalrymen from the Danish military for his campaigns in Ireland and the Netherlands.[18] According to the agreement, the English government would pay 240,000 *riksdaler* to transport the troops to an English port or 325,000 *riksdaler* if William III chose to transport the troops to an Irish port. Half of the money was to be paid after the ratification of the treaty and all of the troops had been loaded on to the ships. The remaining sum would be paid when the troops arrived at the designated port. In regard to the soldiers' salaries, William III was to be responsible for their financial upkeep and the soldiers were to receive the same pay as the other troops in William's service. Additionally, William III was to provide the Danish king with monetary compensation for each soldier lost during the campaigns.[19] Finally, the treaty stipulated that the troops were to be released from English service within three months if the Danish kingdom was attacked, and vacancies within the ranks would be filled by William III with the recommendation of the Danish commanders.[20]

For the Danish king and his councilors, the conclusion of the treaty held many benefits. With the heightened tensions in the Baltic region throughout the 1680s over the Holstein-Gottorp question, the Danish king had been forced to maintain his army almost at wartime levels. Sustaining the army at these levels had proven, however, to be extremely difficult given the financial difficulties of the Danish crown. Throughout the later half of the seventeenth century, the Danish kingdom had faced an economic crisis similar to that of other European kingdoms, which historians have classified as "the general crisis of the seventeenth century."[21] Due to a rapid expansion of the state's bureaucratic and military institutions, the traditional fiscal system, which assumed that the king could live off the income of the royal estates, was abandoned. In its place emerged a system of state finance based upon direct and in-direct taxation.[22] Rapidly rising taxes combined with a century of almost continuous warfare, much of which was fought on Danish soil and much of which led to the loss of Danish territory to Sweden, left the Danish economy in a severely weakened state and the Danish peasantry in a position where they could not afford to support continued expansion of the military.[23] As the English diplomat Robert Molesworth described the situation:

> The King of Denmark has been but too apt a Pupil to such a Master [the French king] and has endeavoured even to exceed his Original; which he finds to his cost at this day, in raising more men than his country can maintain. Soldiers are, through I know not what mistaken Policy, esteemed the Riches of the Northern Kings, and other German Princes; for when they make an estimate of each others Wealth, it is not by the usual and ancient manner of Computation, the fertility or extent of the Territory, the Traffick, Industry, Number, or Riches of the People; but by so many Horse and Foot.[24]

Thus, allowing foreign rulers to hire regiments of the Danish army brought such benefits as freeing the Danish king from having to pay troops he could no longer afford while at the same time bringing into the kingdom much needed financial support, which could be used to bolster the economy.[25] The agreement also had military benefits for the Danish kingdom as the soldiers' battle readiness was maintained through continuing to fight in campaigns and perhaps improved by serving under new leadership and under different battlefield conditions.[26]

Danish Soldiers in William III's Army

The soldiers chosen to enter William III's service consisted of three cavalry regiments and nine infantry regiments, totaling 7,155 men.[27] This force represented a sizable contingency of the Danish army as it constituted about one-fifth of the Danish cavalry and about one-fourth of the Danish infantry.[28] The majority of the officers and soldiers were foreigners, which would not have been unusual. Throughout the seventeenth-century, the Danish monarchs hired foreign regiments to fill out the ranks of the military due to the kingdom's small population that was insufficient to defend the realm's many far flung territories. The officer corps' foreign makeup particularly increased after the introduction of absolutism in 1660 when the kings showed a preference for hiring foreign officers as a means to weaken the political influence of the native Danish nobility. The foreign element within the army became so strong after 1660 that German became the language of command within the Danish army.[29] Robert Molesworth described the foreign makeup of the Danish army in the following manner,

> The Foot, both Officers and Soldiers are for the most part Strangers of all Countries, whom Choice, or Fortune, brings thither; Germans, Poles, Courlanders, Dutch, Swedes, Scotch, Irish; and now and then an English Seaman, whom they make drunk after a long voyage, and inveagle him by fair Promises in that humour to take some of the King's money.[30]

Embarkation of the troops was planned for September 22, but due to delays in gathering the forces, the soldiers did not sail until November 6, 1689. Given the late starting date, the ships ran into storms in the North Sea, which scattered the vessels. Five ships were driven into Norwegian ports and did not set sail again until January, 1690. French privateers captured one ship containing four companies from the Queen's Regiment. These soldiers were sent to France where they were incorporated into the French army.[31]

The remaining ships landed in various ports in England and Scotland during November, 1689. The majority of the vessels, including the one carrying the commanding officer, Ferdinand Wilhelm, Duke of Würtemberg, landed near Hull. The soldiers had suffered greatly due to the rough passage and to the fact that they had consumed all of their provisions. Additionally, many of their horses were sick, weak, or had died, which had forced the soldiers to dispose of eight horses by throwing them overboard.[32] The local commanders quickly sent requests to the Privy Council in London seeking advice about what to do with the soldiers and where to send them. For as one commander stated:

> I think it will not be proper to have too many of these Forces within Garison, for we are but Weake our selves and tho thay are our very good friend, and that I use them with all Civility imaginable, yet it will be a hinderance to many disorders that may be Committed, for I well know, that Strange Troops Seldome agree well together.[33]

Although these were allied troops, having too many armed, hungry, discontented men within one region could strain local supplies and lead to problems with both the civilian population and the native forces stationed in the area.

Another problem that quickly confronted the English commanders was the language barrier that existed between them and the foreign troops. One of the English officers lamented that 119 Danish soldiers had unexpectedly arrived in his region. They were rank and file soldiers who did not have an officer accompanying them. The English commander wanted officers to be quickly sent to the region in order to "awe them in their March" and suggested that action to move the soldiers along be taken quickly since "we find them very troublesome here."[34] In order to accomplish this goal, he urged the government to send an interpreter because "there is not one amongst them yt. can speak English."[35]

 Given the disorganized landing, the forces went into winter quarters with the cavalry settling around Glasgow and the infantry near Chester. The Danish regiments finally sailed for Ireland in March, 1690.[36] During the ensuing war in Ireland, the Danish forces played a major role in William III's campaigns to subdue the Irish supporters of James II. In terms of numbers, the Danish regiments constituted about one-sixth of William's forces in Ireland.[37] Additionally, they participated in all of the major campaigns and sieges that restored English control over Ireland. Most notably, the Danish troops fought valiantly at the Battle of the Boyne in July, 1690, when William III's forces routed those of James II, who were trying to prevent the English advance toward Dublin.[38] According to Würtemberg, the Danish forces forded the Boyne River through a deep, boggy section with the water coming up to their armpits. As they exited the water, an enemy dragoon squadron charged them, but the Danish soldiers successfully pushed them back.[39] The day after the battle, William III gave a speech to his officers where he particularly thanked his most trusted soldiers the Dutch, the Danes, and the Huguenots for their brave service the day before.[40]

Although the Battle of the Boyne represented a devastating defeat for the Jacobites and led to James II fleeing Ireland for France, the fighting continued into 1691. As the conflict dragged on, the Danish forces were gradually decimated through disease, which spread quickly among the soldiers due to inadequate housing and a lack of supplies. Particularly when they entered winter quarters in October 1690, disease rapidly spread among the Danish regiments due to poor quarters "in which half of them have no beds."[41] Compounding the soldiers' suffering was the fact that by October of 1690, the English government owed the members of the Danish regiments 6 months of back pay.[42] In April 1691, Würtemberg reported that he was short 1,300-1,400 men as a result of "Our troublesome crossing, together with the difficulties of transport, winter marches and the rough country."[43]

Although the Danish forces were weakened during the winter of 1690-91, they continued to fight for William III in Ireland throughout the spring and summer of 1691. After the Irish war ended in 1691, the Danish regiments were transferred to Flanders where they fought in the Dutch campaigns against Louis XIV's army. They returned to Denmark in 1698 after the signing of the Treaty of Ryswick, which brought the Nine Years' War to an end.[44] Of the roughly 7,000 soldiers who sailed to England in 1689, about 1,500 returned to Denmark in 1698, the others having died or deserted during their military service.[45]

Conclusion

Although the Danish kingdom lost a large portion of the soldiers it sent abroad in 1689, the policy to hire these regiments to a foreign ruler provided many benefits. First, as Gunner Lind has suggested, the Danish kingdom during the seventeenth and eighteenth centuries was the most militarized state in proportion to its population in Europe.[46] With its territories stretching from northern Norway to Schleswig-Holstein, the Danish monarchs needed a sizable force to preserve and maintain their sovereignty in these widely scattered areas. Compounding this challenge was the constant military threat exerted by the Swedish kingdom throughout the seventeenth century as the Swedish monarchs sought to secure and expand their empire in the Baltic region.[47] These military commitments, however, placed severe strains on the resources of the Danish kingdom as the country struggled to recover from constant invasions during the middle decades of the seventeenth century and to deal with the limited natural resources available within the kingdom. In an era when military support consumed roughly 66% of the monarchy's budget during peacetime and upwards of 88% of the budget during periods of war, the opportunity to have a foreign ruler maintain the kingdom's troops must have provided a welcome respite to the economic woes of the kingdom.[48]

Second, the hiring out of Danish regiments also provided significant diplomatic advantages. Throughout the seventeenth century, the Danish kingdom's political position in the Baltic declined in the face of the buildup of the Swedish empire. A consequence of this trend was that the Danish kingdom was less capable of exerting its influence in European affairs. Forging ties with the Maritime Powers through the use of its military, thus allowed the Danish monarchy to continue to play a role in European diplomacy and to help affect the outcome of European military conflicts without compromising its already weakened political and economic position.

ENDNOTES

1. Mark A. Thomson, "Louis XIV and William III, 1689-97," in Ragnhild Hatton and J.S. Bromley, eds., *William III and Louis XIV: Essays 1680-1720 by and for Mark A. Thomson* (Toronto: University of Toronto Press, 1968), 24-5.

2. Stewart P. Oakley, *William III and the Northern Crowns during the Nine Years War 1689-1697* (New York: Garland Publishing , Inc. 1987), 10-1.

3. For example, see Steven Murdoch, "The House of Stuart and the Scottish Professional Soldier 1618-1640: A Conflict of Nationality and Identities," in Bertrand Taithe and Tim Thornton, eds., *War: Identities in Conflict 1300-2000* (Stroud, Gloucestershire: Sutton Publisher, 1998), 37; Thomas Riis, *Should Auld Acquaintance Be Forgot...Scottish-Danish Relations c. 1450-1707* (Odense: Odense University Press, 1988), 81-112.

4. For a comprehensive account of the seventeenth-century wars fought between Denmark and Sweden, see Stewart P. Oakley, *War and Peace in the Baltic 1560-1790* (New York: Routledge, 1992), 27-110. For a discussion of Danish involvement in the Thirty Years' War, see Paul Douglas Lockhart, *Denmark in the Thirty Years' War, 1618-1648: King Christian IV and the Decline of the Oldenburg State* (Selingrove: Susquehanna University Press, 1996).

5. For an account of the warfare in the Baltic region during the 1650s, see Robert I. Frost, *The Northern Wars: War, State and Society in Northeastern Europe, 1558-1721* (Harlow, Essex: Pearson Education Limited, 2000), 169-183. For a comprehensive account of the creation of Sweden's Baltic empire, see Michael Roberts, *The Swedish Imperial Experience: 1560-1718* (Cambridge: Cambridge University Press, 1979), 1-42.

6. Oakley, *War and Peace in the Baltic*, 97-101.

7. Jonathan Israel, *The Dutch Republic: Its Rise, Greatness, and Fall 1477-1806* (Oxford: Clarendon Press, 1995), 316-8.

8. Lars Christensen, "The Foreign Policy of Hannibal Sehested 1660-1666," in *Scandinavian Journal of History* 24, no. 1 (1999), 117; Yngve Lorents, *Efter Brömsebrofreden. Svenska och Danska förbindelser med Frankrike och Holland 1645-1649* (Uppsala. Almqvist & Wiksells Boktryckeri, 1916), 8-18, 93-8.

9. Ragnhild Hatton, "Gratifications and Foreign Policy: Anglo-French Rivalry in Sweden during the Nine Years War," in Hatton and Bromley, *William III and Louis XIV*, 70-1. Also see Oakley, *William III and the Northern Crowns*, 29-30.

10. Oakley, *William III and the Northern Crowns*, 30-1.

11. Preben Torntoft, "William III and Denmark-Norway, 1697-1702," in *The English Historical Review* (January, 1966): 2-3.

12. Ibid., 2.

13. Oakley, *William III and the Northern Crowns*, 33.

14. Torntoft, 3.

15. Stewart P. Oakley, "The Interception of Posts in Celle, 1694-1700," in Hatton and Bromley, *William III and Louis XIV*, 98.

16. Oakley, *William III and the Northern Crowns*, 46-8.

17. Ibid., 79.

18. Copy of a Treaty with Denmark, regarding 6000 foot and 1000 horse, August 15, 1689, Additional Manuscripts 40799, British Library, London.

19. K. Danaher and J. G. Simms, *The Danish Force in Ireland 1690-1691* (Dublin: Stationery Office for the Irish Manuscripts Commission, 1962), 8-9.

20. Oakley, *William III and the Northern Crowns*, 82-4.

21. For a discussion of the European wide crisis during the seventeenth century see Niels Stennsgaard, "The Seventeenth-Century Crisis," in Geoffrey Parker and Lesley M. Smith, eds., *The General Crisis of the Seventeenth Century* (New York: Routledge, 1997), 32-56.

22. Knud J. V. Jespersen, *Danmarks historie*, Vol. 3, *Tiden 1648-1730*, Søren Mørch, ed. (Copenhagen: Gyldendal, 1989), 109-44. Also see Knud J. V. Jespersen, "Absolute Monarchy in Denmark: Change and Continuity," in *Scandinavian Journal of History* 12 (1987), 309.

23. Thomas Munck, *The Peasantry and the Early Absolute Monarchy in Denmark, 1660-1708* (Copenhagen: Landbohistorisk Selskab, 1979), 28-37.

24. Robert Molesworth, *An Account of Denmark as it was in the Year 1692* (London, 1694), 124-5, Wilson Library, Special Collections, University of Minnesota, Minneapolis, MN.

25. K. C. Rockstroh, *Udviklingen af den nationale hær i Danmark i det 17. og 18. aarhundrede*, Vol. 2, *Tiden 1670-1708* (Copenhagen: Det Schønbergske Forlag, 1916), 341.

26. Danaher and Simms, *Danish Force in Ireland*, 7.

27. List and Number of the Danish Forces, Egerton 3337, British Library, London.

28. Danaher and Simms, *Danish Force in Ireland*, 12.

29. Gunner Lind, "Military and Absolutism: The Army Officers of Denmark-Norway as a Social Group and Political Factor, 1660-1848," in *Scandinavian Journal of History* 12 (1987), 226-31.

30. Molesworth, *An Account of Denmark*, 135.

31. Danaher and Simms, *Danish Force in Ireland*, 12.

32. George Barrett to the Marquis of Caermarther, Lord President of his Majesty's Privy Council, Hull, November 10, 1689, Egerton 3337, no. 119, British Library, London; Fairfax to a member of the government administration [individual's name unknown], Egerton 3337, no. 125, British Library, London; Fairfax to Marquis of Carmarthen, Lord President of his Majesty's Privy Council, Hull, November 19, 1689, Egerton 3337, no. 131, British Library, London.

33. Fairfax to Marquis of Carmarthen, Egerton 3337, no. 131, British Library, London.

34. Admiral de Cardo to William Blathwayt, Additional Manuscripts 35155, no. 161, British Library, London.

35. Ibid.

36. Duke of Würtemberg to Christian V, Belfast, March 13, 1690, in Danaher and Simms, *Danish Force in Ireland*, p. 31.

37. C. O. Danachair, "The Danish Corps in Ireland, 1690-1691," in *The Irish Sword* 5 (1961-62), 1.

38. For a detailed description of the battle, see Pádraig Lenihan, *1690 Battle of the Boyne* (Stroud, Gloucestershire: Tempus Publishing Limited, 2003), 147-208.

39. Würtemberg to Christian V, near Dublin, July 5, 1690, in Danaher and Simms, *Danish Force in Ireland*, 42-3.

40. Lenihan, *Battle of the Boyne*, 226.

41. Würtemberg to Christian V, Waterford, November 12, 1690, in Danaher and Simms, *Danish Force in Ireland*, 91.

42. Würtemberg to Christian V, Waterford, October 29, 1690, in Ibid., 90.

43. Würtemberg to Christian V, Waterford, April 4, 1691, in Ibid., 104.

44. Danachair, "The Danish Corps in Ireland," 8-9.

45. Ibid., 9.

46. Gunner Lind, "Den dansk-norske hær i det 18. århundrede. Optimering, modernisering og professionalisering," in *Historisk Tidsskrift* 86, no. 1 (1986), 28.

47. Lind, "Military and Absolutism," 222.

48. Jespersen, *Danmarks historie*, 112.

CHAPTER 8

THE FASHION FOR PHYSICS: PUBLIC LECTURE COURSES IN ENLIGHTENMENT FRANCE

Michael R. Lynn

On 21 November 1754, a French newspaper, the *Affiches de Paris*, announced the beginning of a new lecture course in experimental physics by the famed savant and long-time popularizer Jean Antoine Nollet. This course—covering such topics as electricity, mechanics, optics, and magnets—was but one in a myriad of similar endeavors all aimed at disseminating Enlightenment science to the people of Paris. Hundreds of popularizers offered thousands of public lecture courses and demonstrations throughout the eighteenth century. Nollet himself gave well over 150 classes in the course of his 35-year career.[1] Parisians went wild over science, a predilection reported by the celebrated writer, François-Marie Arouet, called Voltaire, as early as 1735. Everyone, he noted, was "beginning to act like a geometer and a physicist."[2] By the end of the century, this trend had expanded exponentially, causing one social commentator, Jean-Baptiste Pujoulx, to claim that "savants roamed the streets, and our boulevards have become schools of physics."[3] As a common cliché suggested, in the eighteenth century "science was for everyone."[4]

During the course of the Enlightenment, science expanded from private laboratories and royal academies and entered popular culture. No longer limited to elite savants, science became an object of popularization and commodification as the general public began to see it as something worth spending its time and money to acquire. "The taste for physics is so spread out in the world today," wrote the author Jean Ferapie-Dufieu, "that it seems necessary . . . to have at least a smattering of it."[5] Many people pursued knowledge in order to sprinkle their conversations with scientific metaphors and references or perhaps even to utilize and incorporate this newfound knowledge into their lives. Science as cultural capital took on a whole new role as knowledge of scientific language, methods, goals, and discoveries became a necessary and significant part of eighteenth-century culture. Public lectures on a number of topics such as natural history, experimental physics, chemistry, and mathematics drew in an extraordinary array of men and women from a variety of social, economic, and educational backgrounds. However, these lectures have received little attention from historians of eighteenth-century France who have focused instead on the study of movements like Mesmerism or technological innovations like ballooning. Most of the historiography on French popular science centers are on the work of the intellectual elite. The relationship between science and popular culture, however, has rarely been addressed for Enlightenment France.[6]

This essay uses experimental physics as a case study to examine the nature and process of popularization in eighteenth-century France and explains its place within the larger cultural milieu of the public sphere and urban scientific culture. Disseminators employed a variety of methods when taking science out of elite academies and laboratories and putting it into the hands of the general public. While most historians of French science have focused on printed popularization, this essay examines public lecture courses and their significance within the urban cultural milieu. Those venues provided Parisians with access to elite scientific activities and gave people an opportunity to influence the ways in which science was made available for a commercial audience. Public lecture courses, like salons, scientific and literary clubs, reading societies, freemason lodges, and provincial academies, provided locations where interested amateurs could appropriate science. Most important, the rise of public lecture courses indicated a conceptual shift in the way people viewed science. The attraction of science did not come about because of some dramatic change in the content of science or because the Enlightenment philosophes asserted that it was important.

The idea of popularizing science for amateurs did not suddenly appear in the eighteenth century. Instead, some people, members of high society in particular, already had some access to scientific dissemination beginning in the seventeenth century. Part of this work appeared at the behest of nobles and other elites. The French physicist and educator, Jacques Rohault, for example, earned a considerable reputation throughout Paris for the regular meetings he held in his home from 1659 until his death in 1672, during which he disseminated Cartesian physics to a general audience. These so-called "Cartesian Wednesdays" earned praise from savants such as Christiaan Huygens and were well-attended by the fashionable women of the seventeenth century. Every Wednesday, persons of "all ages, both sexes, and all professions" could meet to watch Rohault as he strove to provide an experimental base for the philosopher René Descartes' physics.[7] Rohault's educational mission was taken up by one of his followers, a savant named Pierre Sylvain Régis who, reputedly, lectured to the "most prominent ladies" of Toulouse and Montpellier before he settled in Paris.[8] The existing educational system also had a role in the early formation of scientific dissemination. Pierre Polinière, for example, performed experiments outside the classroom for students interested in watching concrete demonstrations of the physical principles they learned in their philosophy classes. Polinière was not attached to any specific college but worked instead as a free-lance demonstrator of natural philosophy. His courses offered "a complete, but also amusing, course of study [that] strongly appealed to the tastes of the young men." This smattering of popularization activities, for the elite and for students, was supplemented by other efforts as well.[9]

So much scientific dissemination took place in the first half of the eighteenth century that by the 1730s, nearly every type of science imaginable was undergoing some kind of popularization. At the same time, in addition to an increase in the subjects begin popularized, the lecturers began to target a much broader spectrum of society. Even a cursory examination reveals the large number and variety of lecture courses offered in Paris. In 1765, for example, the *Affiches de Paris*, a periodical aimed at middle class men and women, printed advertisements for classes on general mathematics, experimental physics, natural history, botany, geometry, chemistry, and pharmacy. The same journal also promoted numerous non-scientific classes offered on topics such as commerce, history, geography, art, architecture, and foreign languages. By the 1780s, the opportunities for satisfying intellectual needs and desires had risen still further both in overall numbers and in variety. In 1785, over 100 public lecture courses were advertised in the *Affiches de Paris* alone.[10]

Now people could attend classes in navigation, physical astronomy, electricity, French writing and pronunciation, the properties of air, vocal and instrumental music, midwifery, surgery, Latin, the vegetable kingdom, the structure of the eye, the painting and sculpture of animals, Hebrew, poetry, optics, mineralogy, and agriculture. Moreover, the courses offered did not merely water down elite science for an unlearned audience. Auditors taking Monsieur Dupont's mathematics class in 1779, for example, studied such advanced subjects as differential and integral calculus.[11] Few individuals today, after already finishing their schooling, would be likely to voluntarily take a calculus class, but Dupont's classes were perennial favorites in Paris for well over a decade. Experimental physics, broadly defined by contemporaries, holds an important place amid these many courses and provides a broad look at the fashionable side of science.[12]

Part of the problem in trying to understand, describe, and analyze the place of popular science in eighteenth-century France lies in the confusion over the precise definition of popular science. The perennial question is "popular compared to what?" Frequently, this problem is overcome by negative definitions; popular science earns its title because it is not elite or official science. Of course, popular science can be produced by elite savants, who occasionally felt the need to address their ideas to an audience larger than that of their immediate intellectual peers, but this sort of popularization usually took the form of polemical works written with the intent to persuade others to accept a particular scientific position. Nonetheless, not only did some elite savants create popular science works and participate in the process of popularization, but the trend worked the other direction as well. A few popularizers wrote books intended for an elite scientific audience. Mathurin-Jacques Brisson, for example, taught popular science courses for several decades while simultaneously producing advanced works on ornithology and physics. Jean-François Pilâtre de Rozier published several articles in the *Journal de Physique* on such topics as gases, even as he offered a series of popular lecture courses to the Parisian public.[13] The line between elite and popular, therefore, was by no means clear nor does drawing a dichotomy between elite and popular science clarify the situation.

Popular science is sometimes differentiated from elite science by calling it fringe or marginal science, indicating just how difficult many historians of science have found the problem of defining popular science. Should all types of science be classified by comparison to some standard of elite science? If it is not elite science, then it must be outside of the mainstream and therefore merely marginal? The problem lies in the fact that popular science is only marginal if compared solely with elite science. In fact, popular science is directly within the mainstream of urban culture, and arguably figured as prominently in the lives of Parisians as elite science. The average urban dweller in eighteenth-century Paris was more likely to see some form of popular science than he or she was to interact with academicians or attend one of the public meetings of the Royal Academy of Sciences. Taken from this point of view, popular science occupied the dominant position in society while elite science found itself located on the cultural margins. Popular science, then, should be located more centrally. Taken from the perspective of urban culture, elite science was the marginal science.[14]

To avoid the problem of comparing popular science to elite science at one end of a spectrum and charlatan science at the other, some historians have suggested an analysis that situates popular science as public science in the public sphere. However, popular science was not necessarily public science. A great deal of science occurred in the public eye but not all of it was designed to appeal to the masses. For example, the Royal Academy of Sciences, an institution deeply concerned with its public image and devoted to the publicity of its actions held the biannual public meetings. Those sessions were certainly public since they were open to those other than academicians and were held in a public setting. Much of the information presented at those meetings was set at a level comprehensible to the expanded audience. But the focus of these sessions rarely lay on the science itself; the goal of the academicians centered on social and political legitimization. The science introduced at the public sessions aided the members of the academy in demonstrating their worth, both to the state that gave them pensions as members of a royal academy and to the public who made them heroes.[15] Frequently science found in that arena was being popularized, at least in the sense that it was being diffused or watered down for a non-scientifically educated audience; but that was rarely the point of the exercise. The academicians chose their topics carefully, at least partially based on what they thought might be appreciated by the people watching and listening. Science certainly underwent dissemination here, and it was certainly public science, but its popularity was hardly the issue. In fact, the elite and exclusive audience at these meetings was severely limited and those present had little control over the content of the meetings. A minimum definition of a popular science must include a much larger and more involved audience base.[16]

The general public found some popular science exceptionally easy to observe. Ballooning offers the supreme example of public performance from the eighteenth century. Aeronautic experiments were frequently held directly in the public eye, often before mass audiences comprising just about anybody, as contemporary descriptions and depictions indicate. These demonstrations almost had to be performed in a large public arena due to the nature of the work involved. Launching a balloon required, first of all, lots of space. Equally important, it required lots of money; tickets were sold to people so that they could view the launch from close quarters with the price of the tickets increasing relative to one's proximity to the balloon. Thus, the public not only watched, it also directly funded the experiments. Tickets were a form of subscription and people who paid in advance got first access to the demonstrations. The public, in this case, acted as both witnesses to the experiments and as patrons of the work; science cannot achieve a much more public status. Ballooning achieved a rare position within mass culture. The crowds involved themselves so completely in ballooning launches that failed experiments could even lead to riots, as in the case of the unfortunate Abbé Miollan whose botched attempt to take off in a balloon resulted in his being run out of Paris. Of course, popularizers rarely sought out such a large audience and few tried to teach all segments of the population, such as the *sans-culottes* (that is, the working classes) about science.[17]

Popular science, then, dealt with topics in such a way that a general audience could understand and grasp some of the basic concepts and important applications. The information was not necessarily diffused or watered-down science but one that had been explained in a largely oral and visual way that did not require a detailed knowledge of mathematics or mechanics. The techniques involved drew upon both elite and charlatan scientific presentations and occupied an important space between the two. The composition of the audience remained theoretically open, much more so than some public science. But limitations, usually economic, did operate to reduce the pool of potential audience members; participation in popular science courses required a level of income higher than that of the average urban worker. The popularizers themselves were not opposed to elite savants; indeed, some popularizers were themselves elite savants. Instead, the work of dissemination should be placed within a larger spectrum ranging from the charlatanesque at one end to elite science at the other, with the recognition that any one individual could conceivably appear at several different places on the spectrum depending on the kind of work in which he was engaged.

Historians most often associate the practice of popularization with books, such as Bernard de Fontenelle's *Conversations on the Plurality of Worlds*, Francesco Algarotti's *Newtonianism for Ladies*, and Voltaire's *Elements of the Philosophy of Newton*, which he wrote with the considerable assistance of Emilie du Châtelet. Alternately, scholars have studied popular science through periodical publications, such as the *Mémoires of the Académie Royale des Sciences*, the *Journal de Physique*, and the *Journal des Savants*.[18] In a few instances, other periodicals, aimed at an amateur, middle-class audience, also included scientific information; these include the *Avant-Coureur*, the various affiches such as the *Affiches de Paris* and *Affiches de Province*, and the *Journal de Paris*. These journals, and especially the *Affiches*, targeted an elite and middle class audience.[19] However, a more widespread form of popularization has hitherto been neglected within the French context—namely, the public science course, a venue that offered a very different kind of popularization than the more literary forms.

First of all, popularizers were more intimately concerned with their audience than were authors since the work of popularization more directly contributed to their livelihood. Voltaire, du Châtelet, Algarotti, and Fontenelle all had other sources of income, such as government offices and money through marriage or family, and did not need or try to earn a living through the popularization of science. Disseminating science was merely a sideline for these individuals and was usually undertaken as a means to persuade their peers to a certain philosophical position. The people who taught public lecture courses usually practiced popularization as a full-time job. These professional disseminators, of course, utilized a number of methods to popularize science, including books, but a common denominator existed in the form of a public lecture course. When lecturers wrote books, the format usually followed the public lectures closely so that an audience member could follow along with the lecture in the book or, alternately, so amateurs could duplicate the experiments on their own. The number of such courses grew steadily over the course of the eighteenth century.[20]

Disseminators who offered public lecture courses furnished their audiences with, arguably, the easiest access to popularized science. By not requiring a learned audience, they opened themselves up to a very wide group of possible auditors. Many lecturers targeted women, who typically suffered from fewer educational opportunities than their male counterparts. In addition, public lecture courses varied both in terms of length and the necessary level of intellectual acumen. Courses could range from one-day only demonstrations to much lengthier affairs lasting as much as three or four months. At the same time, the content varied greatly as well, with some offering much more advanced information; this included the popularization efforts of Pagny, a popularizer who eventually managed to get the attention of the French royal family, and whose course on experimental physics included an analysis of the varying scientific explanations of gravity.[21] Other disseminators admittedly concentrated on only the most appealing and descriptive experiments. The broad selection of courses offered in eighteenth-century Paris enabled the interested public to shop around and only take those in which they had a specific interest. Courses were offered both during the day and at night and could be fairly expensive; at the high end a series of lectures might cost as much as 72 livres. On the other hand, a single course could cost less than one livre or about the cost of a one-day's supply of bread. Since a reasonably well-off artisan could make 10 to 15 livres each week, it is certainly possible that some of his income might go towards a single lecture or demonstration. Popularizers might target a specific social or intellectual group or might open the class to a more general audience. They might aim at a more intellectually oriented group or hope to reach a more uneducated segment of the population. This marketplace reality encouraged a certain level of competition among popularizers and made them extremely responsive to the wishes of their potential students.

The enduring popularity of the professors and demonstrators who worked in and around Paris testified to their ability to capture the admiration and loyalty of their audience. In addition, they took quite seriously the appellation many of them used; "science for everyone." Nollet noted that because of the general interest in physics, it was fitting for him to describe its principles "at the level of everybody."[22] Men and women from a wide variety of social, economic, and educational backgrounds found themselves the targets of innumerable advertisements designed to lure them into attending public lecture courses. The combined breadth and depth of public lecture courses made them into a sort of oral and visual *Encyclopédie*, covering nearly all aspects of knowledge as more and more options becoming available throughout the eighteenth century. In many respects, these public lecture courses were the most up-to-date presentations available in terms of content, rivaling periodicals in this respect. Audiences watched the unveiling of new instruments and experiments and gained access to the latest theories and ideas in experimental physics. Popularizers were on the cutting edge in terms of scientific activity during the Enlightenment and could take advantage of their positions as mediators of that knowledge to present new trends as they developed.

The popularizers left little doubt that their chief goal was to teach people about the utility of science. They hoped, or at least claimed, that their courses would aid in the intellectual development of their audience and would thus contribute to the overall rationalization of society promised by the Enlightenment. In this fashion, popularizers implicitly linked their work to that of the Enlightenment in general. This connection, however, is certainly tenuous at best, composed as much of propaganda as it was of fact. Professing that a course in experimental physics would be useful proved easier than explicitly demonstrating that utility to the audience. In order to strengthen the impression of usefulness, many popularizers emphasized the entertainment factor in their demonstrations. Experiments could become so theatrical, in fact, that often the science seemed to be lost. Such is certainly the case with one of Giuseppe Pinetti's experiments, during which he used electricity to make an artificial spider move.[23] Although Pinetti apparently performed this trick with great skill and enthusiasm, its scientific purpose eludes the modern reader. However, the real utility lay in obtaining scientific knowledge, in this case about electricity, and at least a moderate claim to enlightened rationality.

To make these links between Enlightenment utility and the spectacle of science, some courses specifically used eighteenth-century icons, especially the English physicist and mathematician Isaac Newton and the various forms of Newtonianism. In the 1760s, a teacher and demonstrator of experimental physics named Allard began offering a course that purported to explain all the principles of Newton's natural philosophy. His advertisements claimed that he performed a great number of "interesting and curious" experiments designed to confirm Newton's theories.[24] The savant Antoine Deparcieux likewise concentrated his efforts on Newtonian astronomy and optics for the physics course he established during the 1780s. One classic Newtonian experiment performed by Deparcieux (and many others) dealt with the division of sunlight into the color spectrum with a prism. In addition, he applied Newtonianism to his explanations of other phenomena, such as electricity and magnetism.[25] In 1783, Jean-François

Pilâtre de Rozier appropriated some of Newton's theories and "most entertaining experiments" for a series of lectures on optics.[26] But, for every lecture course that focused on Newtonianism, there were many more that proposed other theories. The abbé de la Pouyade, for example, proselytized the natural philosophy developed by the amateur cosmologist and natural philosopher Jacques-Charles-François de la Perrière de Roiffé. This system rejected Newtonian gravity in favor of a theory of impulsion whereby astronomical bodies moved through an outside force, rather than through some mysterious attraction.[27]

Some popularizers favored their own theories over those of other savants. Jean Paul Marat, later to become a martyr of the French Revolution, thought that his own work in such fields as optics had surpassed Newton's and "changed the face" of science. As a result, he offered several courses advocating his theories over those of other savants.[28] In 1753, Charles Rabiqueau, a lawyer at the Paris Parlement, published his ideas on electricity in *Le Spectacle du feu élémentaire, ou cours d'électricité expérimentale*, where he described many of the experiments he routinely performed for his students. Rabiqueau clearly hoped to instruct through entertainment. One entertaining experiment utilized electricity to guide a boat around in a bowl of water. Essentially, Rabiqueau argued that electricity was really just a special type of the fire that he believed formed the basic mechanism of the universe. Although Rabiqueau lamented that the Royal Academy of Sciences "refused to accept knowledge" when it was offered, his courses remained fashionable with the public for over thirty years; Parisians knew what they liked, even without the help or the approval of elite savants.[29] The public legitimization of Rabiqueau meant his continued financial and social success, a success maintained in spite of the disapproval of academicians who acted as official arbitrators of good science. Over the course of the eighteenth century, the public not only appropriated science into its cultural milieu, but also gave itself the authority to judge good and bad science. In the public sphere, it was sometimes more important to be thought useful and entertaining than to be officially accepted by the academicians.

While some popularizers were interested only in promoting their own scientific ideas, more often they presented an eclectic blend of various scientific theories. Jean-Antoine Nollet, for example, claimed that he did not limit himself to any particular theory of physics. "It is not the physics of Descartes, nor of Newton, nor of Leibniz, that I propose particularly to follow; but without any personal preference, and without any distinction, it is that which, by the general vogue, and by well attested facts, shall appear to me to be best established."[30] His work combined strong elements of both Cartesianism and Newtonianism. Simply put, Nollet's theories favored the Cartesian worldview, while his emphasis on experimentation relied more on the Enlightenment appropriation of Newtonian methodology. He always emphasized the utility of experimental physics. For this reason, Nollet's views on a variety of scientific phenomena remained well known and accepted long after the "correct" answers had been discovered.[31] Provable theories held less importance in the public arena than did the utility and spectacle of science.

The auditors of such classes accepted the authority of the teachers to create experiments that accurately illustrated good scientific principles. Some of the most entertaining displays, and the ones best known today, came in the field of electricity. In April 1746, for example, Nollet used a Leyden jar to transmit a simultaneous electrical shock to one hundred and eighty of Louis XV's royal guards, all holding hands, while the monarch and his entourage gleefully looked on. Later, he performed the same experiment on two hundred monks, volunteers from a Carthusian monastery located near Paris.[32] It is worth noting that Nollet performed his demonstrations so well, and had such strong support from other savants, that he translated his dissemination efforts into several lucrative posts including teaching science to the children of the king and a position in the Royal Academy of Sciences. Other savants tried to mimic both Nollet's success and his most famous demonstrations. Nicolas-Philippe Ledru, who sometimes went by the stage name Comus (after the Roman god of revelry) put an interesting twist to this experiment by forming his human chain with volunteers taken from the paying audience. This technique literally brought the power of electricity home to the auditors and allowed them to participate directly as both audience and experimental subject.[33] A public easily viewed experiments such as these unaware of the nuances behind complicated scientific apparatus. At the same time, useful generalizations could be drawn from these demonstrations; in the case of the Leyden jar experiment, both the speed and the strength of the electrical shocks could be visually measured. These experiments were good at unveiling the mysteries of science, promoting discussion, and drawing attention to important facts.

Other popularizers placed more emphasis on the spectacular and were less concerned with using their demonstrations to explain scientific principles. For example, the experimental physicist Perrin performed lectures on natural philosophy to wide acclaim even though his experiments did not promote any theory at all. His success as a popularizer rested largely on the strengths of his dog, a spaniel that could "read, calculate, solve problems, and do other physics tricks and games." Perrin's "little savant dog" occupied a central place in the show: women, he claimed, particularly applauded this multi-talented animal that, by 1787, apparently could read both English and French, in addition to its abilities as a demonstrator of experimental physics. Perrin managed to raise himself from relative obscurity, aided by little more than a deft hand and a very talented dog, to become a mainstay in the world of scientific popularization. He gave his short lecture course in the boulevard theaters with a success that was nothing if not remarkable.[34] Perrin, commenting on his achievements, wrote,

> O happy century, where Science
> Is an amusement for everyone!
> Charmed by our intelligence
> Physics has become a very enjoyable subject.[35]

Perrin had every right to be happy with physics, but the relationship between Enlightenment science and this self-proclaimed "mechanic, engineer, and demonstrator of amusing physics" remains obscure. His experiments sound suspiciously like magic tricks or visual conundrums: the "enchanted tower," the "incomprehensible inkwell," the "sympathetic light," and "the dancing rings." This latter experiment was a perennial favorite. It called for rings to be donated by the audience; Perrin would then put them into a glass where, through the application of an electrical charge, they would seem to dance about. Perrin designed his loosely educational experiments in order to maximize their entertainment value. He always struggled to ensure that his "physics games" were also "very instructive."[36] The utility of science, along with its theatricality, became necessary factors in its popularization during the course of the eighteenth century.

But popular science could and frequently did fall into the hands of scientific showmen. One such individual was Giuseppe Pinetti, a professor of mathematics and physics who had earned a pension from the Prussian court, gained membership in many European academies, and could count on recommendations from many of the kings and princes of Europe. He appeared in Paris periodically during the 1780s, often performing his experimental physics show at the royal Théâtre des Menus-Plaisirs. In 1789, he took a definitive step towards turning experimental physics into something as entertaining as it was scientific when he published his book, *Amusemens physiques*. This was just what the public wanted. Contemporaries admired his efforts, one of whom wrote that Pinetti was "a conjurer infinitely superior to Comus."[37] It is interesting to note that while Pinetti's admirers considered him a professor of mathematics and physics, they still referred to him as a conjuror. Pinetti's theatrical style effectively combined science and spectacle with many of his experiences having overtly theatrical names: the "philosophical mushroom" for example, or the "magic table."[38] Intermixed with these experiments were procedures for changing the color of a rose, mathematical calculations with cards, and a method of conjuring an egg under a goblet.

In utilizing a theater for his combination of science and spectacle, Pinetti followed in the footsteps of numerous other popularizers who had taken their courses onto the stage. Many popularizers performed scientific demonstrations and offered courses in theaters, particularly those found on the Boulevard du Temple. In 1785, for example, Perrin worked out of the Salle des Elèves de l'Opéra on the Boulevard du Temple every day from 31 March through 4 April.[39] Perrin and his dog frequently worked out of the boulevard theaters, often for several days in a row, presumably while the actors rehearsed new plays. The general popularity of these theaters probably aided in attracting an audience for the science shows produced there.[40] Although street theaters were scattered all over Paris, the Boulevard du Temple contained several of the most famous such as the Ambigu-Comique and the Variétés-Amusantes. Location, however, did not necessarily affect the lecture style or content but was a natural result of the combination of utilitarian science and spectacular demonstrations. Pinetti's entertaining experiments seem to be a long way from some of the popularizers who strove to disseminate the theories of Newton or Descartes. Nonetheless, he and most other popularizers working in Paris during the Enlightenment employed similar techniques, regardless of whether they aimed at disseminating Newtonianism, exhibiting the usefulness of science, or chiefly trying to be entertaining. Nollet and Perrin, in many ways, occupy the end points of the popular science spectrum. While both claimed to include education and entertainment in their courses, Nollet clearly has a better claim to instruction and Perrin to spectacle. The status of most purveyors of public lecture courses occupied a much grayer middle ground with entertainment and utility both acting as integral parts to the process of popularization.

The role of public lecture courses in the popularization of science in France deserves a central place within the spectrum of scientific activity. As science, especially experimental physics, underwent a conceptual shift within the minds of urban denizens, the significance of popularizers and of the information they disseminated grew enormously. Books alone certainly could not meet such a demand, generated by an ever-expanding audience, and it fell to popularizers and their public lecture courses to satisfy the growing desire for access to the science of the Enlightenment. But what were the results of all of this dissemination? What happened to the popularizers and to their audience? And what happened to the science during all of this activity?

The popularizers gained, at least temporarily, much of what they wanted. In an age of shrinking state patronage and limited opportunities within the royal academies, professional disseminators needed to forge a new path toward intellectual legitimacy and financial solvency; their success depended on the general public rather than the state. At the same time, just as some Enlightenment authors claimed the authority to speak for the public, the new scientifically aware public sometimes availed themselves of the chance to speak out on scientific issues. They spoke, not through philosophical treatises but in a variety of other ways, including through their attendance at public lecture courses. The popularizers they frequented could then claim the full support of the public. At the same time, by paying admission fees, and through their purchase of instruments and books, the public gave popularizers more financial freedom. For their part, the audience for science appropriated their new knowledge into their lives as they saw fit. For some, this meant putting science to work for some utilitarian purpose. Others considered the important place science held among certain circles as a measure of status and so attended courses in order to increase their cultural capital and infiltrate or maintain their social position. Many, of course, attended public lecture courses strictly for their entertainment value. Science was fun, recreational, frequently spectacular, and easily marketable.

Popular science left its mark on the cultural milieu of Enlightenment France in a variety of different ways. Most obviously, a new forum for gaining knowledge, the public lecture course entered forcefully into society and grew in dramatic ways over earlier versions that had been in the exclusive possession of the nobility or universities. Arenas where the public could gain access to science proliferated throughout the century and provided untold opportunities for the general public to participate in the Enlightenment. Similarly, a new and ever-expanding audience came to be the target of this popularization effort. Most importantly, science, and the Enlightenment more generally, came to be a commodity in at least two senses. First, it could be purchased in the form of books, periodicals and, as shown in this essay, in public lectures. Second, it came to hold cultural importance and was an important commodity within urban society.

Whatever the reasons why people took public lecture courses, the relationship between the general public, science, and elite savants changed over the course of the eighteenth century. By the 1770s and 1780s, the general public had gained the right to act as scientific patrons by attending public lecture courses and supporting popularizers. Questions of scientific legitimacy were usually the strict purview of the academicians. But in the last decades of the eighteenth century, the public began to involve itself in debates and to attempt to sway both public and scientific opinion. And just as the French state was forced to address popular opinion in the political sphere, the scientific representatives of the government found themselves compelled to confront a public that had appropriated for itself the role of arbiter of science. Academicians now had to try to win the support of the public in order to win certain scientific arguments. These debates, such as those over the efficacy of the divining rod, drew supporters from among both the general population and elite savants thus moving the debate from its usual spot within the academy and taking it out into the public sphere. [41] Science found itself the subject of general debates with savants and amateurs alike taking sides and expressing opinions in books, journal and newspaper articles, and letters. Science, disseminated by professional popularizers, formed a key component in urban popular culture and the taste for physics maintained a significant place in Enlightenment France.

Michael R. Lynn

ENDNOTES

1. *Affiches de Paris*, 21 November 1754, 717. In 1762, the *Avant-coureur* claimed that Nollet had already offered 147 classes in the previous 26 years; *Avant-coureur*, 8 March 1762, 148-9.

2. Voltaire to Pierre Robert Le Cornier de Cideville, [16 April] 1735, in Voltaire, *Correspondance*, ed. Theodore Besterman, vol. 87 (Geneva, 1965), 132.

3. Jean-Baptiste Pujoulx, *Paris à la fin du XVIIIe siècle* (Paris, 1801), 33-4.

4. This cliché could be found on the title page of many scientific works designed for a popular audience. See, for example, Voltaire, *Eléments de la philosophie de Newton*, in Robert L. Walters and W. H. Barber, eds., *The Complete Works of Voltaire*, vol. 15 (Oxford, 1992).

5. Jean Ferapie-Dufieu, *Manuel physique, ou manière courte est facile d'expliquer les phénomènes de la nature* (Paris, 1758), vii-viii.

6. Pierre Bourdieu, *Outline of a Theory of Practice*, trans. Richard Nice (Cambridge, 1977); Robert Darnton, *Mesmerism and the End of the Enlightenment in France* (Cambridge, MA, 1968); Jean Torlais, *Un physicien au siècle des lumières: L'abbé Nollet, 1700-1770* (Paris, 1954); Geoffrey Sutton, *Science for a Polite Society: Gender, Culture, & the Demonstration of Enlightenment* (Boulder, 1995); Andreas Kleinert, *Die Allgemeinverständlichen Physikbücher der französischen Aufklärung* (Aarau, 1974); René Taton, ed., *Enseignement et diffusion des sciences en France au XVIIIe siècle* (Paris, 1964). For Germany, see Oliver Hochadel, *Öffentliche Wissenschaft: Elektrizität in der deutschen Aufklärung* (Göttingen: Wallstein, 2003).

7. Claude Clerselier, ed., *Lettres de M. Descartes* (1659; reprint, Paris, 1724), vol. 2, preface, unpaginated, quoted in Londa Schiebinger, *The Mind Has No Sex? Women in the Origins of Modern Science* (Cambridge, MA, 1989), 23.

8. Bernard de Fontenelle, "Eloge de Régis," in *Histoire du renouvellement de l'Académie royale des sciences...et les éloges historiques*, vol. 1 (1709; reprint, Brussels, 1969), 179.

9. Anonymous, "Abregé de la vie de M. Polinière," in Polinière, *Expériences de physique*, 5th ed., vol. 2 (Paris, 1741).

10. *Affiches de Paris*, 1785.

11. *Journal de Paris*, 3 November 1779, 1253.

12. See Sutton, *Science for a Polite Society*.

13. See Brisson, *Pesanteur spécifique des corps* (Paris, 1787); for Pilâtre de Rozier, see "Nouvelles Observations sur la Machine Hydraulique de M. Vera," *Journal de Physique* 20 (1782): 132-43; and "Réflexions sur la cause de la Foudre," ibid. 16 (1780): 309-11.

14. Seymour H. Mauskopf, "Marginal Science," in R. C. Olby, et al, eds., *Companion to the History of Modern Science* (London, 1990), 869-85.

15. Mary Terrall, "Gendered Spaces, Gendered Audiences: Inside and Outside the Paris Academy of Sciences," *Configurations* 3 (1995): 207-32.

16. See Jan C. C. Rupp, "The New Science and the Public Sphere in the Premodern Era," *Science in Context* 8 (1995): 487-507; Thomas Broman, "The Habermasian Public Sphere and Eighteenth-Century Historiography: A New Look at 'Science *in* the Enlightenment,'" *History of Science* 36 (1998): 123-49.

17. Charles Gillispie, *The Montgolfier Brothers and the Invention of Aviation: 1783-1784* (Princeton, 1983); on Miollan, see *Journal de Paris*, 26 February 1784, 257-58; ibid., 10 July 1784, 819-20; Henri Decremps, *La science sanculottisée* (Paris, 1793-1794); Henry Moss, "Scientists and Sans-Culottes: The Spread of Scientific Literacy in the Revolutionary Year II," *Fundamenta Scientiae* 4 (1983): 101-15.

18. Fontenelle, *Conversations on the Plurality of Worlds*, trans. H.A. Hargreaves (Berkeley: University of California Press, 1990); Algarotti, *Le Newtonianism pour les dames*, trans. M. Duperron de Cstera, 2 vols. (Paris, 1738); Voltaire, *Eléments de la philosophie de Newton*; *Mémoires de l'Académie Royal des Sciences* (Paris, 1698-1790); *Journal de Physique* (Paris, 1773-1793); and *Journal des Savants* (Paris, 1665-1797).

19. *Avant-Coureur* (Paris, 1760-1773); *Affiches de Paris* (Paris, 1745-1811); *Affiches de Province* (Paris, 1752-1792); and *Journal de Paris* (Paris, 1777-1800).

20. William A. Smeaton, "L'*Avant-Coureur*. The Journal in Which Some of Lavoisier's Earliest Research was Reported," *Annals of Science* 13 (1957): 219-34; on the *Affiches,* see Colin Jones, "The Great Chain of Buying: Medical Advertisement, the Bourgeois Public Sphere and the Origins of the French Revolution," *American Historical Review* 101 (1996): 13-40.

21. *Affiches de Paris*, 30 November 1747, n.p.

22. Nollet, *Leçons de physique expérimentale*, vol. 1 (Amsterdam and Leipzig, 1754-1765), ix.

23. Pinetti, *Amusemens physiques, et différentes expériences divertissantes*, 3rd ed. (Paris, 1791), 35-6.

24. *Affiches de Paris*, 1 December 1766, 919; and *Avant-coureur*, 24 November 1766, 747.

25. Deparcieux was the nephew of the academician of the same name; see *Affiches de Paris*, 25 November 1782, 2722; and ibid., 20 January 1782, 158-59.

26. *Journal de Paris*, 13 April 1783, 429.

27. *Avant-coureur*, 29 December 1766, 823-5; and *l'Année littéraire*, 1766, VIII:142.

28. *Courier de l'Europe*, 14 March 1781, 170-1; and *Affiches de Paris*, 11 December 1784, 3280; see also Clifford Conner, *Jean Paul Marat* (New Jersey: Humanities Press, 1997).

29. Rabiqueau, *Le spectacle du feu élémentaire* (Paris, 1753), 232 and Plate 9, Figure 104. On his view of electricity as fire, see the review of *Le spectacle du feu élémentaire* in *l'Année littéraire* (1755), 8: 277-86; on his critique of the Royal Academy of Sciences, see Rabiqueau, *Manifeste littéraire, Servant de supplément aux Journaux sur le livre du Microscope moderne* (Paris, 1781), 15.

30. Nollet, *Leçons de physique expérimentale*, xviii.

31. R.W. Home, "The Notion of Experimental Physics in Early Eighteenth-Century France," in Joseph C. Pitt, ed., *Change and Progress in Modern Science* (Dordrecht, 1985), 111.

32. John L. Heilbron, *Electricity in the Seventeenth and Eighteenth Centuries: A Study of Early Modern Physics* (Berkeley, 1979), 313-14; on Nollet's version of this experiment, see Joseph Priestley, *The History and Present State of Electricity*, ed. Robert E. Schofield, vol. 1 (1775; reprint, New York, 1966), 124-9.

33. *Journal de Paris*, 4 May 1780, 515.

34. *Journal de Paris*, 12 October 1784, 1208; and Perrin, *Amusemens de physique*, (Paris, 1787).

35. Perrin, *Prospectus* (Paris, 1786).

36. See *Affiches de Paris*, 2 April 1793, 1408; and Perrin, *Amusemens physiques* (Paris, 1789). The "physics games" is found in Perrin, *Amusemens* (1787); idem., *Amusemens physiques* (Paris, 1789); and *Chronique de Paris*, 9 April 1790, 396.

37. *Mémoires secretes pour servir à l'histoire de la République des Lettres en France depuis 1762 jusqu'à nos jours*, vol. 24 (London, 1784-89), 90.

38. Pinetti, *Amusements physiques*, 50-1, 68-70.

39. See the *Affiches de Paris*, 31 March 1785; ibid., 1 April 1785, 864; ibid., 2 April 1785, 872; ibid., 3 April 1785, 887; and ibid., 4 April 1785, 896.

40. Michele Root-Bernstein, *Boulevard Theater and Revolution in Eighteenth-Century Paris* (Ann Arbor, 1984), esp. 41-75; Robert Isherwood, *Farce and Fantasy: Popular Entertainment in Eighteenth-Century Paris* (Oxford, 1986), 167-97.

41. Michael R. Lynn, "Divining the Enlightenment: Public Opinion and Popular Science in Old Regime France," *Isis* 92 (2001): 34-54.

CHAPTER 9

REBELLIONS AND NON-EVENTS IN LATE TOKUGAWA AND MEIJI JAPAN

Neil Waters

Three thousand two hundred and twelve *ikki* (struggles) wracked the Japanese countryside during the 278 year period from 1590 to the end of the Tokugawa (1603-1868) era, and 499 more in the first ten years of the Meiji period (1868-1912), according to the compilations of Aoki Koji's *Hyakusho ikki sogo nenpyo*. That number was amended slightly by Yokoyama Toshio in 1977 to 3,001, a figure that, he assures us, is unlikely to grow by any significant number because local historians all over Japan have pursued the traces of *ikki* with such unrelenting energy that few if any could have escaped their efforts.[1]

Indeed, local historians in Japan with whom I have dealt have expressed a sense of actual shame when their own regions produced a dearth of *ikki*. The historiographical conditions which gave rise to what amounted to a local competition for evidence of peasant revolts has been noted elsewhere.[2] For *minshu* (people's) historians, *ikki* are evidence of communitarian values later destroyed by modernization; for Marxists, of class solidarity foully thwarted. For still others without an ideological ax to grind the Edo era *ikki* helped to create the mental climate for the overthrow of the Tokugawa shogunate (Harootunian, Walthall), and serve as evidence that conflict, not continuity, marked the transition from Tokugawa to Meiji.[3]

There may be some truth in all of these positions, but the single-minded zeal with which historians, especially in Japan, focus on *ikki* can obscure two critically important facts: most Japanese never experienced *ikki*, not even in the latter years of the Tokugawa period, when conditions that affected their lives altered with blinding rapidity, and most *ikki* were legal, non-violent, or both. Historians must therefore look to other explanations for how ordinary Japanese coped with one of the world's most dramatic social and economic transformations while keeping their identities, and the nation, intact. Readily available statistics can serve to demonstrate that the role of the *ikki* needs to be sharply downgraded.

First, what is an *ikki*? The *Nihonshi yogo daijiten* defines its Tokugawa incarnation as a *toso* (strife, struggle, conflict, combat) directed against the *ryoshu* (proprietor—usually a *daimyo, daikan* (*shogunal* deputy), *hatamoto* (bannerman), temple, or representatives of these). That leaves a lot of room. Aoki Koji, recognizing this vagueness, divided *ikki* into seven types. From least to most violent these are *fu-on* (meetings to air grievances), *shuso* (legal petition—follows prescribed channels), *osso* (illegal petition), *chosen* (flight), *uchikowashi* (destruction of buildings; usually aimed at rice merchants, pawn brokers etc), *goso* (sometimes called direct petition; the *ryoshu* is pressured by force to accept a petition) and *hoki* (large-scale insurrection, can involve whole provinces).

Even if we accept, momentarily, that all seven of these classifications can be usefully grouped under a single term, it becomes quickly apparent that they should not all have equal weight. A *fu-on* may involve a simple discussion in one village about the possibility of drafting a complaint against an increase in the annual rice-tax; a *hoki* may involve mass destruction and some loss of life over a sizable region, involving hundreds of villages. The former was not even illegal, although it could on occasion escalate into illegal activity, yet it gets equal weight with a genuine *hoki* in most of Aoki's statistical summaries.

Again, Yokoyama tried to ride to the rescue. To make *ikki* statistics more reflective of scale and degree of violence, he gave three forms of *ikki, fu-on, shuso* and *chosan* a weight of one event; *osso, uchikowashi* and *goso* were worth two each, and an insurrection counted as three.

Using these numbers he derived a more useful statistic: incidents per ten thousand *koku* of assessed rice production (one *koku* is about 4.6 bushels of rice, theoretically enough to feed an adult male for one year). He used this figure to rank the *kuni* of Japan in order of their "activity level." This led to a substantial change in the rankings; Musashi, for example, which ranked eighth most active on Aoki's list, ranks, at 1.1 incidents per 10,000 *koku* of assessed production, 44th among Japan's 74 *kuni* (provinces) on Yokoyama's adjusted tables.

Yokoyama's coefficients provide in some ways a better picture of the seriousness and geographical distribution of *ikki* than Aoki's less processed numbers, but they are by no means perfect. A full-scale *hoki* is still worth more than three times the average *fu-on*. It could in fact be argued that since most (not all) *fu-on* were legal, they shouldn't be termed *ikki* at all. The same can be said of *shusho*, or legal petitions. While some escalated into illegal confrontations, most did not. The two classifications together total 950 incidents, or about one -third of the total of all incidents from 1590 to Meiji 4 (1871).[4] Clearly, the difficulty of weighing very disparate events remains.

Moreover the *kokudaka* (annual rice-production)-pegged coefficient could lead one to believe that *ikki* are simply an index of immiseration. It is possible, however, that fairly large numbers of *ikki* could occur in relatively prosperous areas because of rising and frustrated expectations. The *kokudaka* coefficient would be diminished by high productivity, masking any such phenomenon. Yet we know that 1) virtually all petitions in the Tokugawa era calling for a change in *ryoshu* sought to become *tenryo* (lands held directly by the shogunate); none ask to switch from *tenryo* to the status of a private holding—say a *hatamoto*—or a daimyo-controlled holding. And 2) there were overall more *ikki* on *tenryo* than on *han* or *hatamoto-ryo*. So why did people ask to be switched to what appears to be a more desperate condition? I suspect it is because the administrators of *tenryo* were on the whole less strict, and *ikki* on *tenryo* were on the whole more expressive of expectations than desperation.[5]

We still lack any real sense of the odds that an average Japanese peasant would experience an *ikki*, in large part because an *ikki* could involve a portion of a single village, or hundreds of them. We can probably get a rough idea by a sort of order-of-magnitude estimate: there were an average of about 60,000 villages in Tokugawa Japan; *ikki* averaged, roughly, 6 villages per incident (glancing over Aoki's statistics suggests an average of 4-8, with one the most common number); 3,001 *ikki* thus affected about 18,000 villages at one time or another over a period of 278 years. So (barring repeats) on average one-third of Japan's villages experienced some sort of activity once in the whole 278-year span. Since one-third of these were legal, only one-fifth were ever involved in anything illegal. A Japanese peasant living 45 years had roughly one chance in thirty of seeing his village, or a portion of it, involved in an illegal act. His chance of witnessing an illegal act involving physical force or corporal punishment was, if Yokoyama's tables are approximately correct, less than half of that.

I have made a rough check on these numbers by counting and classifying the *ikki* occurring in a single province (Musashi, Japan's highest in rice production) during the period from 1830 to 1871. This 41-year period, fairly close to an average peasant lifespan, is not typical. Nationally, more than one-third of all *ikki* (1,028 out of 3,001) took place in this period; in Musashi the same proportion holds (32 incidents out of a total of 90, in Aoki's unweighted figures, for the 1590-1871 period). One of these, moreover, was the 1866 *Bushu* insurrection, which affected, albeit briefly, a total of approximately 300 villages.[6]

In short, if ever a Musashi commoner were to experience an *ikki*, it was most likely during this period. What were the odds? Again, I cannot claim precision, but any errors will tend toward overestimating the amount of *ikki* participation; when the number of involved villages is unclear, I pick the number 15, which I believe to be high. In 1834, Musashi contained a total of 3,042 villages, with an assessed *kokudaka* of 1,281,000 *koku*. In Meiji 4, (1871) the count stood at 3,004 villages, and 44 *cho* (towns), with an assessed *kokudaka* of 1,273,540 *koku*.[7]

Excluding the 1866 uprising, village involvement in *ikki* is as follows, by my count:

Type	Incidents	Involved villages
fu-on (legal gatherings)	10	41
shuso (legal petitions)	5	60
osso (unauthorized pet.)	5	82*
chosan (flight)	1	1
uchikowashi (demolition)	5	32
goso (force used to get acceptance of petition)	5	47
totals	31	263

*Includes 66-village irrigation association

The figures jump considerably when the Bushu uprising is added, indicating that for Musashi, Yokoyama's weight of three for such events is off by more than an order of magnitude:

Type	Incidents	Involved villages
Hoki	1	300
Grand Total	32	563

Without the Bushu uprising, a Musashi peasant living in Japan's most volatile era since the *sengoku* (warring states) period would have one chance in 12 of living in a village involved in an *ikki*; the odds would slip to about one in 20 if legal *ikki* are excluded. With the Bushu uprising the odds rise to one village in 5½. That, of course, assumes no repeats, but the Bushu uprising affected primarily the portions of Musashi most heavily dependent on silk worm raising (generally counties with 70% or more of farming households were involved in silk worm raising); for a variety of reasons these areas seemed to have been more active than others. Hence one can presume lots of repeats in the Bushu areas, and a relative paucity of *ikki* in the rest of Musashi.

There are, of course, other sorts of disputes; Aoki chronicles village struggles aimed not at the *ryoshu*, but at rural merchants, landlords or others within the village. But these seldom involved more than a single village at a time. Aoki lists 105 village disturbances from Tempo (1830) 1 to Meiji 10 (1877) in Musashi, or about 1 village out of 30. In addition there are urban disputes, also aimed internally, usually at rice merchants, money lenders or pawn brokers. Musashi was heavily afflicted with these, largely because of the growth of Yoko-hama and other urban centers. Aoki records 18 such events between Tempo 1 and Meiji 4. Of these 5 were *so-on*; the rest were *uchikowashi*. While some of the *cho* were repeatedly involved, it is apparent that a town resident was far more likely to witness a disturbance (not aimed at the *ryoshu*) than a villager.[8]

Despite the imprecision in these numbers (exacerbated no doubt by the unspoken assumption that villages have approximately equal populations), it is reasonable to assert that the vast majority of Japa-nese went through the traumatic years from 1830 through early Meiji without experiencing an *ikki*. This is not to suggest that the transitions of this tumultuous era were easy, or that Japanese commoners simply shuffled along in abject obedience to authority, or even that *ikki* were not significant. I do suggest however that to rely on Aoki's data to some extent sucks us in to the world of the *ikki*, and makes us forget the range of action outside of that world. Once inside we tend to see open conflict with authority as the dominant means by which com-moners in Japan dealt with changes that affected their lives—from the price of rice to changes in taxation to the impact of a new and scarcely understood market economy. We still think of *ikki* as rebellion, and tend to forget that only a minority of *ikki* involved force.

So what? Scholarship that focuses on commoners in the late Tokugawa and early Meiji eras has tended to make everything or nothing of the *ikki*, and in the process miss the range of action in the middle ground. I learned in earlier studies of about 80 villages in what is now the city limits of Kawasaki that a lot could be done without direct confrontation of authority. There were no illegal *ikki* in that area between 1830 and 1871. Yet the villagers, used to governing their own daily affairs in the Tokugawa period, were not passive recipients of change. They combined in multi-village units at the drop of a hat to plan how to deal with special levies, changes in the land tax, Meiji-era changes in administration, the draft, the initiation of a modern school system and even marauding peasants. They found all sorts of methods short of rebellion for blunting the impact of changes they did not like—including procrastination, alteration of instructions, and of course, legal forms of what Aoki terms *ikki*. They also facilitated reforms that they did like. In short, they fully exploited a middle ground between the poles of outright capitulation to feudal lords or Meiji reformers and open rebellion.

If this range of activity has been largely missed by those who focus solely on the *ikki*, it has also been missed by those who discount the *ikki* completely. Those who look at the *ikki* world from the outside (mostly American Japanologists) have noted its tendency to claim too much, and have in the past tended to dismiss it entirely, emphasizing instead themes of continuity. Beginning around 1959 with the publication of Thomas Smith's monumental *Agrarian Origins of Modern Japan*, many western scholars, more concerned by then with discerning the roots of Japan's post-war successes than the causes of its wartime failures, began to re-examine the late Tokugawa and early Meiji periods. Under this scrutiny, the spread of a market economy in the Tokugawa era was not perceived as a source of new problems; it was instead a solution to "feudal remnants" that impeded progress. The focus was no longer on peasant rebellions; instead we see politically passive peasants, benefiting from the growth of the market, using family-centered by-employments to ride out the transition to a full market economy. Their growing economic differentiation meant an opportunity to rise or fall; early exposure to such vicissitudes helped Japan face the rigors of the modern transformation.[9]

This genre proved to be a useful counterweight to the immiseration and class solidarity portrayals of Tokugawa and Meiji commoners by Japanese historians caught up in the desire to explain the roots of Japan's "failure" to undergo a true revolution that would have, presumably, obviated the militarization that led Japan to defeat in World War II. Yet most of its practitioners did not regard commoners as historical actors; few looked at localities below the level of prefecture at all. The merit of the village-dwelling commoner was little more than a function of his preparedness and willingness to be integrated into a new national polity.

Perhaps inevitably, this stance, too, evoked a reaction—a growing feeling among historians beginning in the 1970s that the theme of smooth continuity between Tokugawa and Meiji had been overstated, and that conflict had been buried beneath an over-arching emphasis on modernization.[10] Part of the reason for this shift was undoubtedly the permeation of ongoing Japanese scholarship on peasant uprisings, *seikatsushi* ("daily life" history), and the psychological costs of rapid change into the consciousness of American Japanologists. The result was a flood of books and articles in English about peasant protest—many of them focusing on specific regions.[11]

To say that this work was balanced would be to claim too much. The very fact that it focuses almost exclusively on peasant protests re-creates the distorted impression that protest normally accompanied the economic, political and social changes that accompanied the Tokugawa-Meiji transition.

Yet the focus on protest has acted as a corrective to the passive peasant approach of earlier years, and it has brought local studies to center stage. Moreover, most of the new studies of protest are free of the strictures of rigid ideological commitment that marked such work in Japan in the 1950s and 1960s. They have added to the debate about how ordinary people get through extraordinary times in a variety of ways. Despite their over emphasis on conflict, I think that they are beginning to achieve a rough consensus about *ikki* in late Tokugawa and early Meiji Japan that will lead to a broader understanding of the ways that Japan's commoners and authorities dealt with and manipulated each other.

The consensus is in terms of the Scott vs. Popkin framework of peasant behavior which most of these studies utilize. This framework is undoubtedly old hat to most readers, but it may bear reiterating. James C. Scott, in a study entitled *The Moral Economy of the Peasant: Rebellion and Subsistence in Southeast Asia*, maintained that in peasant society the imperative of insuring subsistence is far preferable to the risks that might be incurred by pursuing personal profit through a market economy.[12] Instead, peasants accepted a condition of dependence, with the understanding that it would ensure their subsistence and that of the village as a whole. Attempts from the outside to introduce a market economy, with its attendant threat to the subsistence contract, could provoke rejection on moral grounds. Rebellion against the status-quo takes place only if landlords push peasants so far that physical survival is threatened. In 1979, Samuel Popkin took a radically different stand in *The Rational Peasant: The Political Economy of Rural Society in Vietnam.*[13] He argued that peasants, far from passive, constantly calculate how best to maximize their own gain. Participation in a market economy is not seen as an evil, but as a possible way to gain. Even rebellion is a tool to extract gain, not necessarily an act of desperation.

Although we must have reservations about applying studies of peasants in Southeast Asia to all times and all places, the Scott vs. Popkin framework in this country has a certain resonance with the immiseration question in Japan: it addresses the controversy over whether *ikki* stemmed from economic problems or from improved economic circumstances that permitted protest to be included in the arsenal of the calculating peasant.

Susan Hanley and Kozo Yamamura can be said to represent the Popkin pole for the Tokugawa period; Richard Smethurst does the same for the Meiji and Taisho periods. Scott advocates are a bit less strident; they include Stephen Vlastos and Patricia Sippel; their works have already been cited. There is a vector sum to their positions that lies between Scott and Popkin, leaning a bit toward Popkin. That is, some level of economic grievance, although seldom sufficient to threaten actual survival, underlies the majority of protests in late Tokugawa- and Meiji-era Japan. Scott-like, grievances are always stated in moral terms, whether the protest is stimulated by local, and presumably correctable, lords or landlords, or by "impersonal" market economy forces. Yet there seems to be no evidence of peasant allergy to market relations *per se*. There is repeated evidence that the moral language of petitions is calculated to produce very specific results, with escalations or de-escalations of rhetoric and action following, according to rational calculations about what is likely to be effective.[14]

For Japan, then, the Scott vs. Popkin controversy seems to be reconcilable. Whether protests stem more often from economic crisis or empowerment, both involve a reaction to perceived divergences from what "ought" to be. The notion of "oughtness" here is not far from Irwin Scheiner's concept of the "covenant" (referring to Tokugawa times) and Smith's "right to benevolence" (status justice, referring to worker appeals between 1890 and 1920). Oughtness of course includes subsistence, but is not limited to it; it can be expanded to include expectations of a better life. It is ensured by the "benevolence" of one's superiors, a concept malleable enough to include a daimyo granting a reduction in the rice tax and a factory providing institutional entitlements to its workers. Saito Osamu, Thomas Smith in recent writings, and Michael Lewis have all noted, with some amazement, similarities between Tokugawa peasant uprisings, Toyama rice riots in the Taisho (1912-26) era, and factory strikes: they get underway not necessarily in response to intolerable conditions, but from a sense that those who should be doing something are not; they all involve petitions written in moral language; they all employ similar methods to protect leaders from punishment.[15]

The moral economy persists, but is seldom concerned solely with subsistence; the rational peasant (and even the rational worker) is always in evidence, but never just concerned with individual gain.

One implication is that in much of Japan the transition to a market economy, even in its accelerated version after the opening of Yokohama and other ports, was not as abrupt as might be supposed, and that some of the tools developed for dealing with problems in a pre-modern setting may have retained some effectiveness throughout the Meiji period, and perhaps even longer. This implication involves a re-emphasis on the theme of continuity. For the peasant-farmer in Tokugawa and Meiji Japan, and in some parts of the country much later, action meant practicing the art of the possible within an openly paternalistic system.[16]

How do the *ikki* fit in? They were in their most confrontational forms, of course, actions of last resort, deemed to be worth risking if chances of punishment were low, or the degree of anticipated punishment was mild, or the numbers punished were limited, or if circumstances were desperate. But *ikki* were only part of the arsenal to be used in practicing the art of the possible. A range of action short of rebellion, from procrastination to subversion of orders to the lesser forms of what Aoki calls *ikki* constituted the most common forms of protest for late Tokugawa and early Meiji commoners.

122

ENDNOTES

1. Aoki Koji, *Hyakusho ikki sogo nenpyo* (Tokyo: San'ichi shobo, 1971), 33; Yo-
    koyama Toshio, *Hyakusho ikki to gimin denso* [Nihonshi 85] (Tokyo: Kyoikusha
    rekishi shinsho, 1977), 143.

2. Neil Waters, *Japan's Local Pragmatists* (Cambridge: Harvard Council of East
    Asian Studies, 1983), 3-30.

3. Harry Harootunian, "Ideology and Conflict," in Tetsuo Najita and J. Victor Kos-
    chmann, eds., *Conflict in Modern Japanese History* (Princeton: Princeton Uni-
    versity Press, 1982), 59-61; Ann Walthall, *Social Protest and Popular Culture in
    Eighteenth Century Japan* (Tucson: University of Arizona Press, 1986), 221-6.

4. Yokoyama, *Hyakusho ikki to gimin denso*, 38.

5. Aoki Koji, Kobayashi Shigeru, and Oishi Shinzaburo, "Hyakusho *ikki* towa nan-
    na no ka," *Rekishi koron* 4.6 (June, 1978): 31; Yamanaka Kiyotaka, "Hyakusho
    ikki no jidaisei to chi-ikisei," *Rekishi koron* 4.6 (June, 1978): 52.

6. Yamanaka, *Hyakusho ikki to gimin denso*, 55. Figures for Musashi are distilled
    from Aoki et al, "Hyakusho *ikki* towa nanna no ka," 222-365. On Bushu insur-
    rection, see Patricia Sippel, "Popular Protest in Early Modern Japan: The Bushu
    Outburst," *Harvard Journal of Asiatic Studies* 37.2 (1977): 273-322.

7. Kimura Motoi, *Kyudakakyuryo torishirabecho. Nihon shiryo sensho* 3 (Tokyo:
    Kondo shuppansha, 1980), 3-4.

8. Aoki et al, "Hyakusho *ikki* towa nanna no ka," 391-409, 532-620.

9. See, in addition works by Smith, William Jones Chambliss, *Chiaraijima Vil-
    lage: Land Tenure, Taxation and Local Trade, 1811-1884* (Tucson: University of
    Arizona Press, 1965).

10. This reaction is specifically stated in the preface, and more tediously in the in-
    troduction, to Tetsuo Najita and Koschmann, *Conflict in Modern Japanese His-
    tory*.

11. These include William Kelly, *Deference and Defiance in Nineteenth Century Ja-
    pan* (Princeton: Princeton University Press, 1985); Anne Walthall, *Social Protest
    and Popular Culture in Eighteenth-Century Japan* (Tucson: University of Arizona
    Press, 1986); Stephen Vlastos, *Peasant Protests and Uprisings in Tokugawa Ja-
    pan* (Berkeley: University of California Press, 1986); Roger Bowen, *Rebellion
    and Democracy in Meiji Japan* (Berkeley: University of California Press, 1980);
    Herbert Bix, *Peasant Protest in Japan, 1590-1884* (New Haven: Yale University
    Press, 1986); Michael Lewis, *Rioters and Citizens: Mass Protest in Imperial Japan*
    (Berkeley: University of California Press, 1990).

12. James C. Scott, *The Moral Economy of the Peasant: Rebellion and Subsistence in Southeast Asia* (New Haven: Yale University Press, 1976).

13. Samuel Popkin, *The Rational Peasant: The Political Economy of Rural Society in Vietnam* (Berkeley: University of California Press, 1979).

14. These generalizations are a distillation of themes from protest studies by Walthall, Hanley, and Yamamura, Waswo, Sippel, Lewis and Kelly, all cited above.

15. See Irwin Scheiner, *Christian Converts and Social Protest in Meiji Japan* (Berkeley: University of California Press, 1970); Thomas C. Smith, *Native Sources of Japanese Industrialization* (Berkeley: University of California Press, 1988), 11-3, 236-70; Saito Osamu's review of Smith in *Journal of Economic History* 49.4 (Dec. 1990): 992-98; Lewis, *Rioters and Citizens*, 55-69.

16. Lewis, *Rioters and Citizens*, 176-7, is an excellent discussion of paternalism in Japan.

CHAPTER 10

If this is Democracy, then Democracy is Ugly: Posting Columns and the Berlin Landscape, 1918-1936

Molly Loberg

The news of their defeat in the First World War after four years of brutal combat, winters of near starvation, and millions of casualties, came to Germans in different ways: in the figures of soldiers who demobilized themselves by walking away from the front towards home, as rumors told by neighbors and strangers in shops and on street corners, and as black and white newspaper headlines.[1] In the capital city of Berlin, defeat inscribed the urban landscape in the form of governmental proclamations glued to *posting columns* on busy streets and intersections.[2] The announcement of the anticipated abdication of the emperor was pasted over by the declaration of a ceasefire and a people's republic. Another layer of glue and paper explained positions of the new government such as voting for women, protection of workers, and an end to censorship. Thus, world historical events and dramatic political transformation manifested themselves as a thick crust of pasted texts on posting columns and the anxious, milling crowds which surrounded them.

On November 17th, 1918, an artist depicted such a scene for the cover of the *Berlin Illustrated Newspaper*.[3] Berliners of both sexes, diverse classes, and all ages gathered around a posting column with expressions of intense interest to read a governmental proclamation. The perceived mood, however, was most strikingly expressed by the flames and trembling letters of a theatrical advertisement above their heads. It read, "*Die Welt geht unter*:" the world is falling apart. Despite the dramatic tone, this image contained several ambiguities. The proclamation bore the same heading as the Kaiser's declaration of war on 6 August 1914: "An das Deutsche Volk." But the leafless trees suggested a November date and the proclamation of the last wartime chancellor, Max von Baden, anticipating war's end. Nevertheless, it remained unclear whether the apocalypse referred to war itself, war's end in defeat, the Kaiser's abdication, or the democratic future. The artist rendered another tension in this image: the casual placement of a theatrical advertisement so near a declaration of great import, whose message the *advertisement* expressed more clearly. The intention was perhaps satire, but the depicted incongruity was nevertheless factual: even in times of political rupture, commerce and entertainment struggled on and competed with politics for public attention.

This image from the *Berlin Illustrated Newspaper* introduces the subject of this essay—the posting column and its political, commercial and social uses and implications in Berlin from 1918-36—and four major themes. The diverse crowd at the base of the column suggests the first. In this essay, I argue that the advertising column represented a major structure of the public sphere and, in comparison to newspapers, radio, or film, was the media perhaps most deserving the designation of "mass." Secondly, this essays seeks to contextualize political propaganda and commercial advertising, so often studied as independent texts, by situating them in the dynamic urban environment in which they appeared. Neither political propaganda nor commercial advertising appeared in isolation but rather as piled up, pasted over, competing sources of information. The governmental stationery of the proclamation exemplifies the third theme: the advertising column as a symbol and instrument of power. By law, the state had special rights to certain symbols for its stationery and publications (e.g. the Prussian coat of arms and the color red). The columns themselves were the property of municipal authorities. And lastly, I argue that space in the city was a limited and important commodity, which, by its limited nature, could not meet all of the demands placed upon it. This was especially true in a time when economic crisis, political fragmentation and changing patterns of urban use magnified the volume and intensity of demands on public space. As a result, the attempts by various commercial and political groups to use or even control the advertising columns made them a major site of conflict, sometimes even violence. This story is about how public space was constructed, who could access it, and, in the end, who was pushed out.

It is ironic that a leader of the social democratic party used the advertising columns to assert the end of the emperor's authority, because the advertising column itself emerged in the period after the 1848 revolutions as a means of repressing democratic and socialist agitation while at the same assuring business profits. The 1851 Press Law strictly forbade the pasting, nailing, affixing, mounting, erecting or calling out of any advertisements of a non-commercial nature.[4] Licit materials, including notices about commercial activities, public amusements, approved gatherings, even lost and found items, still required police permission. In 1855, the printer Ernst Litfass offered the municipal authorities a device for better containing the information exchange in public: columns erected throughout the city, particularly in high traffic areas, to draw the "wild placarding" off houses, fences, trees and lampposts. The columns were multi-purpose: they contained street cleaning equipment, encased the pipes for watering fountains, even hid pissoirs.[5] But the operator of the monopoly concession, Litfass, and the grantor of this concession, the Berlin police chief, shared a common understanding of the chief function of the column: to organize diffuse and disorderly postings into centrally managed locations that would promote above all commercial activities, specifically the interests of Litfass Publishing's clients.[6]

Advertising columns quickly became Berlin landmarks. They can be found in almost all illustrations of Berlin street life from oil painting to comic sketchings. They were a popular source of local information, particularly for travelers and those who did not have newspaper subscriptions. Columns also fostered the development of modern commercial advertising and the graphic arts by providing a reliable broad surface, whose contents, by law, could not be meddled with or defaced. The police also came to rely on the columns for communicating with the public, or as was more often the case, warning them.

But the columns also produced contradictions and tensions, as suggested by the famous notice of Police Chief Jagow from 1910. Responding to an upsurge in demonstrations, it read "The street serves traffic alone. Resistance will result in the use of weapons. *I warn the curious.*"[7] The first statement is simply untrue, the street in Berlin never served a single purpose but rather was a site for working, buying, selling, playing, socializing, demonstrating, breaking the law, and enforcing it. The police used the columns and the streets for their own purposes, in this case suppressing agitation. By investing these columns with the authority of state power, the state had also created a visible target for challenges to authority. After the First World War, the collapse of the imperial government and tenuous hold of the new government created an authority vacuum in public space and thousands of voices of varied interests rushed in to fill it. The state of affairs was perhaps most vividly expressed in the layers of paper that covered Berlin streets in 1918 and 1919, despite the rationing of paper.

Berliners experienced the transition from war to peace time, from empire to democracy through their physical environment and the changes in these urban surfaces registered as several different kinds of shock. The first was that of democracy itself. Restrictions on political advertising prior to the war and the silences created by four years of civil truce had left Berliners ill-prepared for the ensuing "orgy" of propaganda. Nor was this peaceable, as bill stickers, leaflet distributors and carriers of political placards were often beaten up by the opposition. Perhaps most disconcerting was the perception that this mess was *what democracy looked like*, and it was only just beginning. Secondly, ubiquitous images of sex and violence, which now sold everything from political parties to feature films to cookware, produced a moral and aesthetic panic. Critics worried about the effect on the public, especially on young men, who (quoting from one critic) upon seeing "the fantastic depictions of robbery and murder scenes" might be driven to "shameful deeds."[8]

But perhaps the most common reaction to the changing landscape was that of information overload. One commentator for the advertising journal "Die Reklame" complained he had actually seen bill stickers standing in line to post over the same wall space in the Friedrichstrasse subway station, each one covering the poster of the person before him, boxing beat out a winter ball which had discreetly hidden a beer ad.[9] Words and images piled up without any sense of hierarchy. Political and commercial advertisements alternated so quickly that the paste didn't even have time to dry. As ads covered ads, many Berliners complained that the city's appearance had become unreliable. On the other hand, advertising journals published articles that claimed there simply wasn't enough space to handle all the new information.[10] Some bill stickers took it upon themselves to claim new spaces including on other people's shop windows, public buildings, even police stations.[11]

The perception, however, that censorship had ended with the empire, was simply that, a perception. Many of the rules for governing public space still appeared in the books in their 1851 form. It was public perception about the rules that had changed. In their statements to the police after being fined or arrested, bill stickers claimed that they were acting in accordance with their new rights and powers as citizens. The space to inform, advertise, agitate was up for grabs and no one had more rights than anyone else to it, or so they believed.

It was not an opinion that the municipal government in Berlin would tolerate for very long. Throughout the 1920s, it began to reassert its ownership and authority through regulations, policing, the formation of new organizations, and, after the political assassinations in the early twenties, bans on seditious public expression. All of these tactics claimed the cause of public good and public order. Sometimes bill stickers, advertisers and political organizations respected the new order and sometimes they challenged it through public denunciations of the city, by simply ignoring the rules, and, as the political environment radicalized at the end of the 1920s, with vandalism and violence.

One concern of the city was financial, as it made no money off the "wild" postings of the bill stickers who hung their signs without fees or permits. And post-war Berlin was broke. The municipal government was charged with paying a third of the compensation to private citizens for damages caused by rioters and revolutionaries in 1918-9, as well as increased welfare responsibilities for citizens, plus basic expenditures for street cleaning, road and sewer building, police forces, and so on. The mayor was left desperately seeking additional sources of revenue. In 1921, the government cancelled all leases on the columns and formed a mixed private-public company to manage them, Berliner Reklamewesen or in its bureaucratic acronym BEREK. BEREK took on the task of suppressing all unpaid advertising. But its task was not to suppress advertising in general, as the critics of the city's postwar appearance had hoped. The city simply couldn't afford it. Instead BEREK increased the number and the size of columns. New advertising structures such as kiosks, waiting halls, bus stops, sign posts, even first aid booths crowded into the streets. The pressure on public spaces for advertising reached a high point during the currency inflation in 1923, a fact which revises the dual image of 1920s Berlin as either a city darkened by poverty, mass unemployment and political radicalism or illuminated by film glamour, avant-garde theater, and bold modern advertising. The blossoming of advertising was actually a symptom of an impoverished municipal government and a reflection of the desperation of various interests to reach out to a mass audience.

I argue above that the columns deserved to be called a mass media more than other iconic media of the 1920s such as radio and film. The columns were an urban phenomenon, a means of spreading information in a large and anonymous population. They were different from film, radio, and newspapers in that there was no financial barrier to their use. Reading the postings was free. But perhaps most important was how they engaged their audience. The columns met the public on the street, where they moved as part of city traffic. It was a unique opportunity to engage diverse, urban masses. As a result, advertisers developed a style of address that emphasized color and image and aimed for arousing distracted minds at the subliminal level. Finding the crowd was critical, thus commercial advertisers and political parties fought for columns in highest traffic areas to assure maximum exposure. This fight for exposure and the city's demand for revenue established a hierarchy of interests in public space, in which the bigger trademark companies, especially cigarette, liquor, and mouthwash companies, acquired the most desirable urban spaces while smaller operations were condemned to quiet streets out from the center of town.[12] Smaller operations accused BEREK of greed and favoritism.

A second conflict emerged literally at the intersection between advertisers' attempts to reach the masses and the municipality's concern for public order. Automobiles, which had practically vanished during the war, were now back in the city and behind the wheel sat many inexperienced drivers exhilarated by high speeds. Traffic volumes overwhelmed the street policeman already distracted by crime and political violence. Berlin papers reported an alarming rise in accidents. Private automobile owners were by far the worst offenders of any vehicle category. In response, the first traffic light in Europe was erected at the city's main intersection, Potsdamer Platz, in 1923. Schools and newspapers launched educational series for teaching unruly Berliners how to cross the street. An image from a 1925 issue of the *Berliner Illustrated Newspaper* presented some of the difficulties in crossing a street now cluttered with so many advertising structures.[13] Below an illustration of a woman pushed to the edge of the curb by an advertising column and threatened by an approaching car, the caption warned pedestrians not to stand on street corners where running boards and door handles might tear them off the sidewalk. Citing the danger of traffic, the city began clearing street clutter, especially removing unprofitable advertising structures from the early 1920s. Some advertising columns were torn down, but a more modern version reappeared a meter further back from the curb. Traffic had modified but not eliminated an important source of municipal revenue.

Economic stabilization in the mid-1920s translated into a highpoint in municipal authorities' assertion of power in public space in managing use and traffic. But, by the end of the decade, radical political organizations, in particular communists and national socialists, challenged the integrity of the columns by making them targets in a bigger fight *in* the streets *over* control of the streets. The Weimar Constitution of 1919 had committed itself to the freedom of assembly and expression. But the government was unprepared for such intense resistance and agitation against the republic. Attempts to contain political violence, such as the 1922 Law for Protection of the Republic and numerous emergency decrees, evidenced a growing gap between a commitment to no censorship in principle and real censorship in practice. By the end of the 1920s and the early 1930s, the communists and the national socialists were the major targets of such measures.

Bans had been imposed on fighting units. Slander and violent language was forbidden as was the extensive use of the color red in posters, which otherwise might cause confusion over which postings were issued by the government and which postings were put up by parties aspiring to governmental control.[14] Perhaps the most effective form of censorship against these groups was through the city's manipulation of space. The police refused to approve posters presented to them for public distribution and BEREK simply refused to put up many of those which had passed police inspection.

Intensifying restrictions on columns enhanced their status as symbols of power. Organizations chasing power thus claimed the columns in several different ways. One method was symbolic, with communists and Nazis creating alternative public spaces in which the column serviced their ambitions. For example, a neighborhood communist newspaper, *Der Rote Reporter*, confiscated by the police in 1932, depicted an advertising column on its front page. But the column was idealistically reimagined covered in soviet icons and anti-fascist language, something impossible in real public space. The Nazi publication *Der Angriff* entitled its events calendar section Die Plakatsäule (the poster column), a space in which they could more freely inform their readership, including giving them tips on dealing with the police.[15] Acts of vandalism in real public space also claimed columns. Posters of oppositional parties or the police were ripped down. Postings were also put up without permission, especially when their content crossed the line of permissible speech. BEREK found this practice particularly insidious as it damaged valuable advertising put up by paying clients. But far worse for BEREK were the arson attacks of 1932 in which dozens of columns in working class areas of the city were torched.[16] In both cases, BEREK suspected the communists, but those arrested were released on insufficient evidence. I would argue here that acts of vandalism against the columns fit into a broader culture of using violence to claim public space. When the so-called "pasting platoons" (Klebekolonne) went out illegally to post, they went out armed with brass knuckles, guns, knives, even screwdrivers and ready for a fight. The goal was to disrupt public space and destabilize authority.

This points to the uniqueness of the columns as a medium, both its possibilities and its dangers. Today we exist in a media world which increasingly carves out niche markets and fosters separate publics. The columns were very different: they reached out to a diverse, mass public, but were also exposed to this diverse, mass public. They could be acted upon or even attacked. The danger was an increasingly violent and fragmented public as oppositional groups fought each other over the columns' surfaces, especially at election time. The possibility was the resistance to authority and power. In his second set of decrees as chancellor in February of 1933, Hitler suspended the right to freedom of opinion and expression with severe penalties for violators. From this point on, the answer to who had the right to access the columns would be the national socialist regime.

So who wins control of public space in 1933 is who we expect to win. But even when the winner in this struggle seems clear, the victory was complicated by diverging interests and confusion over message. BEREK often resisted the exploitation of the columns by the party—not because of their commitment to a free and democratic public space, but rather because the political postings were crowding out their commercial contracts and they were becoming a money losing enterprise. The government itself struggled throughout the 1930s to balance its ideological commitments and its concerns about the economy and its image abroad. Photographs taken of posting column during the state-proclaimed boycott of Jewish businesses in April 1933 show how posting columns were mobilized for excluding Jews from commercial life. Posters urged pedestrians "don't buy from Jews!"[17] Due to concerns about domestic disruptions and international repercussions of a counter-boycott, this action was quickly declared a success and called off. For the time being, "grass roots" boycotts against department stores and other businesses were prohibited as detrimental to the sense of safety of the public and their consuming impulses. In early to mid-1930s, more moderate factions within the government sought to alter the image Germany projected abroad, especially in preparation for the 1936 Olympics. Berlin and its columns received a make-over, including the removal of kitschy advertising and all anti-semitic signage along tourist paths. Public space was meant to appear harmonious, attractive and safe. The exclusion and violence was below the surface and around the corner.

ENDNOTES

1. It is estimated that up to a million German soldiers became "shirkers" (avoiding duty, absent without leave) after the spring offensives in 1918. See Richard Bessel, *Germany After the First World War* (Oxford: Clarendon Press, 1993), 46.

2. In this essay, I use the term "posting column" to refer to a built structure that has several different names in German: *Anschlagsäule* (posting column), *Plakatsäule* (poster column), *Litfasssäule* (Litfass column, after its Berlin inventor). The sources use these term more or less indiscriminately. I use the term "posting column" because it expresses the purpose of the column rather than the format or content of the material, which varied markedly. While the term Litfass columns is still used by many Berliners, several different companies succeeded the Litfass publishing company as operators of the concession.

3. "Schicksalstage," *Berliner Illustrierte Zeitung* (17 November 1918), cover page.

4. Preussisches Ministerium des Innern, *Der kleine Ratgeber für die polizeiliche Behandlung von Versammlungen, Druckschriften, Plakaten und Waffen: Ein Handbuch für die Praxis* (Berlin: Gersbach und Sohn Verlag, 1931), 37.

5. Landesarchiv Bilderabteilung 08 Str., II, 3764.

6. Various versions of posting columns appeared in England and France in the early 19th century. Litfass is accredited with being the Berlin "inventor" since he was able to acquire a monopoly concession from the Berlin chief of police. See Franz M. Feldhaus, Berlin-Friedenau, "Zur Geschichte der Plakatsäule," *Das Plakat* (March 1919), 235. Feldhaus published this research again as Dr. Ing. H.C.F.M. Feldhaus, "Zur Geschichte der Plakatsäule," *Die Reklame* (1 January 1926), 22.

7. As quoted in Thomas Lindenberger, *Strassenpolitik: Zur Sozialgeschichte der öffentlichen Ordnung in Berlin 1900 bis 1914* (Bonn: J.H.W. Dietz, 1995), 11. "I warn the curious" subsequently became a popular phrase in Berlin dialect.

8. Kurt Jahnke, "Berlin Plakatterror," *Die Reklame* (1919), 109.

9. Max Lang, "Plakatierung," *Die Reklame* (1919), 139.

10. D. Jans Meyer, "Mehr Anschlagfläche!" *Das Plakat* (1919), 303.

11. "Die Wahlpropaganda in Berlin zur Nationalversammlung," *Die Reklame* (1919), 60.

12. Max Pauly, "Höchst merkwürdige Geschichte von den Berliner Anschlagsäulen," *Die Reklame* (1922), 521.

Molly Loberg

13. Fritz Kahn, "Verkehrsgefahren und ihre Verhutung," *Berliner Illustrirte Zeitung* (2 July 1925), 893-5.

14. Preussisches Ministerium des Innern, *Der kleine Ratgeber*, 43.

15. Landesarchiv, Generalstaatsanwalt, A REP 358, n. 1305.

16. Landesarchiv, Generalstaatsanwalt, A REP 358, n. 1140, n. 1256.

17. Landesarchiv, Bilderabteilung, 01 NS, 38401.

CHAPTER 11

HIDING THE NAZI PAST: DENAZIFICATION AND CHRISTIAN POSTWAR RECKONING IN GERMANY

Robert P. Ericksen

As Allied forces moved toward victory in World War II, postwar planners developed two assumptions. First, they assumed that Germany had experienced "nazification," i.e., that the nation had been permeated and thereby tainted by the ideology that had driven the Nazi regime. Americans were convinced that Hitler's ideology had been both pervasive and pernicious. Therefore, the Allies developed a policy of denazification, hoping to achieve a re-education and a cleansing of German society. This first Allied assumption, though still controversial in some quarters, seems to have been accurate. Research has increasingly indicated the widespread and often enthusiastic participation of Germans—doctors, lawyers, architects, engineers, university professors, willing informants to the Gestapo, and "ordinary" killers—in the practices of Hitler's Germany.[1] Nazi crimes occurred with the participation of large segments of the German community and under the umbrella of very broad support for Adolf Hitler, despite the fact that since 1945 these Nazi ideals and practices are seen as the foundation for the Holocaust and have thus received nearly universal condemnation.

The second Allied assumption was that denazification could be undertaken with the cooperation and support of a core group of "good Germans," people especially to be found within the Christian community and among Christian leaders. Churches, it was assumed, had provided a natural foundation of values upon which to oppose Nazi evil. Martin Niemöller, for example, had gained recognition throughout America and England as an opponent and victim of the Nazi state. A Protestant pastor who had been arrested by the Gestapo in 1937, he had spent the next eight years as a "prisoner of conscience."[2] Dietrich Bonhoeffer, though less well known at the time, also represented the right sort of Christian. He had opposed Adolf Hitler from the beginning, and it gradually became known that he had joined in a plot against the Nazi regime, which led to his imprisonment for two years and his execution just weeks before Hitler's suicide and the collapse of the "Third Reich."[3] Both Niemöller and Bonhoeffer seemed to have taken the appropriate Christian stance, opposition to Hitler and his regime based upon their Christian values.

However, the assumption that Niemöller and Bonhoeffer were representative figures or that most Christians had opposed the Nazi state proved far less reliable than the other Allied belief, that much of Germany had been "nazified." Clues to a less attractive understanding of Christian attitudes in Nazi Germany began to emerge in the non-cooperation of church leaders during Allied denazification. Since then scholarship has increasingly shown that Christians in Germany broadly supported Hitler and that postwar Christians systematically misrepresented the past, taking advantage of the benign Allied expectations, making every effort to protect Germans of almost all stripes from Allied punishment, and suppressing the story of their own previous enthusiasm for Hitler and his political ideals.

Martin Niemöller represents a useful place to begin this story. He had voted for and supported Hitler enthusiastically in the latter's rise to power. Martin's younger brother Wilhelm, also a Lutheran pastor, had actually joined the Nazi Party in 1923, when it was still dismissed by many as a fringe organization on the radical right.[4] Together these two brothers had fought against leftists and trade unionists, joining the rightwing *Freikorps* during the tumultuous years after World War I. They were both theology students at the time, and they then took with them into their pastoral careers a set of attitudes shared with the vast majority of Protestant pastors: regret for the collapse of pre-World War I Germany, with its Kaiser and its traditional values; dislike of the democratic Weimar Republic, which had been born in Germany's defeat; and disapproval of the freedom, openness and tolerance which arrived with democracy and which represented to them a breakdown both in proper political authority and in proper moral values.[5]

Many Germans after 1945, trying to explain the evidence of their early enthusiasm for Hitler, blamed it on their idealism. Hitler had promised to unite Germans (except for Jews and communists, of course). He had promised to reestablish traditional values, cleaning the streets of pornography and prostitution, homosexuality and cultural decadence. He advocated taking women out of the workplace and putting them back in the home "where they belonged," offering bronze, silver and gold medals to mothers who produced as many as four, six, or eight children, respectively. He established himself as an opponent of moral breakdown, of modern social decline, and he promised to re-impose the virtue of obedience to authority.[6]

Christians could be made nervous by certain aspects of the Nazi movement, including the hooliganism of storm troopers and/or the violence of Nazi rhetoric. The Catholic hierarchy in Germany even condemned the Nazi ideology prior to Hitler's political emergence, forbidding Catholics the right to join the party. This came about both because the hierarchy supported the rival Catholic Center Party in Weimar Germany and because Nazi racial doctrine—by which they established their prejudice against Jews—was seen to violate the Catholic view that spiritual explanations take precedence over material (racial or biological) modes of analysis.

Both Catholic and Protestant Germans, however, quickly made peace with Hitler once he had been appointed chancellor of Germany in January of 1933. The Center Party voted in favor of the "Enabling Act" in March, legislation which first granted Hitler dictatorial powers. The hierarchy also lifted their ban on Catholics joining the Nazi Party, resulting in a flood of applicants. By the summer of 1933, the Vatican negotiated and signed a Concordat with Germany, a treaty widely seen as giving Hitler international legitimacy.[7] Throughout these early months, Protestant statements of enthusiastic support for

Hitler can be found in almost all sources, including the writings of a leading Lutheran theologian like Paul Althaus, who called Hitler "a miracle and gift from God,"[8] and the editorial pages of the leading Lutheran newspaper, which celebrated even the alleged peacefulness and lack of violence in the rise of Hitler to power (despite the violence now routinely attributed to Nazi street toughs in Hitler's political campaigns).[9]

If Martin Niemöller and other Christians liked Hitler so much, how did this simple pastor end up in prison? He followed a path of gradual disaffection from the regime, beginning already in the summer and fall of 1933, not in response to the politics of the state but in response to an enthusiastic group of Protestants who called themselves *Deutsche Christen* (DC). This term translates as "German Christians," but it means more than simply Germans who happened to be Christian. These individuals, who eventually numbered between one-quarter and one-third of the Protestant church membership in Germany, wanted to make sure that their Christian beliefs merged completely with their support of the Nazi Party. They flew the swastika and wore their brown uniforms in church, and they celebrated Hitler as God's gift to a Germany reborn.[10]

The biggest problem for *Deutsche Christen* lay in the obviously Jewish origins of Christianity. Since Jews earned the absolute contempt of good Nazis, the DC began developing strategies to show their contempt for Jews and their loyalty to Nazi doctrine. First, they proposed the implementation within the church of the "Aryan Paragraph." Hitler had developed legislation in April 1933 to remove Jews from employment by the state, but he had not tried to intervene in the churches. Now the DC wanted to insure that any Christians of Jewish descent who served as clergy or otherwise worked for the church would be removed. This involved only a handful of individuals, of course, but Martin Niemöller vigorously opposed this policy when it passed the synod of the Prussian regional church in September.

Niemöller argued that baptism made all Christians equal, so he called for clergy to join a "Pastors' Emergency League" to express their opposition to the DC program. The battle escalated in November during special Reformation festivities. The year 1933 represented the

450th anniversary of Luther's birth as well as the year of Hitler's rise to power, which prompted many comparisons between the two. DC enthusiasts used a Reformation rally in Berlin to advocate a further dejudaization of Christianity, including the removal of the Old Testament from the Bible. By May 1934, Niemöller and his allies, now including the Swiss theologian Karl Barth, created a statement condemning DC beliefs as heresy. Their document, the Barmen Declaration, became the basis for an alternative movement, the Confessing Church (*Bekennende Kirche*). About one-fifth of Protestant pastors in Germany allied themselves with this Confessing Church, including both Niemöller and Bonhoeffer.[11]

Much of the Allied optimism about "good Germans" had rested on the existence of this Confessing Church, which tended at the time to be viewed as a resistance organization. After 1945, Germans learned to claim connections to the Confessing Church for this reason. Victoria Barnett, for example, describes the story of one woman, part of a group traveling by private automobile in May 1945. American GIs halted the group and learned that both she and her husband had been prominent Nazis, as was her husband's uncle. Things looked bad until she mentioned that she belonged to the Confessing Church and was a friend of Martin Niemöller, at which point the soldiers filled her tank with gas and sent her on her way.[12]

Scholars now recognize that the Confessing Church was not a resistance organization.[13] It is true that some radicals within the group, individuals such as Dietrich Bonhoeffer and Karl Barth, indeed opposed Nazism and had done so from the beginning. Niemöller also learned to oppose the movement he had supported, especially when his right to preach against the DC led to Gestapo surveillance of his sermons and other forms of intimidation. However, the Barmen Declaration had been written carefully so as not to criticize the Nazi state, for fear that good Nazis would not join the Confessing Church on that account.[14] Wolfgang Gerlach has also shown that leaders in the Confessing Church shared most of the Nazi prejudice against Jews and did not focus upon Nazi mistreatment of Jews as a matter of Christian concern.[15]

Almost as soon as the denazification process began, Allied hopes for the assistance of "good Germans" began to disappear. For example, Martin Niemöller raised eyebrows in an interview with Allied reporters on June 5th, admitting that he had been fully prepared to fight for Adolf Hitler's Germany and had even offered to do so. Furthermore, he did not think democracy a form of government suitable for the German people.[16] Other rude shocks came apace, as Clemens Vollnhals has shown. Already on May 2nd, Cardinal Faulhaber of Munich had compared Allied bombing of German cities with Nazi crimes in concentration camps. In June, Faulhaber wrote the clergy in his Archdiocese of Munich as follows:

> For weeks one [meaning the Allies] brought representatives of American newspapers and American soldiers to Dachau, and then they showed slides and movies of the most horrible sights from there, in order to place the disgrace and shame of the German people before the entire world, right down to the last village in Africa [*Negerdorf*].[17]

As the first wave of denazification ensued under military occupation, Faulhaber joined with his Protestant counterpart in Bavaria, Bishop Hans Meiser, to protest the application of blanket sanctions against Nazi party members and members of the SS. They also voiced an appeal for 102 bankers and industrialists who had been removed from their positions. Another leading Protestant, Bishop Wurm of Württemberg, warned in July that the postwar German bureaucracy would be filled by individuals not up to the task and "unsuited in terms of character" for the positions they would now hold. The subtext of his warning was that people suited in character, i.e., church members, were largely being excluded as former Nazis. In October, Wurm attacked Military Government plans more systematically, arguing that loyalty to the church should be the crucial indicator of who could now serve the new Germany, with early membership in the Nazi Party a far less useful criterion. In justifying his critique, Wurm reviewed the circumstances of 1933: the National Socialists promising cooperation with the churches, even the Pope signing a Concordat with Hitler, and the "elemental reaction of the German Volk to the horrible Versailles *Diktat*." "For all these reasons," Wurm suggested, "many of our best within and without the civil service then followed Hitler's call."[18]

There was virtually nothing in these early church responses to Allied victory in 1945 to indicate that Christian leaders acknowledged their actual political stance of 1933 or were willing to rethink their own role in the regime. Each of the individuals mentioned, Niemöller, Wurm, Meiser and Faulhaber, had expressed open enthusiasm for the rise of Adolf Hitler and the National Socialist state, which is only to say that they stood among their peers in positions of Christian leadership. One Protestant statement of guilt did indeed surface in 1945. However, this Stuttgart Declaration was flawed in several ways: 1) It came only under pressure from the World Council of Churches, which virtually demanded such a statement before ecumenical work could begin with German churches. 2) It addressed the problem of guilt in extremely vague terms, apologizing for not acting more courageously in the fight against National Socialism, without mentioning specific victims, such as Jews, or acknowledging extensive Christian efforts in the fight *for* National Socialism. And finally, 3) the Stuttgart Declaration remained highly contested within the church as a whole, with signers often accused of having betrayed Germany by bowing to enemy pressure.[19] In response to Allied plans for denazification, the church was simply unprepared to cooperate. No awareness of Christian guilt, no statement of repentance, and no acknowledgement of the suffering of Germany's victims ever marked the church's side of the dialogue.

I first came across this set of issues while studying denazification at Göttingen University. It seemed remarkable that pastors had written so many of the statements on behalf of the accused, statements derisively known even at the time as *Persilscheine* (that is, "soap certificates" suitable for a whitewash). These clergy vouched for the good character of specific individuals, despite their past membership in the Nazi Party, the SS, or other Nazi organizations. Reference to religious belief or practice often dominated these statements, with the highest value placed on membership in the Confessing Church. Professor Siegfried Wendt submitted into evidence the claim that his family said grace before meals. Although Rudolf Smend, first postwar Rektor at Göttingen, placed Wendt within the "terror group" that had used Nazi politics to dominate personnel matters at the university, and added that he would never again want to have him as a faculty colleague, Wendt's final appeal placed him in Category 5, fully exonerated. His appeal board added the comment: "It is especially his genuine connection to Christianity and the church . . . which must be taken into consideration."[20]

Neither the reliance on clergy for *Persilscheine* nor the reference to religious belief for exculpation should be surprising, actually. In both cases this practice rested upon the belief and/or hope that religious values would in fact serve as a counterweight to Nazi political attitudes, that they had done so before 1945, and that they could be expected to do so for post-1945 Germany. Clergy responded energetically. Frederick Spotts has gone so far as to call the mountain of clergy-written *Persilscheine* "an act of sabotage" against denazification.[21]

Documents in the Central Church Archive in Berlin indicate that this sabotage did not occur by accident. For example, to protect clergy and other employees of the church, the Council of the EKD (acronym for the German Protestant Church) approved guidelines in May 1946, which guaranteed that such employees could ask for and receive a statement verifying their service to the church and their "personal Christian stance."[22] One regional church added this advice about such *Persilscheine*:

> Statements and testimony will have special influence if they draw attention to the early years of National Socialism . . . and if they are able to claim that the official represented the interests of the church in the *Kirchenkampf* (that is, in the conflict with the *Deutsche Christen* and the Nazi totalitarian claims). Other evidence of every sort . . . can be used. . . . The testimony and statements should be clear and convincing, expressing the essential and illustrative details with brevity. Individual details which make an overview more difficult and thereby delay the process and the final decision should be avoided.[23]

This final sentence seems to represent pure prevarication. The "individual details" to be avoided must mean evidence of Nazi memberships or Nazi enthusiasm, likely to render benign assessment of the "overview" less credible.

By September 1946, Bishop Meiser had developed a 12-page packet to advise clergy on how best to conduct their own defense in a denazification hearing. This included a review of the *Kirchenkampf*, to show that this struggle, "although in its deepest essence a struggle over faith, led finally and in reality to *active resistance* [emphasis in the original] against state and party . . ."[24] Meiser noted that clergy must show that they *gave* active resistance and *suffered* actual harm in order to be placed in Category 5 and thus exonerated. His advice was to stress that the *Kirchenkampf* itself represented resistance (a claim which most pastors even then probably would have recognized as fraudulent) and to consider among examples of harm "*spiritual stresses* [emphasis in the original] . . . which led to depression, nervous exhaustion, and similar things."[25]

Alongside this campaign for an effective defense, an occasional document suggests that church authorities recognized the danger of inflated *Persilscheine*. In one case, the Bavarian church had requested that pastors writing statements for their parishioners should submit them first to their dean. A follow-up memo stated,

> [Our] circular was not always understood in its actual meaning. This [procedure] proved necessary through experience, specifically in order to make statements from clergy as effective as possible, but also in the interests of the believability of the church as a whole. The creation of such testimonies should not be left solely in the hands of the individual clergy. Even in cases where the dean can say nothing about the content of a statement in terms of its accuracy . . . he can still draw conclusions from the frequency with which individual pastors write such statements and from the choice of words in which they are written. In some cases this could give occasion for a brotherly word. . . [After noting the extra work for deans, the letter goes on,] Still, experience has shown that this step must be taken. We have had awkward experiences with both German and Military [Government] offices in which we had to be shown the extremely diverse consequences entailed by the willingness of some pastors to produce such statements.[26]

The gentleness of this language seems remarkable. The letter might have said, "You are lying. We know you are lying. Furthermore, the German and Military Government authorities know you are lying and it is making us all look bad." Such clarity, however, would presumably have offended clergy who thought they were lying in a good cause. After all, these cases involved primarily individual members of the Nazi Party, well meaning, idealistic individuals who should not be compared to the true criminals of the regime, or so the church was claiming.

We also have numerous instances, however, in which more significant individuals with more culpability in the Nazi crimes received enthusiastic support from leaders in the church. One such Nazi figure was Professor Otmar Freiherr von Verschuer, the racial scientist who inspired Joseph Mengele in his research on twins at Auschwitz. While director of the Kaiser Wilhelm Institute for Anthropology and Genetics in Berlin, von Verschuer received regular shipment of body parts from Mengele's ample supply. During his denazification process, von Verschuer received startlingly enthusiastic support from his pastor in Frankfurt, Otto Fricke, a former leader in the Confessing Church and a postwar member of the Provisional Leadership of the Protestant Church. In Fricke's words,

> He and his family belong to my confessional congregation and he supported me most energetically during the difficult years of struggle over the Confessing Church and the freedom of the church and its message . . . People of his type and his character are suited to guide the redirection of the German academic world onto a Christian foundation and promote the rebuilding of German life . . . In this my testimony I speak as the responsible leader of the Protestant Church of Frankfurt and as specially commissioned representative of Bishop D. Wurm and Pastor Martin Niemöller.[27]

This claim upon Bishop Wurm's reputation does not seem exaggerated. He too engaged his efforts for the most questionable individuals. For Hans Heinrich Lammers, the head of the Reich Chancellery who signed his name to Hitler's wartime legislation against Jews and other victims, Wurm declared on his behalf that he had taken "a stance beneficial to the church."[28] Regarding SS *Hauptsturmführer* Karl Sommer, of the SS Economic and Administration Head Office (an office entrusted with the financing of the Holocaust operation), Wurm noted that Sommer had spent six years as a member of the Organization of Young Christian Men in Cologne. Ignoring Sommer's withdrawal from the church in 1933, but accentuating his subsequent reading of the New Testament and of devotional literature while in prison at

Nuremberg, Wurm wrote: "I must therefore believe that Sommer, if he really committed crimes worthy of death, must have done so under the pressure of especially unfortunate circumstances, so that . . . [he] as a believing Christian is worthy of a show of mercy."[29] In 1950, Wurm made a plea for Sister Helene Schürg, who had confessed to assisting in the injection death of thirty to fifty children. Although Wurm admitted he knew nothing of her personally, he claimed to have formed "a very favorable opinion" from documents he had been shown, leading to his conclusion "that Sister Schürg in individual cases had sought successfully to protect patients from the murder which threatened them."[30] And so he pleaded for mercy.

There are many similar cases. Eduard Strauch was tried and sentenced to death at Nuremberg. He had been leader of *Sonderkommando* 1b in the Baltic states, that is, head of one of the "mobile killing units" which inaugurated the killing process in the Holocaust. Among other marks against him, he had once accused *Gauleiter* Kube of being too soft on Jews. Kube, who had attended the Wannsee Conference where the Holocaust was planned, had bragged of being among the first to make his region *Judenrein* or free of Jews. If he would be considered soft on Jews, Eduard Strauch must have been very hard indeed. But Heinrich Held, President of the Protestant Church in the Rhineland, pleaded for him. Strauch had, after all, studied theology, and, according to Held, during his trial his susceptibility to epileptic fits may have left him unable to defend himself properly.[31] *Kommandoführer* Waldemar Klingelhöfer of *Einsatzgruppe B* received a *Persilschein* from his pastor which emphasized that he had rejoined the church, had used his opera-trained voice as a soloist on two occasions so far, and, in the view of the pastor, was "a person of upright, honest character, an enemy to all lies and every injustice, . . . the sort of person we need today, outside, among our *Volk*, for a return to health and a rebuilding where so much corruption now prevails."[32] Klingelhöfer had been sentenced to death for the mass murder of Jews in Estonia; however, pleas such as this in support of his "honest, upright character" helped him win a pardon in January 1951.[33]

How could Bishop Wurm and many other clergy find it so easy to make such grand claims for such questionable characters? We find a partial answer in the internal correspondence of the Council of the EKD in 1945 and 1946. It is clear that the church leadership never considered denazification a legitimate undertaking. Not only did leaders such as Niemöller, Wurm, Meiser and Faulhaber oppose Allied denazification in the summer of 1945, the EKD intensified and focused its opposition, especially in the spring of 1946, drafting various arguments against the entire concept that Germany was in need of cleansing.

Ironically, the focal point in 1946 developed around a newly created *German* law, Law 104 for the Liberation from National Socialism and Militarism, as passed by the state governments of Bavaria, Württemberg-Baden, and Hesse in March of that year. Bishop Wurm and the EKD vehemently opposed the law, voicing their opposition directly to General Clay, the American head of Military Government. The irony of EKD opposition to this law consisted not only in attacking the Allied Military Government for a law written and passed by Germans; it can also be argued that the real thrust of this law of 1946 was to create just the effect advocated by the church, i.e., a very minimal removal of alleged Nazis from German public life.

Under Military Government (i.e., Allied) auspices, individuals had been removed from their jobs based upon the actual circumstances of their membership and participation in various Nazi organizations. If they had participated, they were held accountable. The new German law accepted the same categories of responsibility, but with the proviso that mitigating circumstances could be presented. This meant that *apparent* supporters of the Nazi state might prove they were actual opponents or, at most, "fellow travelers" (*Mitläufer*) with the regime. It was this transition which allowed the vast majority of Germans to escape the serious or long term consequences of denazification.[34] They could become the end product of a *Mitläuferfabrik*, a factory in which Nazis could be inserted at one end and mere "fellow travelers" would emerge at the other.[35]

Conflict over this law of March 1946 illustrates the tendency of the church leadership to rise up in immediate opposition to denazification policies. However, it also points to the fact of an early awareness among some church members that there could be an alternative point of view. One of the men responsible for this law, Adolf Arndt of Hesse, illustrates that alternative in his quick response to the EKD stance of opposition. In an essay published by Eugen Kogon in the *Frankfurter Hefte*, Arndt chastises the church for legal hairsplitting and questionable judgment in its attempt to negate denazification. He calls it particularly unseemly that the church should claim that early members of the Nazi Party could not have known the true nature of the regime. In a litany of abuses, he describes how "everyone knew" about the arrest of political opponents, the banning of political parties, and the violence against Jews in 1933; "everyone knew" of the violent and illegal purge by murder in June 1934; "everyone knew" of the burning of synagogues and the violence against Jews during *Kristallnacht* in 1938.[36]

Arndt's critique of the church reads better today than does the church's defense of its own position. Aware as we are of the crimes of the Nazi regime, we may be shocked to find virtually no apology, repentance or rethinking within the church. Instead, we find an almost instinctive protection of Germans against foreign attack, against revenge. That response is far less surprising if we take two simple truths into account. First, church leaders could not accept the cleansing of Nazis from German life, because they had been Nazis. This was literally true for some, such as Wilhelm Niemöller. For many others it was true of their friends and relatives, as we discover in a poignant example involving Bishop Wurm himself. While he led the public fight against punishment of "nominal Nazis," he conducted a private effort on behalf of his son, who had been sentenced to a year in prison for falsifying his *Fragebogen*.[37] Claiming membership in the Nazi Party only from 1938, Hans Wurm had actually joined with the early enthusiasts in 1922. This example from the Wurm family illustrates an obvious reality: Christians had been at home among members and supporters of National Socialism.

The second obvious truth involves those groups which had been least at home within the Nazi state, i.e., leftists and Jews. The public and private comments of church leaders in 1945 and 1946 are filled with the recognition that a thoroughgoing purge of Nazis could only lead to political advantage for the enemies of the church, and it is clear that they reckoned leftists and Jews among those enemies. Thus Wurm worried about those he considered incapable and of inappropriate character. He feared they would now fill the German bureaucracy.

In fact, church fears about a harsh and harmful denazification proved largely unfounded. On the one hand, the most expansive American ideas about cleansing Germany proved simply impossible to implement: Not even that many *Fragebogen* could be read, much less that many Germans removed from the middle and upper ranks of the workforce. The Cold War also impinged, quickly modifying America's passion for cleansing Germany into a quest for allies against communism. Harsh denazification did not fit that new reality.[38]

Left behind in the sad remains of denazification we find the abuse of *Persilscheine*, a willingness to give church support to almost any alleged war criminal, and a tendency to use the terminology of "war prisoners" even when "war criminals" would have been more accurate. At the same time that this story of denazification played itself out, church historians on both the Catholic and Protestant sides sought to tell their story.

Bishop Johannes Neuhäusler developed the first Catholic narrative of the Nazi era. In 1946, he published an account which described Nazi persecution of Catholics in Germany and brave Catholic resistance, without the slightest hint that Catholics had expressed support or sympathy for the regime.[39] Only in the early 1960s did Catholic historians begin to take a more critical look at events, especially when Rolf Hochhuth's play, *The Deputy*, suggested that Pope Pius XII had stood in cowardly silence when he should have spoken out against Nazi atrocities.[40] A vitriolic battle continues to this day on the question of Pius XII, including the bitterly contested issue of whether he should be granted sainthood. However, virtually no one today claims that the story of Catholics and the Nazi state is one of unmitigated honor. Even John Paul II has apologized to Jews, acknowledging Catholic weakness and a portion of Catholic complicity in the crimes of the Nazi regime.

When postwar Protestants set out to write their history of the *Kirchenkampf* (the church struggle), former members of the *Deutsche*

Christen were in disrepute and former members of the Confessing Church were ascendant. Wilhelm Niemöller emerged as perhaps the single most important figure in the writing of this history, because of his connection to his brother Martin and because of his access to Confessing Church documents. He managed to save several important caches of material from destruction and then he constructed an archive on his church premises at Bielefeld.[41] Wilhelm wrote or edited nearly two dozen books dealing with various aspects of Confessing Church history, and he made his archive available to scholars who chose to join in his project. For a full generation, nobody paid much attention to the skeletons in the closet of the Confessing Church. Gradually, however, the heroic story of resistance to Nazism gave way to more critical scholarship somewhat parallel to that undertaken by Catholics.[42]

In the first generation, while Wilhelm Niemöller and Johannes Neuhäusler dominated the early postwar history of churches in Nazi Germany, a minor incident occurred in the career of Otto Dibelius. He had been an important Protestant church leader already in the 1920s. He then became a leader in the Confessing Church, and, after 1945, his career included periods as Bishop of Berlin, President of the Council of the German Protestant Church, and leader of the World Council of Churches. In anticipation of a visit by Dibelius to London in March 1951, *The Observer* profiled him with the following words of praise:

> Immediately after Hitler came to power in 1933, the Protestant members of the Reichstag were sufficiently blind to gather together [in the presence of Hitler] . . . to give thanks in the Nicolaikirche [St. Nicholas Church] at Potsdam. The Bishop exercised his right to preach. In a quiet, but firm, sermon he informed his listeners: "The dictatorship of the total State is incompatible with the will of God. For the sake of the Gospel, we need a democratic state."[43]

Unfortunately for Dibelius, readers of this story in London included one C.C. Aronsfeld, who knew better. He wrote *The Observer* to complain that Dibelius had not only *not* praised democracy so courageously in front of Adolf Hitler, he had also certainly not *believed* in democracy. It turns out that Aronsfeld, a Jewish émigré, had gone to school with Dibelius' son, a youth who covered his school papers with swastikas and other doodles of radical rightwing provenance. Furthermore, Aronsfeld had a printed copy of Dibelius's sermon from 1933, complete with hymns sung and lessons read. As the editor at *The Observer* waffled, attributing the quote to a reputable Swiss newspaper, Aronsfeld discovered that the article in question had been contributed to the Swiss paper by an anonymous "German Protestant." He demanded a correction, since *The Observer* had demonstrably printed an inaccurate quote, whereupon he was told to direct his complaint to Zurich. Although he protested that it was the English speaking world which concerned him, a world which would now mistakenly understand the past of Otto Dibelius, his complaint apparently earned no retraction.

This minor embarrassment in the life of Otto Dibelius illustrates two aspects of the broader story. First, the *actual* stance of most Christians in Germany during the Nazi era could not easily withstand the scrutiny of a postwar world, a world which believed in democracy and condemned the politics of Adolf Hitler. Secondly, various stratagems were undertaken by Christians in Germany to distort the past. They did so in hopes of earning a respectable place for churches within that postwar world. Denazification represents one corner of the carpet under which we must look to find what was swept away. A more careful and honest practice of historical inquiry will show us who handled the broom.

ENDNOTES

1. A brief list of such studies might include Christopher R. Browning, *Ordinary Men: Reserve Police Battalion 101 and the Final Solution in Poland* (New York: Random House, 1992); Robert Gellately, *The Gestapo and German Society: Enforcing Racial Policy 1933-1945* (Oxford: Oxford University Press, 1990); Norbert Frei and Johannes Schmitz, *Journalismus im Dritten Reich* (Munich: C.H. Beck Verlag, 1989); Ingo Müller, *Hitler's Justice: The Courts of the Third Reich* (Cambridge, MA: Harvard University Press, 1991); Benno Müller-Hill, *Murderous Science: Elimination by Scientific Selection of Jews, Gypsies, and Others, Germany 1933-1945* (Oxford: Oxford University Press, 1988); and Robert Jay Lifton, *The Nazi Doctors: Medical Killing and the Psychology of Genocide* (New York: Basic Books, 1986); as well as Robert P. Ericksen, *Theologians under Hitler: Gerhard Kittel, Paul Althaus and Emanuel Hirsch* (New Haven: Yale University Press, 1985).

2. See James Bentley, *Martin Niemöller, 1892-1984* (New York: Free Press, 1984), and Jurgen Schmidt, *Martin Niemoller im Kirchenkampf* (Hamburg: Leibniz-Verlag, 1971).

3. See Eberhard Bethge, *Dietrich Bonhoeffer: Theologian, Christian, Contemporary* (London: Collins, 1970). Bethge studied under Bonhoeffer, became his closest friend, and then joined the family by marrying a niece. He is responsible for making Bonhoeffer known to the postwar world by editing and publishing Bonhoeffer's writings, and he is a reliable interpreter of Bonhoeffer's life.

4. See Schmidt, *Martin Niemöller*, 91, note 127.

5. See Bentley, *Martin Niemöller*, 24-5 and 39-43. See also Ericksen, *Theologians under Hitler*.

6. See Claudia Koonz, *Mothers in the Fatherland: Women, the Family and Nazi Politics* (New York: St Martin's Press, 1987), and Claudia Koonz, *The Nazi Conscience* (Cambridge, MA: Harvard University Press, 2003).

7. See, for example, Guenter Lewy, "Pius XII, the Jews, and the German Catholic Church," in Robert P. Ericksen and Susannah Heschel, eds., *Betrayal: German Churches and the Holocaust* (Minneapolis: Fortress Press, 1999), 129-48.

8. Paul Althaus, *Die deutsche Stunde der Kirche*, 3d ed. (Göttingen: Vandenhoek & Ruprecht, 1934), 5.

9. See Wilhelm Laible's editorials in the weekly editions of the *Allgemeine Evanglische-Lutherisch Kirchenzeitung*, especially "Nationale Revolution," AELKZ 66:18 (5 May 1933), 424.

Robert P. Ericksen

10. See Doris Bergen, *Twisted Cross: The German Christian Movement in the Third Reich* (Chapel Hill: University of North Carolina Press, 1996).

11. This assessment of one-fifth can be found in Wilhelm Niemöller, "The Niemöller Archives," in Franklin H. Littell and Hubert G. Locke, eds., *The German Church Struggle and the Holocaust* (Detroit: Wayne State Press, 1974), 43.

12. Victoria Barnett, *For the Soul of the People: Protestant Protest against Hitler* (New York: Oxford University Press, 1992), 3-4.

13. See Robert P. Ericksen and Susannah Heschel, "German Churches and the Holocaust," in Dan Stone, ed., *The Historiography of the Holocaust* (London: Palgrave Macmillan, 2004), 296-318.

14. See Robert P. Ericksen, "The Barmen Synod and its Declaration: An Historical Synopsis," in Hubert G. Locke, ed., *The Church Confronts the Nazis: Barmen Then and Now* (New York: Edwin Mellen Press, 1984), 27-91.

15. See Wolfgang Gerlach, *And the Witnesses were Silent: The Confessing Church and the Persecution of the Jews* (Omaha: University of Nebraska Press, 2000).

16. Clemens Vollnhals, *Evangelische Kirche und Entnazifizierung, 1945-1949. Die Last der nationalsozialistischen Vergangenheit* (Munich: Christian Kaiser Verlag, 1989), 13. Another book on the topic of the churches and denazification is Gerhard Besier, *"Selbstreinigung" unter britischer Besatzungsherrschaft. Die Evangelisch-Lutherische Landeskirche Hannovers und ihr Landesbischof Marahrens 1945-1947* (Göttingen: Vandenhoek & Ruprecht, 1986).

17. Quoted in Ernst Klee, *Persilscheine und falsche Pässe: Wie die Kirchen den Nazis halfen* (Frankfurt am Main: Fischer Taschenbuch Verlag, 1991), 11.

18. The details and quotations in this paragraph can be found in Vollnhals, 52-7.

19. See, for example, Gerhard Besier and Gerhard Sauter, *Wie Christen ihre Schuld bekennen. Die Stuttgarter Erklärung 1945* (Göttingen: Vandenhoeck & Ruprecht, 1985).

20. Wendt's file is in the Niedersächsisches Hauptstaatsarchiv Hannover, Nds. 171 Hild, 18531. Wendt's religious beliefs and practices are praised in letters from Günter Schweitzer (9.11.46), Heinrich Markwort (19.11.46), and Prof. Dr. Martin Dibelius (attached to Wendt's *Fragebogen* of 18.1.47). The opinion expressed by his appeal board is in the "Entnazifizierungs-Entscheidung, Rechtskräftig am 18,2,1949." See also Robert P. Ericksen, "Religion und Nationalsozialismus im Spiegel der Entnazifizierungsakten," *Kirchliche Zeitgeschichte*, 7:1 (1994), 93-5.

21. Frederick Spotts, *The Churches and Politics in Germany* (Middletown, CT: Wesleyan University Press, 1973), 99, note 2.

22. "Richtlinien zur Durchführung der Selbstreinigung der Kirche," approved at Treysa on 2 May 1946, Evangelisches Zentralarchiv in Berlin (EZA), 2/318, 228.

23. Landeskirchenamt an die Herren Pröpste und Dekane d. Ev. Landeskirche v. Kurhessen-Waldeck, 24.6.46, EZA, 2/318, 171.

24. Evang.-Luth.Landeskirchenrat, An die sämtliche Dekanate der Bayerischen Landeskirche, 10.9.46, EZA, 2/321, 85. The entire document is found on pages 85-90, front and back.

25. Ibid.

26. Evang-Luth. Landeskirchenrat an sämtliche Dekanate, 1.6.46, EZA, 2/318, 281.

27. Quoted in Ernst Klee, *Persilscheine und Falsche Pässe*, 128.

28. Quoted in Ibid., 95.

29. Quoted in Ibid., 101.

30. Quoted in Ibid., 122-3.

31. See Ibid., 99.

32. See Ibid., 99-100.

33. Ibid., 99.

34. This picture can be extracted from files in the EZA, especially in correspondence between Adolf Arndt and EKD headquarters. See, for example, EZA, 2/318, 185-99. See also Vollnhals, 60-8.

35. See Lutz Niethammer, *Die Mitläuferfabrik. Die Entnazifizierung am Beispiel Bayern* (Berlin, 1982).

36. Adolf Arndt, "Quo vadis?" in EZA, 2/318, 185-99.

37. The "Fragebogen" was an Allied questionnaire in which Germans were asked to list all memberships in and connections with Nazi organizations.

38. See Robert P. Ericksen, "Religion und Nationalsozialismus im Spiegel der Entnazifizierungsakten der Göttinger Universität," *Kirchliche Zeitgeschichte* 7:1 (1994), 83-101.

39. Johannes Neuhäusler, *Kreuz und Hakenkreuz. Der Kampf der Nationalsozialismus gegen die katholische Kirche und der kirchliche Widerstand* (Munich: Katholische Kirche Bayerns, 1946).

40. See Rolf Hochhuth, *The Deputy* (New York: S. French, 1964), and Hans Müller, *Katholische Kirche und Nationalsozialismus* (Munich: Nymphenburger Verl.-Handlung, 1963) for early examples of a critical view.

41. See Wilhelm Niemöller, ed., *Die vierte Bekenntnissynode der Deutschen Evangelischen Kirche zu Bad Oeynhausen* (Göttingen: Vandenhoek & Ruprecht, 1960), 5.

42. See Robert P. Ericksen, "Wilhelm Niemöller and the Historiography of the *Kirchenkampf*," forthcoming in Manfred Gailus and Hartmut Lehmann, eds., *Nationalprotestantische Mentalitäten in Deutschland, 1870-1970* (Göttingen: Vandenhoek & Ruprecht, 2005).

43. "Profile—Dr. Dibelius," *The Observer*, 4.3.51, as found in the Dibelius Personal File, Wiener Library, London. The following correspondence between C.C. Aronsfeld and The Editor of *The Observer* is found in the same file.

CHAPTER 12

HISTORY, MEMORY, AND IDENTITY IN W. G. SEBALD'S *AUSTERLITZ*

Gerald A. Fetz

An extensive amount of recent scholarship has focused on the themes and related problematics of history and memory in German-language literature, especially in literature that deals either with the Holocaust and the period of the Third Reich and the Second World War, on the one hand, or with the East German (GDR) experience up to the unification of Germany in 1990, on the other.[1] At the center of much of this scholarship and the discussions of the literary works and issues it has sought to understand and explain, one can find numerous recurring questions, several of which have also occupied professional historians and others who concern themselves with these historical periods in serious ways: Whose history gets to be written, by whom, and from whose perspective? How reliable are the traditional assumptions about the possibility of historical objectivity? What purposes does historical writing, including literature about history, serve, and who is allowed to decide which purposes should prevail? What is the relationship between historical writing and the political or social agendas of the present? How reliable is memory in the writing of historical accounts, particularly of autobiography and so-called eyewitness accounts? How valid are the various kinds of historical documentation? And what is the relationship between historical writing, whether of the scholarly or literary sort, and the events, their interpretations and the significances which society chooses to privilege, remember, believe, believe in, and thereby declare: *this* is the history that matters (to us)? These and related questions, then, have (pre)occupied many historians, literary scholars, and writers of fiction at least since the highly publicized *Historikerstreit* (Historians' Debate) of the 1980s and the flurry of re-assessments of GDR history in the early 1990s, right up to the present, as the recent controversy-laden discussions surrounding Martin Walser's novel *Ein springender Brunnen* (1998), Günter Grass's recent work, *Im Krebsgang* (2002), or Sebald's own collection of essays under the title *Luftkrieg und Literatur* (1999)[2] vividly illustrate.

In this modest contribution to the collection of essays in honor of Professor Phil Nordquist, in whose courses I sat, learned, and became a history major between 1963 and 1966, I intend to focus on W.G. Sebald's literary responses to some of the questions suggested above in his last completed work before his tragic death in December 2001, that is, in the masterful novel *Austerlitz*.[3] Sebald's fascination with the intertwining complexities of history, memory, and identity is clearly evident in many of his earlier scholarly essays, but it is in his more fictional works that this fascination yields consistently discernible attitudes, strategies, and even, we might assert, a *Sebaldian* attitude toward history. Already in those literary and literary historical essays, collected most notably in the volumes *Die Beschreibung des Unglücks* (1985)[4] and *Unheimliche Heimat* (1991),[5] Sebald showed that his historical interest was not so much in major events or figures, in the so-called victors or victories, in the perceived "high points" or "turning points" of history, even of literary history, but rather, in the usually deleterious effects which those events had on those who (often barely) survived them. As the title of the first of those two collections suggests, Sebald pursued stories and cases of *Unglück* (misfortune), of what one commentator has termed the "stille Katastrophen" (quiet catastrophes) that result from the great calamities of history.[6] The writers and literary characters he investigated, wrote about, and felt an obvious kinship to were talented, but often side-tracked and under-appreciated sufferers; writers, artists, and intellectuals who were displaced and pushed to their societies' periphery, to loneliness, and, often, to suicide; pushed there by mainstream society, by circumstances, disease, poverty, by major historical events—most notably and most frequently by the Holocaust—by *history*, as we usually understand it. Even when Sebald wrote about the lives of more famous writers, thinkers, and artists, he appeared far less interested in their successes than in their failings, failures, and, finally, in their suffering. Judging solely from his choice of writers, works, and topics for his scholarly essays, regardless of the period of history dealt with, one can sense even there a strong tendency toward a melancholic and quite pessimistic view of the world and about history.

In *Die Ausgewanderten,* his first work translated into English (although other at least partially fictional works preceded it in German),[7] Sebald substantiated that impression by focusing his attention on the lives of four talented sufferers, who, even though they had managed to escape or survive the major European calamities of the first half of the 20ᵗʰ century, eventually succumb to the psychological wounds and pain which that *modern* era in history had inflicted upon them. They may have physically survived the events which uprooted and scattered them into foreign parts of the world, but the aftermath, the "afterschock,"[8] as one critic has aptly termed it, and the traumatic legacy of their history, and of Europe's history, ultimately do them in.

Jacques Austerlitz, the protagonist in the work that carries his name, possesses numerous similarities to the main characters in the four sections or stories that constitute *Die Ausgewanderten*: Henry Selwyn, Paul Bereyter, Ambros Adelwarth, and Max Ferber. Austerlitz, too, it turns out, was uprooted by calamitous historical events—in his case, the annexation of Czechoslovakia by Hitler's Third Reich in 1938; he, too, *survived* the physical brutality of that regime, thanks to his being sent to England and then to Wales via a *Kindertransport* in the following year; but in ways similar to the fates of those Sebaldian precursors, that physical survival came at the price of his identity and of his wholeness as a human being. The lives of all of these Sebaldian characters, including Jacques Austerlitz, are characterized by displacement and enormous loss, which, even when successfully repressed or just held consciously at bay, results in a numbing emptiness, isolation, debilitating melancholy, and alienation. Robbed of their *initial* and *essential* connections in life, they become incapable of connecting elsewhere, to others, and even to themselves. Their lives are eerily ghost-like.

I will return to the novel *Austerlitz* in a moment, but let me first attempt to extract from these Sebaldian *post*-lives a little more insight into his view of history. The majority of Sebald's characters are not caught up in the dramatic events or moments of history, as profoundly as these events ultimately affect those lives; in fact, Sebald is much less interested in or concerned with those events than he is in what happens to the so-called survivors in their aftermath. The portions of the lives of the Selwyns, Adelwarths, Ferbers, and Austerlitzes on which Sebald sheds some light are those which they lead not so much *in history*, but, as many current theorists would call it, in *post-history*. Virtually everything in the worlds and times that Sebald's characters, including his narrators, inhabit has already happened. They are populated not by flesh-and-blood contemporaries who, in the midst of their own lives occasionally look back and reflect on history, or by a vital present time, but by ruins and remnants; empty streets (except for apparitions and illusions perceived by the narrators and protagonists) and abandoned estates; dusty books and remote, quirky museums; by dead and perhaps unfairly forgotten individuals and submerged villages; even nature has been rendered mute and is generally devoid of vitality. As one American commentator on *Austerlitz* asserted, Sebald's world approximates "a memoryscape—a twilight fogbound world of half-remembered images and ghosts."9

Sebald's works are most frequently set, like *Austerlitz*, in the final decades of the 20th century. It is, as several critics have pointed out, generally a *post-World War II* world, and many of the protagonists, if not the narrators, are Jewish. As such, their world is distinctly *post-Holocaust*, and it is that horrible history with which they primarily struggle and by which they are chiefly haunted. When more distant history enters the narrative in Sebald's works, usually it is of the 19th century, a history that, from Sebald's perspective, was overwhelmed, covered over, and rendered obsolete and lifeless by 20th century modernity in all of its gargantuan and destructive aspects. But the narrators, and some of the other characters as well, are frequently fascinated by the fragments and remnants of that pre-20ᵗʰ century world which they stumble across or consciously seek, much in the way that archaeologists search for and occasionally uncover illuminating fragments from past times. In fact, more than one critic has likened Sebald's approach to history to that employed by archaeologists. Sigrid Löffler, in reference to *Die Ausgewanderten,* expressed it this way in an essay from 1993:

> In accord with his temperament, the melancholic [Sebald, for instance] is the custodian of the ruins of the past; he is a de-coder of forgotten, submerged texts; he is a collector and investigator on the rubbish fields of times past. The sedimented unsimultaneities in the world have captivated him. His archaeoligising vision recognizes the ruins of the past in the present, above all, the ruins caused by the past's violent destructions. [My translation][10]

And Arthur Lubow, relying on the same basic comparison, suggested that "like an archaeologist reconstructing a pot from a couple of shards, [Sebald] worked in a way that he characterized as 'extremely tenuous and unreliable.'"[11]

This last point is especially important to note, because, despite the tremendous archaeological efforts, no clear picture of any historical past is achieved by Sebald's characters or his works. The historian Saul Friedländer has distinguished two basic poles in the historical writing about the Holocaust, ". . . i.e. precise factual information offered within strict limits and usually around a central idea that gives it coherence OR an outburst of pain and despair that, in principle, rejects the possibility of order and coherence. Whereas the first one means closure, the second indicates an open-minded process of remembrance."[12] Since Sebald is not interested in supplying anywhere close to complete portrayals of any past, especially of any aspect of the Holocaust, and since he rejects the possibility of closure, again about any aspect of history and especially of the Holocaust, he approaches all historical material with a skepticism that rejects the notion that facts can be collected and re-assembled into a continuous or coherent whole from which reliable meaning can be extracted. As he stated more than once when asked about his "view" of history, Sebald put far more stock in the insights to be gained from reflection on the shards of history or on the fragments of memory, and from the metaphors and allegories that emerge from such reflection, than on any traditional historical monograph-like or purportedly factual rendition that would lay claim to the possibility of genuine understanding or "closure."[13]

As I hope to show in the remaining discussion about Sebald's remarkable book *Austerlitz*, he approaches the historical subject matter he chooses to emphasize with curiosity, empathy, and a strong belief in the importance of his project; yet, his approach is likewise characterized by the realization that his effort will be futile, ultimately, if judged by the usual expectations for historical writing, and no clear picture or convincing understanding will result. And since he rejects the historian's general faith that such goals are attainable, Sebald also chooses to approach his subject matter differently: "obliquely" rather than "frontally," as one critic has put it, or "crab-wise," to use another's term.[14] On several occasions, Sebald stressed that he felt he had to deal with the Holocaust *indirectly*, by focusing not on the events themselves but on their *post-historical* ramifications: "I don't think you can focus on the horror of the Holocaust. It's like the head of the Medusa: you carry it with you in a sack, but if you looked at it you'd be petrified. I was trying to write the lives of some people who'd survived – the 'lucky ones.' . . . But I didn't see it; I only know things indirectly."[15]

For anyone unfamiliar with Sebald's *Austerlitz*, the following very brief synopsis of its content will have to suffice for the purposes of this essay. The four-year old Jewish boy Jacques Austerlitz was taken to England and then to Wales, where he was raised by an otherwise childless and austere Calvinist minister and his wife. After a few letters from his mother, Jacques never heard from his parents again, was given the Welsh name Dafydd Elias, and gradually lost all conscious memory of his origins, even though he always felt somehow "out of place" in his Welsh life. His rather stark childhood was eventually lightened somewhat by his boarding school experience, where he evidenced both academic and athletic talent, even though the overall regime of the school was repressive. At school he developed a friendship with a younger boy whose family took him to their country estate during numerous holidays, and Dafyyd was introduced there to a wide range of eccentrics and their (mostly natural history-related) pastimes. While in his mid-teens, first his adoptive mother died, of a broken heart, it would seem, and then his adoptive father went insane and was committed to an asylum where he, too, soon died. At the boarding school, Dafydd was subsequently told that his real name was Jacques Austerlitz, but little more.

The reader of this book learns about Jacques' life, including his later years as an architectural historian in London and his frequent peripatetic wanderings as an older adult throughout Europe, mostly for the alleged purpose of conducting research on massive historical structures for a planned, but never completed study, all of this re-lated by a younger Sebaldian narrator who meets Austerlitz in 1967 in the central train station in Antwerp, Belgium. The two meet in a fashion clearly reminiscent of several Thomas Bernhard narrators and their older, eccentric "teachers," at various sites in Europe, sometimes by design, sometimes by accident, at both short and long intervals right up to the mid-1990s. Some of what Austerlitz tells the book's narrator about his life and thoughts happened prior to their initial meeting, some of it, however, during the years of their "friendship." We learn about his life, as does the narrator, in piecemeal fashion, in fragments and in irregular installments. Interspersed with the re-tell-ing of Austerlitz's monologues about his life are the narrator's first-person descriptions and reflections, of and on Austerlitz, but also of and about his own existence that leads him, as well, to frequent solo wanderings through Europe. The basis of their relationship appears to be in part their shared melancholic temperaments and their mutual interest in fragmentary history and some of its more quirky artifacts. The narrator, it is clear, is also an exceptionally attentive listener, and that quality doesn't escape the usually isolated Austerlitz, who appreci-ates that quality and chooses him, therefore, to be the recipient of his still evolving "story."

Not surprising to any Sebald reader is the fact that Austerlitz's "story" is related, both to the narrator and, through him, to the read-ers, in choppy and non-linear fashion. Chronology has to be con-structed by the readers, and we also have to draw our own connec-tions between and among the narrated pieces of Austerlitz's life and the assorted treatises, architectural observations, and philosophical or artistic reflections which also constitute a large part of what he tells the narrator. Perhaps the most significant turn in Austerlitz's adult life, and in the narrator's task of re-creating what Austerlitz tells him, occurs when Austerlitz gradually begins to awaken from his amnesia about his pre-Wales past, an awakening sparked by a short radio interview he casually overhears with two women who had been sent to England on a *Kindertransport* at the end of the 1930s. The resulting stutter-steps toward remembering, as incomplete as that is, which the women's rec- ollections and a sudden vision of himself as a child in the Liverpool Street Railroad Station trigger in Austerlitz, lead him to Prague, to an unexpected and very lucky reunion with his mother's best friend, who had also been Jacques' nanny, and finally to Theresienstadt, where he searches in vain for even a miniscule piece of evidence that his mother had been there.

In spite of the forward motion of his *remembering* slowly who he had been and where he had come from, Austerlitz is in many ways a reluctant and clumsy rememberer: "Ich merkte jetzt, wie wenig Übung ich in der Erinnerung hatte und wie sehr ich, im Gegenteil, immer bemüht gewesen sein musste, mich an möglichst gar nichts zu erinnern und allem aus dem Weg zu gehen, was sich auf die eine oder andere Weise auf meine mir unbekannte Herkunft bezog" (*Austerlitz*, 201).[16] Despite his former nanny's loving assistance in his effort to re- connect with who he had been, this world of partial memory which he re-enters in Prague, and for which he seeks clues in Theresienstadt, was nonetheless frightening, inhabited by ghosts; and it led him to a conclusion that most likely caused his subsequent nervous break- down: "Irgendwann in der Vergangenheit, dachte ich, habe ich einen Fehler gemacht und bin jetzt in einem falschen Leben" (*Austerlitz*, 302).[17] Austerlitz's re-awakened memory proves to be unwieldy and labyrinthine. He has difficulty distinguishing among dream-worlds, memories, and the present. He suffers from the gap between who he is and has been and who he might have been, even should have been. Finally, the confrontation with his losses—family, home, and iden- tity—and the confusion caused by his very belated journey toward glimpses of his lost self overwhelm him, at least temporarily.

Austerlitz's perceptions about the intertwined realities of past and present, of the worlds of the dead and the living, suggest, I would assert, some of the basic features of Sebald's view of history and of the relativity of time:

> Es scheint mir nicht, sagte Austerlitz, dass wir die Gesetze verstehen, unter denen sich die Wiederkunft der Vergangenheit vollzieht, doch ist es mir immer mehr, als gäbe es überhaupt keine Zeit, sondern nur verschiedene, nach einer höheren Stereometrie ineinander verschachtelte Räume, zwischen denen die Lebendigen und die Toten, je nachdem man zumute ist, hin und her gehen können, und je länger ich es bedenke, desto mehr kommt mir vor, dass wir, die wir uns noch am Leben befinden, in den Augen der Toten irreale und nur manchmal, unter bestimmten Lichtverhältnissen und atmosphärischen Bedingungen sichtbar werdende Wesen sind . . . (*Austerlitz*, 265).[18]

Such an intermingling of past and present and the implied denial of the usual demarcation between the realms of the dead and of those alive is underscored already at the beginning of the novel when, during their first encounter in 1967, Austerlitz points out to the narrator certain characteristics of the giant clock on the wall of the Central Railroad Station in Antwerp, located beneath the old and rather tarnished coat-of-arms of the former Kingdom of Belgium, where "…eine mächtige Uhr, an deren einst vergoldetem, jetzt aber vom Eisenbahnruss und Tabaksqualm eingeschwärztem Zifferblatt der zirka sechs Fuss messende Zeiger in seiner Runde ging" (*Austerlitz*, 12).[19] Timeworn, yet timeless, somehow obsolete and out-of-place, the clock still functioned nonetheless, marking both the passing of time and the continuing presence of the past. It should be acknowledged that the book *Austerlitz* is replete with spatial constructions and artifacts—numerous train stations or the fortresses that later became concentration camps, Breendonk and Theresienstadt, for example—that also serve as powerful metaphors for Sebald's notion about the fluidity of history, about the simultaneous transitoriness of the past and, contradictorily, its continuing, if ghostly presence in the present.

There is certainly a lot more one could say about *Austerlitz*, Sebald, and the topic of this brief essay. But allow me to offer a few concluding remarks. In reference to this work, the *FAZ* critic Thomas Steinfeld asserted shortly after its initial publication that Sebald "…

[hat] vor allem ein Buch über die Theorie verfasst, wie man Geschichte zu schreiben hat, und diese Theorie ist weder logisch noch widerspruchsfrei."[20] Michael Rutschky, writing at the same time, claimed that *Austerlitz* ". . . praktiziert eine 'Poetik der Erinnerung,' die ganz wesentlich von Walter Benjamins schwarzer Geschichtsphilosophie beeinflusst wird."[21] And Iris Radisch postulated in her review in *Die Zeit* that "Sebald eigentlich kein Erzähler . . . [ist] . . . , sondern eine Art materialistischer Geschichtsmetaphysiker, ein Virtuose des Zettelkastens, Stimmenimitator, Konservator und Archivar."[22] My repeated readings of and extensive reflections on the book and its author make me tend to agree with all of those rather cryptic assertions. *Austerlitz is* a literary work that clearly reflects a Benjaminian pessimism about European, even Western history in general; it *is* a literary work that suggests a metaphysics of history in which access to the past can be gained only to a very limited extent, and then only through a veritable mélange of fragmentary material artifacts, assorted documents, including photographs, dreams, even, and the strenuous process of remembering, rather than in traditional scholarly fashion; and it *is* a literary work that illustrates Sebald's apparent theory of historical writing that denies the validity of chronology, linear time, and the possibility of achieving by any means a complete and accurate re-creation of the past, while at the same time admitting contradictions, the illogical, and the relativity of time and place.

Yet, in spite of all those reversals that seem to mock the historian's quest and the historian's craft, Sebald took history and its enormous importance for the present very seriously. He demonstrates through the character of Austerlitz what happens when history is repressed or forgotten; he asserts the alienation and falseness that prevail when one fails at least to try to remember where one came from, what one has lost, and those who have been lost. One of Sebald's self-appointed tasks was to recover pieces of the past, clue by clue, anecdote by anecdote, shard by shard, transport them in all their fragmentariness into our present, and provoke us into acknowledging some of what has been lost through the calamitous events of the 20th century and into seeing some of the ghosts that wander right next to us through the streets, in and out of the buildings and places that they used to inhabit and that we have continued to use. In a way, Sebald's view of how to treat history and how history remains active in the present is, as he asserted shortly before his death, ". . . an old notion . . . Where I grew up, in a remote village at the back of a valley, the old still thought the dead needed attending to—a notion so universal it's inscribed in all religions."[23] *Austerlitz* is a book which makes a compelling case for attending to the dead as well as to those who are alive around us.

Gerald A. Fetz

ENDNOTES

1. See, with regard especially to the challenges of writing about the Holocaust, the following studies as selected examples: Saul Friedländer's article "History, Memory, and the Historian: Dilemmas and Responsibilities," *New German Critique* (Spring/Summer 2000), 3-15, or the volume of essays he edited, *Probing the Limits of Representation. Nazism and the 'Final Solution'* (Cambridge, MA & London: Harvard U. Press, 1992); Gillian Banner, *Holocaust Literature. Schulz, Levi, Spiegelman and the Memory of the Offence* (London & Portland, OR: Valentine Mitchell, 2000); the essay collection edited by Berel Lang, *Writing and the Holocaust* (New York & London: Holmes & Meier, 1988); the collection edited by Michael L. Morgan, *A Holocaust Reader. Responses to the Nazi Extermination* (Oxford & New York: Oxford University Press, 2001); Dominick LaCapra, *Representing the Holocaust: History, Theory, Trauma* (Ithaca: Cornell University Press, 1994); Caroline Wiedmer, *The Claims of Memory. Representations of the Holocaust in Contemporary Germany and France* (Ithaca & London: Cornell University Press, 1999); Andrea Reiter, *Narrating the Holocaust* (London & New York: Continuum, 2000); Ernestine Schlant, *The Language of Silence. West German Literature and the Holocaust* (New York & London: Routledge, 1999); or Jeffrey Herf, *Divided Memory. The Nazi Past in the Two Germanys* (Cambridge, MA & London: Harvard University Press, 1997).

2. W.G. Sebald, *Luftkrieg und Literatur* (Munich & Vienna: Carl Hanser Verlag, 1999). Translated by Anthea Bell into English as *On the Natural History of Disaster* (New York: Random House, 2003).

3. W.G. Sebald, *Austerlitz* (Munich & Vienna: Carl Hanser Verlag, 2001). English translation by Anthea Bell, *Austerlitz* (New York: Random House, 2001).

4. *Die Beschreibung des Unglücks* (Salzburg & Vienna: Residenz Verlag, 1985).

5. *Unheimliche Heimat* (Salzburg & Vienna: Residenz Verlag, 1991).

6. Renate Just, "Stille Katastrophen," in Franz Loquai, ed., *W.G. Sebald* (Eggingen: Edition Isele, 1997), 25.

7. *Nach der Natur. Ein Elementargedicht* (1988) and *Schwindel. Gefühle* (1990).

8. Lynne Sharon Schwartz, in "A Symposium on W.G. Sebald," *The Threepenny Review* (Spring 2002), 19.

9. Michiko Kakutani, "Life in a No Man's Land of Memories and Loss," *New York Times* (October 26, 2001).

10. "Seinem Temperament nach ist der Melancholiker [Sebald, for instance] Kustode der Ruinen der Vergangenheit, er ist Dechiffrierer vergessener, versunkener Texte, er ist Sammler und Spurensucher auf den Trümmerfeldern abgelebter

Zeiten. Die sedimentierten Ungleichzeitigkeiten in der Welt haben es ihm angetan. Sein archaeologisierender Blick nimmt im Bestehenden die Trümmer des Vergangenen wahr, vor allem die Trümmer vergangener Verheerungen." Sigrid Löffler, "W.G. Sebald, der Ausgewanderte," in S.L., *Kritiken, Portraits, Glossen* (Vienna: Deuticke, 1994), 74-75.

11. See FN #4, "A Symposium on W.G. Sebald," 21.

12. See FN #1, 4-5.

13. See Sigrid Löffler, "'Wildes Denken:' Gespräch mit W.G. Sebald," in Loquai (FN #3), 137. Sebald says here, for instance: ". . . erst in der Metaphorisierung wird uns Geschichte emphatisch zugänglich," and, "Was die historische Monographie nicht leisten kann, ist, eine Metapher oder Allegorie eines kollektiven Geschichtsverlaufes zu produzieren." ("'Wild Thinking': An Interview with W.G. Sebald." ". . . only by making history metaphorical can one really gain access to history," and, "What the historical monograph cannot accomplish is to produce a metaphor or allegory of a collective course of history.")

14. See Maya Jäggi, "Recovered Memories," *The Guardian* (London, September 22, 2001). The critics referred to and cited by Jäggi are Michael Hoffmann and A.S. Byatt, respectively.

15. Quoted by Jäggi, see FN #12.

16. English edition of *Austerlitz*, translated by Anthea Bell (New York: Random House, 2001). This passage reads (p. 139): "I realized then, he said, how little practice I had in using my memory, and conversely how hard I must always have tried to recollect as little as possible, avoiding everything which related in any way to my unknown past."

17. Ibid., 212: "At sometime in the past, I thought, I must have made a mistake, and now I am living the wrong life."

18. Ibid., 185: "It does not seem to me, Austerlitz added, that we understand the laws governing the return of the past, but I feel more and more as if time did not exist at all, only various spaces interlocking according to the rules of a higher form of stereometry, between which the living and the dead can move back and forth as they like, and the longer I think about it the more it seems to me that we who are still alive are unreal in the eyes of the dead, that only occasionally, in certain lights and atmospheric conditions, do we appear in their field of vision."

19. Ibid., 8: ". . . a mighty clock . . . with a hand some six feet long traveling round a dial which had once been gilded, but was now blackened by railway soot and tobacco smoke."

20. Thomas Steinfeld, *Frankfurter Allgemeine Zeitung* (March 20, 2001): ". . . has written above all a theoretical book about how history should be written, and this theory is neither logical nor void of contradictions." (My translation)

21. Michael Rutschky, *Frankfurter Rundschau* (March 21, 2001): ". . . practices a 'poetics of memory,' which has been influenced very crucially by Walter Benjamin's dark philosophy of history." (My translation)

22. Iris Radisch, *Die Zeit* (April 5, 2001): "Sebald is actually not a teller of tales, but rather a kind of materialistic metaphysician of history, a virtuoso of the index box, an imitator of voices, a conservator, an archivist." (My translation)

23. Quoted by Jäggi, see FN #12.

CHAPTER 13

NIXON AND THE CLERGYMEN: POLITICS, RELIGION AND THE ANTI-COMMUNIST THREAT, 1953-1960

Laura J. Gifford

Having completed his oath of office, newly minted President Dwight D. Eisenhower approached the lectern and began to speak to the assembled audience. "My friends," he began on the afternoon of January 20, 1953, "before I begin the expression of those thoughts that I deem appropriate to this moment, would you permit me the privilege of uttering a little private prayer of my own." Inserting listeners into this "private prayer," he added, "And I ask that you bow your heads." With this unconventional act, the former general initiated the American public into eight years of American life characterized by increasing religious influence in the public realm and in popular culture.

In the West Wing, Eisenhower convened his first cabinet session with a pause for silent prayer, a practice he would continue throughout his administration. In the halls of Congress, Congress passed legislation in 1954 adding the words "under God" to the Pledge of Allegiance. In 1956, it passed a joint resolution declaring "In God We Trust" to be the official motto of the United States, and added the phrase to U.S. paper currency beginning in 1957.[1]

While the Eisenhower administration indoctrinated the religious into government culture, this heightened dedication to religion was at least in part a response to trends well underway in the United States. By the late 1940s, the Roman Catholic Church was baptizing one million babies every year, and by 1949, over a billion dollars of Protestant church construction was underway. Bible sales doubled between 1947 and 1952, and by the time Eisenhower ran for reelection in 1956, 62 percent of the American public claimed membership in a religious congregation, with that figure reaching a high-water mark of 69 percent at the end of the decade. Previously, church membership had never stepped above 50 percent of the population. A 1954 survey showed that nine out of ten Americans believed in the divinity of Jesus Christ, and almost two-thirds believed in the existence of the devil.[2]

With religion's increasingly important role in government and in American society, the influence of the ecclesiastical made its way into popular culture. On the television airwaves, Bishop Fulton J. Sheen's "Life is Worth Living" (1952-57) became the only religious television program ever to be commercially sponsored and compete for ratings.[3] Sheen beat out luminaries including Jimmy Durante, Arthur Godfrey, Lucille Ball and Edward R. Murrow for the 1952 Emmy as Most Outstanding Personality, thanking his writers—Matthew, Mark, Luke and John—in his acceptance speech.[4] In the nation's civic auditoriums and sports arenas, the Reverend Billy Graham built upon the initial success of his first Los Angeles crusade in 1949, gaining crowds and influence in the United States and around the world. His 1953 book, *Peace With God*, became a best seller, and the young evangelist sent one of the first copies to President Eisenhower.[5] In Manhattan's Marble Collegiate Church and around the country, the Reverend Norman Vincent Peale's enthusiastic advocacy of *The Power of Positive Thinking* (1952) gained adherents to a program of "applied Christianity; a simple yet scientific system of practical techniques of successful living that works."[6]

In the midst of all this religious fervor resides an individual whom contemporary, Watergate-disillusioned Americans might consider an unlikely connection: Eisenhower's vice president, Richard M. Nixon. Despite his popular portrayal as amoral, opportunistic or downright deceptive, Richard Nixon in his vice presidential years displayed an amazing tendency to draw leading religious figures into his circle of friends and advisers. His connection to these "men of the cloth" illustrates the key to the religiosity of the 1950s: the Communist threat.

Nixon represented the refined arm of the anti-Communist crusade, a young, polished and intelligent "fighting Quaker" who lacked the bombast and crudeness of Joseph McCarthy. Nixon's credentials as the man who brought down Alger Hiss played a major role in his selection as the Republicans' vice presidential nominee, and throughout the decade he continued to serve as the Republican Party's (less embarrassing) anti-Red point man. America in the 1950s was a society struggling to lay a foundation that could withstand an ideological threat. For many Americans, a popular—and even populist—Christianity was the ultimate weapon against "atheistic Communism." In such an environment, Christian leaders gained a great deal of influence in the political realm. Nixon's dealings with two major figures, in particular, and their dealings with him, serve to elucidate major themes of this deceptively tumultuous "consensus" period. They also demonstrate the dangers of mixing the political with the ecclesiastical—for the pastors, at least. Religion remained a contentious issue for Americans even as it provided a shield for Cold War fears, and with the election of 1960, the presumptive civil religion of the 1950s came under fire.

This paper will chronicle the relationships Nixon enjoyed with Father John F. Cronin, S.S., of the National Catholic Welfare Conference, and evangelist Billy Graham. Graham is an obvious choice for his visibility and influence in the 1950s—and for the depth of his relationship with Nixon. Cronin, while less visible than many other Catholic leaders at the time, was nonetheless a longtime influence in labor and anti-Communist circles and is notable for the strength of his ties to Nixon. Other prominent Catholics maintained polite, formal contacts with Nixon throughout the 1950s, though some notables, like the above-mentioned Monsignor Sheen, remained outside the political realm despite his anti-Communist messages.[7] Cronin, however, exercised no such caution, and his involvement as a Nixon adviser also helps to complicate the picture of civil religion in the 1950s. The threat of 'atheistic Communism' trumped religious differences to the extent that the world's best-known Protestant and a politically prominent Catholic alike threw their support behind the man who brought down Alger Hiss.

John Francis Cronin (1908-94) was ordained in 1932 as a member of the Society of Saint Sulpice, a Roman Catholic order devoted primarily to the education of priests.[8] Before his nomination as assistant director of the National Catholic Welfare Conference's Department of Social Action in 1945, Cronin taught economics and philosophy at St. Mary's Seminary in Baltimore. The young priest began his career as a student of the Progressive priest Father John A. Ryan, and through his influence became involved in the labor movement, working as an organizer for the CIO.[9] This new, industrial union movement was popular with American Catholics desiring to fulfill Pope Pius XI's 1931 *Quadragesimo Anno* advocating the creation of a society where members of all industries and professions would belong to associations and cooperate for the common good.[10]

Over the course of his involvement with the CIO, however, Cronin became increasingly conscious of the presence of Communism within the federation. Even during the Popular Front years of the 1930s, Catholic labor activists tended toward anti-Communism, influenced by Pope Leo XIII's 1891 *Rerum Novarum* urging Catholics to organize Catholic-led unions as an alternative to the socialist labor movement.[11] Historians Judith Stepan-Morris and Maurice Zeitlin have demonstrated that some allegedly Communist-aligned unions actually led the way in terms of union democracy. Nonetheless, one-quarter of CIO unionists belonged to unions with Communist-aligned leaders in the 1940s.[12] At some point in the early 1940s—scholars have cited dates ranging from 1940 to 1943—an FBI special agent approached Cronin about sharing information on the Communist threat in labor organizations. By the end of World War II, the priest had become a prominent authority on Communist espionage, leading a campaign to educate Catholics and other workers in the dangers of Communism and authoring a secret 1945 report for Catholic bishops on the Communist threat in trade unions.

Scholars including Athan Theoharis and John Stuart Cox have argued that Cronin's report helped to solidify anti-Communist attitudes among the Catholic hierarchy.[13] Cronin himself claimed that Maryland was the only industrialized region in the country to experience a drop in Communist Party membership in 1944, when his worker education program was well underway.[14] In December 1945, he ghost-wrote a second report titled "Communist Infiltration in the United States" for the U.S. Chamber of Commerce, which published it under the name of Francis Matthews, a Chamber official.[15] Cronin's FBI files indicate that even after the war ended he was in semi-regular contact with the FBI and a rather skeptical J. Edgar Hoover, but the evidence indicates that Cronin's attempts to aid the Bureau were not always welcome.

Cronin lobbied the Bureau for assistance in pulling together an organization to publish an anti-Communist newsletter that would "ferret out fact" and "thus help to awaken the American public to realities."[16] He was the topic of interdepartmental memos among FBI brass as he made speeches claiming Communists held federal jobs, prompting Hoover to remark in his distinctively bold handwriting that "I think the Reverend Father is making the mistake so many others have made—popping off too *prematurely* and thereby giving his enemies basis for branding him a 'red-baiter.'"[17] Over the course of a week in March 1946, Cronin was warned off the idea of hiring his own private investigators and instructed by the Bureau to confine his activities to research and stop making speeches. By June, following the revelation that Cronin had told Cardinal Spellman about his magazine idea—and Spellman had in turn informed the Pope—Hoover showed considerable exasperation: "There must be no further cooperation with Father Cronin as it is obvious he twists contacts into different meanings."[18]

Despite Hoover's frustration with his priestly union insider, it is clear that the Bureau had few reservations about using Cronin for its own devices when advantageous. In 1950, Cronin sought information that he could use in writing a scathing interview of Max Lowenthal's recent book on the FBI, and an interdepartmental memo advised that "consideration be given to furnishing Father Cronin any derogatory information contained in the Bureau's files of a public source nature regarding Lowenthal and also data indicating factual errors in the book."[19] The Bureau used information it received from Cronin's union involvement, as seen in the 1946 admonition to stick to his research. Most importantly, by the time Cronin first met Richard Nixon in 1947, he had viewed 1939 and 1945 memos containing information about the Bureau's interviews with ex-Soviet spy Whittaker Chambers.[20]

It is important to note, however, that Cronin's expertise was not limited to anti-Communism. A prolific author, he expounded a philosophy of moderate government involvement in the workings of the economy, based once again upon papal writings such as *Rerum Novarum* and ideals of natural law. An analysis of wage structures Cronin prepared early in his career, for example, concluded that individuals possessed a series of natural rights—the right to marriage, the right to decent living conditions and the right to dignity among them. An individual's wages must be sufficient to allow these rights to be fulfilled.[21] In his 1939 economics textbook, *Economics and Society*, he wrote, "it is assumed . . . that some social adjustments are necessary and that the problem confronting the modern world is that of an intelligent choice of objectives and means."[22]

Cronin was initially introduced to Nixon in 1947 by Wisconsin Congressman Charles Kersten, who felt the priest would be a helpful source of information on Communism and labor unions during the debate over the Taft-Hartley Act.[23] Nixon did not divulge details of their relationship during the 1940s in either of his memoirs dealing with the period, *Six Crises* and *RN*. In fact, he revealed little about their relationship throughout his life. Herbert Parmet, perhaps, scored the biggest coup on the topic from the Nixon end when he got the ex-President to admit in an interview that the priest "became one of our most intimate friends during the Vice Presidential years" and was often a guest in the Nixon household.[24]

The Chambers interviews Cronin had access to included information about the activities of the infamous Alger Hiss, and Cronin's 1945 report to the American Catholic hierarchy included a reference to the then-State Department official.[25] In the late 1960s, Cronin alleged that he was the first person to inform Nixon of Hiss' Communist connections, telling Garry Wills, for example, that he had named names to Nixon as early as eighteen months before Chamber's testimony to the House Committee on Un-American Activities. He also told Wills that the FBI fed information to Nixon throughout the Hiss case, using Cronin as an intermediary.[26] Scholars including Theoharis,

Kenneth O'Reilly and Thomas Spalding have cited this interview.[27] By 1990, however, he told Nixon biographer Jonathan Aitken that he hadn't discussed the case with Nixon until after Hiss first made his public denial.[28] More recent historians, including Herbert Parmet and Irwin Gellman, have concluded that Nixon could not have known about Hiss prior to Chambers' testimony.[29] Cronin biographer John Donovan has questioned Cronin's later memories and Gellman's use of appointment calendars to prove that Cronin and Nixon did not discuss Hiss before the trial. Any information about Hiss that Cronin gave to Nixon would have come from confidential sources, Donovan argues, and would not therefore have been noted in Nixon's records. Instead, the consistency of Cronin's story in interviews from 1958 to 1974—that he did give Nixon information about Hiss—is most persuasive. Ultimately, however, Donovan points out that hard evidence does not exist to support either conclusion.[30]

By 1948, Cronin was in contact with Nixon regarding legislative business, sending him, for example, analyses of the Mundt-Nixon Subversive Activities Control Act of 1948. During the 1940s, Cronin signed his letters "John F. Cronin, S.S." By 1959, however, he sent Nixon a birthday card signed "John F. C., Anastas I. M., Nikita S. K." and including the note "DICK: How about broadening this competition to a quiet poker game in the Kremlin some evening.—K."[31] Clearly the intervening period saw a great deal of interaction, and in fact the paper record demonstrates a consistently growing relationship between the priest and the politician.

Records of interviews with Cronin indicate that his relationship with Nixon did not develop beyond the realm of Communism-related consultations until 1954, when he "got a call from Rose [Mary Woods, Nixon's longtime secretary] saying, 'The boss would like to see you.'"[32] Archival records, however, demonstrate that the priest's memory was faulty in this regard. By at least 1950, Cronin had begun his trademark practice of sending itemized memos of recommendations and advice to Nixon. While the frequency of these memos picked up from about 1955 onward, as early as Nixon's 1950 senatorial campaign the congressman received a two-page list of "Suggestions for Mr. Nixon" covering such varied topics as agriculture, inflation, labor, liberalism and social security and the Catholic vote.[33] In 1952, a three-page Cronin memo outlined a range of topics, from "Probable Mistakes So Far" to a long list of recommendations on various issues. Taft-Hartley, he reminded the nominee, was meant to protect workers from Communist labor leaders; to disseminate information on foreign policy and Communism, Nixon should not depend on "closed circles of longhairs in New York and Washington." Throughout this memo, Cronin betrayed a central concern with Communism, whether dealing with the issue directly or tying it in to topics ranging from labor to newspaper support.[34]

As the two men's relationship grew, however, Cronin's advice began to reflect more fully the diversity of his interests and his intellectual background. Perhaps Cronin later felt that Nixon had taken his advice to hit hard on the Communism issue too much to heart, because by 1953 he had moderated his tone on the subject. In January, he sent the Vice-President-Elect a draft of an editorial the priest had written for *Sign* magazine. "It is about time to state bluntly," Cronin wrote, "that there is no Red revolution in the making. The American Communist Party could not overthrow the New York police department, much less our nation." While the article did not minimize the dangers of Communist espionage and sabotage—or of the influence of anti-anti-Communism in "that twilight world of the confused liberal"—Cronin advocated a "pin-point" approach to fighting espionage and sabotage, relying heavily on the FBI.[35] Here he sounded more like the man who proposed a reasoned, three-pronged response to the threat of Communism in the 1945 Catholic bishops' report: "denunciation and avoidance," a positive agenda to increase the appeal of the anti-Communist position, and "counter organization" in labor and other realms.[36]

Cronin's advice to the vice president on foreign policy matters was even more circumspect. In an April memo further discussing a conversation the two men had with Ambassador William C. Bullitt at a party, Cronin displayed considerable, if measured, optimism about the new Khrushchev regime. Repeatedly stressing the term "finesse," he advocated remarkably specific measures in light of his status as assistant National Catholic Welfare Conference (NCWC) director

speaking to a vice president. Cronin's "three-level approach" for dealing with the Soviets included

> 1) stopping the war in Asia and removing potential causes of war by a
> fair German and Austrian settlement, etc. 2) concomitant with these
> moves, definite steps towards universal disarmament, both in conven-
> tional and atomic weapons; 3) seeking of pledges to use part of the
> resources thus released for fighting poverty at home (propaganda value
> in Soviet Union, France, Italy, etc.) and in less developed countries
> (propaganda value in Asia, Africa, and Latin America.[37]

Clearly, Cronin was working to gain as much influence as possible.
The year 1953 also brought evidence of social ties between the priest
and the Nixon family. On April 27, 1953, for example, Cronin sent
Pat Nixon a handwritten note thanking her for "a delightful evening
Saturday" during which he "met some wonderful people."[38]

As the years went by, Cronin seemed to place increasing value
on his relationship with Nixon. Many of his notes and memos can be
viewed as grooming the vice president for bigger and better positions
to come. In late 1955, Cronin cautioned Nixon against tagging Democratic programs as "Socialistic," arguing that "the public is seeing you
now as mature, constructive, and above petty partisan politics—the
very image that they seem to admire so much in the President."[39] By
May 1956, the priest was attempting to prepare Nixon to look presidential—sooner, perhaps, than later:

> It may be objected that the above [plan for campaign talks] sounds
> more like a lecture series than a campaign program. There is no ele-
> ment of attack or partisanship involved. Yet, in the climate that the
> opposition will probably create, this may be the most effective possible
> approach. As each audience waits for the slashing, hysterical attack
> promised by the opposition, there will be immediate feelings of dis-
> appointment at the quiet, sensible discourse offered. But the second-
> thought reaction, fed by commentators, will be that here is a sound,
> thoughtful, mature, statesmanlike approach. Surely we have nothing
> to fear from such leadership, *should Providence decide to shorten the life
> of our President* [emphasis mine].[40]

As early as 1956, also, came evidence that perhaps Cronin's superiors
were less than thrilled by his dedication to the vice president and the
world of politics. On September 13 of that year, Rose Mary Woods

instructed Nixon's staff that any materials mailed to Cronin during the campaign period should be mailed in a plain envelope. Callers to Cronin's office were to identify themselves in messages by name alone—"do not say that the Vice President's office is calling," the memo stated.[41]

Nixon's sole reference to Cronin in his memoirs states that his "old friend" provided "some valuable help" on Nixon's acceptance speech at the 1956 Republican Convention in San Francisco.[42] Cronin told Garry Wills in the late 1960s that "from 1953 to 1960, I was his only speech writer."[43] A quick survey of files relating to other Nixon aides and confidantes easily disproves this claim—a 1956 draft of a speech on atomic energy by James Shepley, for example, or evidence of writing done by Gabriel Hauge during the 1960 campaign.[44] Archival records do indicate, however, that Cronin served extensively as a speechwriter for the vice president, especially during his second term. Straying beyond the bounds of Communism-related topics, the priest drafted speeches, notes and memos on subjects including labor, race relations, economics and foreign policy. He served as a moderate influence in Nixon's circle of advisers, again displaying something of a contrast since the early days of the two men's relationship.

This moderation could reflect Cronin's own changing views, or his developing preoccupation with heightening the stature and appeal of the politician in whose hands he had placed his influence. More likely, however, this simply reveals Cronin's true colors once he moved beyond his initial, one-issue relationship with the vice president. While he had drifted toward the GOP by the late 1950s, Cronin, it turns out, was a Democrat![45] Nixon's willingness to listen to the advice of a registered Democrat indicates his own views were more moderate, or at the very least open-minded, than his liberal opponents were generally willing to concede. Donovan points out, for example, that on one occasion, Nixon asked Cronin for more information on race relations than Cronin, a civil rights advocate, initially provided.[46] Nixon, then, was both open to and encouraging of Cronin's ideas and analysis.

On the subject of labor, in particular, Cronin was able to serve as a helpful resource. The priest was one of the clergymen called in to help negotiate the ugly Kohler strike in 1957. Providing updates from

Wisconsin, Cronin attempted to use his connections to help both Nixon and his own cause. In February, for example, he wrote Nixon and mentioned that the vice president's association with a possible settlement could be very helpful for both sides. For Nixon, he argued, it could be "what Bill Rodgers [sic] called the 'man of action' approach." For the negotiations, "if some face-saving is needed by the Company for any concession that they said they would not make, an appeal by you would give them an out." "You need not worry about getting ideas to solve these problems," Cronin concluded. "If face-saving is needed, we will have the formula and all you need to do is approve it."[47] In March, Cronin again asked about the possibility of a Nixon intervention.[48] The clergy-mediated talks broke down April 26 upon the company's rejection of a four-point union offer.[49] No record was found of a Nixon decision for or against intervention before then.

Even with regard to the little things, Cronin was always ready to lend a hand. In 1957, he showered Nixon with memos prior to his trip to Italy, arranging a tour of the North American College in the Vatican and recommending good restaurants.[50] Betraying his deep concern with the way Nixon presented himself and the reception he would receive, he advised the vice president to check on the pronunciation of Theodore Roosevelt's name prior to delivering a speech in Oyster Bay in 1958: "We always pronounced it 'RU' and FDR as 'RO.' It might be a sensitive point in the Oyster Bay area."[51]

Cronin's devotion to his political friend did not cease in 1960—Nixon's office kept extensive clippings, for example, on the reaction to Cronin's 1962 book *Communism: Threat to Freedom*.[52] His advice seems to have been accepted by Nixon as he planned his 1960 slate of advisers. A July 28 article in the New York *Times* on Nixon's advisers refers to his "egghead contingent" as including one Charles Lichtenstein, political science professor at the University of Notre Dame, and in mid-1959 Cronin had recommended this very individual to Nixon staffer Bob Finch as a possible asset.[53] He also assisted Nixon with detailed speech material early in the campaign. A raft of memos and speech excerpts relating to Nebraska in late March provides an excellent example of the detail into which Cronin delved—"On a True Conservatism," "Race Relations," "Medical Care for the Aged," "School Construction."[54]

The article that demonstrated Nixon's willingness to accept Cronin's advice on staffing, however, might also have led to Cronin's exposure and downfall. As early as April, Cronin had begun to express unease about the level of his involvement with the vice president. Nixon's public comments regarding the provision of birth control to underdeveloped nations, in particular, caused concern on Cronin's part that the vice president was trying to make a deliberately "Protestant" impression in contrast to Kennedy's Catholicism.[55] On April 28, Cronin sent Nixon a letter explaining that the NCWC could not "take a partisan position in relation to our government and its political parties." While Cronin's work for Nixon was personal and apart from his work with the NCWC, "an extremely different interpretation would be given" to their relationship in a presidential race. Therefore, while he was still willing to serve in a consultant's capacity, he would no longer be able to write campaign speeches or visit the vice president's office "unless the reason for my presence were governmental rather than partisan."[56]

The July 28 *Times* article reported, however, that Nixon's group of academic advisers included, on an " 'as-needed'" basis, two Harvard professors—and "the Rev. John F. Cronin, an economics and philosophy teacher now on the staff of the National Welfare Conference [sic] in Washington."[57] The very next day, Cronin sent Nixon his congratulations on his acceptance speech at the Republican convention in Chicago. "As I watched the proceedings in Chicago, naturally I felt a desire to be with you," he wrote. "However, in God's Providence, I feel sure I can do you more help by prayer and faithful adherence to the instructions of my superiors here about refraining from purely partisan activity."[58] The politico priest, it seems, had been caught. Muzzled by his superiors, and by his own concern for the integrity of his organization, the flow of activity from Cronin ground to a halt. The archival record preserves no further indication of contact between the two men until Cronin sent Nixon a letter of consolation in November—and a thank-you note for his Christmas present from the Nixons in December.[59]

A man who needs little introduction anywhere in the world, Billy Graham (1918-) began his independent evangelical ministry in 1949 and was internationally prominent by the mid-1950s. While the evangelist did send Nixon a wire of congratulations following the 1952 election, the bulk of evidence points toward a relationship beginning in the mid-1950s and intensifying throughout the remainder of the decade. As with Cronin, a progression is visible in the language Graham uses—the man who was "Dear Mr. Vice President" in 1955 was "Dear Dick" by the end of 1956.

While Cronin's interactions with the vice president were primarily political, only occasionally drifting into the realm of religious tone or content, Graham's relationship with Nixon was grounded in, and constantly referred back to, the issue of religious faith. Much of this, of course, is due to the two men's differing vocations. Cronin was a teacher, a labor activist and an administrator in a social welfare organization; Graham was a Baptist evangelist, charged with the mission to preach the Good News to the masses. This might also, however, reflect the weight of religious differences, as Nixon's Quaker faith was Protestant—if not evangelical.

Despite his privileging of religious issues above the political, Graham's correspondence with Nixon betrays a strong concern with the Communist menace. In October 1955, for example, he expressed to the vice president his concern that the Soviets' recent expressions of goodwill posed an insidious danger to the United States. ". . . the basic issues between Communism and the West have not changed," he cautioned, "and the Communists are now beginning to gain ground rapidly. They have learned that a smile means more than a big fist."[60] In November 1956, Graham advocated action in Hungary, pointedly reflecting that he hoped the United States would not make "a serious mistake at this hour of history." It was difficult for him to see the morality in standing aside while "Russian steel crushes the Hungarian people," particularly after Radio Free Europe and the Voice of America had devoted so much time to propagandizing the Hungarian people.[61] By couching his argument in moral terms, Graham was using his position of greatest influence.

On the domestic front, Graham filled Nixon in on events like his appearances at Yale University in February 1957. His meetings were well attended and his altar calls well received, Graham reported. "Let us pray that the bewildered, confused and frustrated students on the

campus today will turn to Christ rather than Marx!"[62] Conversation
on issues of Communism went both ways. In August 1957, Nixon
passed along to Graham a report he'd received from "a reliable source
closely associated with the Communist party." This source, referring
to Nixon's appearance at Graham's 1957 New York Crusade, referred
to Nixon, Graham and crusade attendees as "stupid half-wits" and
"dirty capitalists." "I think you will agree with me," the vice president
concluded, "that as long as the name calling to which we are sub-
jected comes from that source we are probably all right!"[63] This note
is particularly revealing because it demonstrates Nixon placing Graham in the anti-Communist fight alongside himself. Graham's role
was recognized and, one could argue, encouraged by this letter. Nixon
understood the importance of religious support, and he devoted time
to developing this connection between religion and politics.

The 1950s were a busy decade for Graham's international evangelical missionary organization, and Graham made good use of his
political connections to smooth his journeys abroad. In late 1955, he
asked whether Nixon might write a letter of introduction for him to
Indian Ambassador John Sherman Cooper in preparation for his In-
dia crusade.[64] Having received a friendly response from the vice president, Graham further pressed his political connections, confiding to
Nixon in January 1956 that he was "particularly anxious to have a few
minutes with Mr. Nehru." He also provided a list of other countries
he planned to visit, including the Philippines, Hong Kong, Formosa,
Korea and Japan. Letting the vice president know he would do any
favors asked of him in these places, Graham closed out his entreaty
with a rousing "Still thinking you are the greatest Vice President in
history and following you with my daily prayers in this crucial year of
your career."[65] Whether predisposed to grant the favor or buoyed by
the evangelist's flattery, Nixon once again responded in the affirma-
tive, cabling Ambassador Cooper regarding Graham's request. By the
end of the month, an appointment had been made for Graham to
meet with Nehru on February 4.[66] The vice president offered similar
assistance during preparations for Graham's trip to Australia in 1958
and his Africa trip in 1959.

Amusingly, however, while Graham saw Nixon as a resource, at least one member of the American public saw things differently. In an exchange that demonstrates just how high the evangelist's profile was in the 1950s, a Mrs. L. Diers of Richmond Hill, Long Island, New York, wrote to the vice president, asking him to make her an appointment to see Graham! "I know you are a close friend of Mr. [?] Graham," she wrote. "I thought if you would write and ask him to make a personal appointment for me to ask him for guidance I hope this won't be asking too much."[67] Nixon staffers exchanged memos on what to do about this issue, and finally the vice president's executive assistant, Robert E. Cushman, wrote Mrs. Diers back, thanking her for her correspondence and politely suggesting that she might consider writing to Dr. Graham personally.[68]

Throughout the period under discussion, Graham gently prodded Nixon to be more forthcoming about his religious faith. He connected political discussions to evangelical ideas, advocating, for example, a dispensational approach when looking at the conflict in the Middle East.[69] He reminded Nixon of the talk the two men had with Florida Senator George Smathers regarding Biblical prophecy and "highly significant" happenings in the region "from a Biblical point of view."[70] Graham repeatedly suggested the vice president attend church more regularly, arguing in late 1959 that "I am convinced that you are going to have the backing of the overwhelming majority of the religious minded people in America. It would be most unfortunate if some of your political enemies could point to any inconsistency."[71] A letter Nixon wrote to Graham during the 1960 presidential campaign indicates he took the evangelist's advice seriously—but with dubious consequences. Since the primaries, he reported, the press covered his every move, including his visits to church with Pat and his daughters "virtually every week." Evidently a Kennedy supporter complained to one of Nixon's friends that Nixon was deliberately introducing the religious issue by allowing his picture to be taken attending church. "This shows that you just can't win on that issue!"[72]

Probably Graham's greatest triumph in terms of getting Nixon to connect himself visibly to spiritual concerns came in July 1957, when the vice president attended the evangelist's New York Crusade and spoke briefly to the assembled throng. Graham was ecstatic, but the flood of letters pouring into Nixon's office demonstrated a de-cidedly mixed reaction on the part of the American public. Some writers responded quite positively to the event. Adelaide Benner of Quakertown, Pennsylvania, for example, wrote, "We are so thank-ful that the president and vice-president of our beloved country are God-fearing men—men who make their decisions in their prayer closets with God."[73] Not everyone, however, was as thrilled. Dorothy Redfern of Bellaire, Michigan admonished Nixon to "leave the tub-thumping to the cults and the quacks and the Billy Grahams of the world," and even before Nixon's appearance Robert Scott of Los Ga-tos, California complained that the vice president would be violating the First Amendment.[74] A third group of people objected to Nixon's actions, but not on the basis of separation of church and state. Ella Kern Rhoads of Hatboro, Pennsylvania, for example, wrote that it was "most appropriate" that the vice president should attend the crusade, "but as a repentant down front 'with repentant heart to find salvation and forgiveness through Jesus Christ.'"[75] And Mrs. M. W. Rowland of Dallas, Texas lamented, "how could you afford to pass up such an opportunity to say *just one* good word for Jesus?"[76]

Graham's involvement with the Nixon campaign for the presi-dency in 1960 followed a trajectory somewhat similar to that of Fa-ther Cronin's, albeit with different levels of involvement and a slightly different timeline. It is clear that Graham threw his support behind Nixon long before the race. An undated slip of U.S. Senate stationery stuck in the midst of early 1958 archival materials states "Billy Gra-ham—Come out for RN before Democratic National Convention."[77] While there is no way to ascertain whether this was actually written in 1958, by August of that year Graham expressed to Nixon his be-lief that he would win the Republican nomination.[78] May 20, 1960, Graham made a statement to the Southern Baptist Conference that at a time of tension in the world, "I don't think it is the time to experi-ment with novices,"[79] and a May 23 office memo to Nixon stated Gra-ham had decided to come out for Nixon publicly.[80] Graham offered Nixon advice on subjects ranging from the U-2 incident, on which he believed the vice president should stay quiet, to potential running mates, advocating first Walter Judd and then Nelson Rockefeller.[81] He even indicated in late August that he had written a letter to the Billy Graham Evangelistic Association mailing list, urging members to "organize their Sunday school classes and churches to get out to vote."[82]

Despite his behind-the-scenes advocacy, however, and his promise to come out for Nixon publicly, Graham never actually followed through with a public statement of support. As Kennedy continued to gain strength and won the Democratic nomination, the "religious question" began to present a challenge to clergymen interested in expressing their opinions without being drug into the allegations of bigotry, real and imagined, swirling around the campaign.

The Reverend Norman Vincent Peale, another Nixon associate who would grow closer to the vice president and his family after their move to New York City in the 1960s, fell afoul of public opinion regarding the "religious question" in a rather spectacular way. Peale was active in a variety of anti-New Deal and anti-Communist political organizations from the late 1930s through the early 1950s, but by 1960, he was long past his years of greatest involvement in political activity. While vacationing in Switzerland, however, he became involved, along with Graham, in a summit meeting of evangelical leaders at Montreaux. At the same time, the National Association of Evangelicals had convened a campaign interest group called the Citizens for Religious Freedom. The Montreaux group asked Peale to arrange a meeting between Nixon and evangelical leaders, and also decided to schedule a larger, public meeting to talk about issues relating to the 1960 campaign. The large meeting was scheduled for September 7 in Washington, D.C., perhaps with the idea that Peale and the religious leaders would meet with Nixon in the next few days. As it happened, this planned meeting would become an extraneous note.[83]

While he was not among the leadership of the September 7 conference, Peale was chosen to speak to the press at the conclusion of the meeting, and was cast as the head of the National Conference of Citizens for Religious Freedom in the press. The group released a five-point statement stating, among other things, that "it is inconceivable that a Roman Catholic President would not be under extreme pressure by the hierarchy of his church to accede to its policies with respect to foreign relations in matters, including representation to the Vatican."[84]

Peale was pilloried. The New York Times ran excerpts from Catholic newspapers decrying his actions—including a comment from Richard Reid of the *Catholic News* that "the anti-Catholicism is enough to make the angels weep and the Communists rock with glee."[85] Union Theological Seminary theologians Reinhold Niebuhr and John C. Bennett denounced the statement, arguing it had "loosed the floodgates of religious bigotry."[86] Peale renounced his membership in the organization and issued a statement clarifying his participation in the meeting, arguing he had nothing to do with setting up the meeting and "was merely present as an invited guest." He avowed that he was "strongly opposed to any admixture of religious discussion and political partisanship" and cited his long record of interfaith activity. He also stated, however, that he felt it was "perfectly appropriate for a group of Protestants or any other group to meet to discuss and consider the possible impact of the election of a Catholic President upon religious liberties in the United States."[87]

The fallout from the event struck Peale so deeply that he offered his resignation, though refused, from the Marble Collegiate Church and refused speaking engagements for quite some time. He was gravely concerned he had done irreparable harm to Nixon's election chances. Nixon took care after the election to write Peale and thank him for his support and friendship, adding that if Peale was concerned about having lost Nixon the election "you should banish such thoughts from your head once and for all."[88] Nixon's letter evidently came as a great relief to the minister. "I must confess that I was literally broken-hearted by the turn of events," he wrote, "especially the possibility that I, who love you and believed in you so deeply, might have contributed in any way to the defeat." He went on to eulogize Nixon's campaign in words that sum up the tone of the beliefs each of these religious figures demonstrated with regard to the vice president:

> You are the truly great man in this whole dramatic episode of history. Never once in the slightest degree have you failed to demonstrate the nobility which is so marked in you. You pitched your campaign on the high level of a Christian and a gentleman and a statesman.[89]

By September, having witnessed Peale's verbal flogging and subsequent trauma, Graham appeared chastened. "Not only would [the press] crucify me, but they would eventually turn it against you, so I must be extremely careful."[90] Continuing to waver, Graham went so far as to pen an October article in favor of Nixon for *Life* magazine, speaking in glowing terms of the man, his qualifications, and their friendship. At the last minute, however, it was temporarily pulled to await a parallel response from Niebuhr, and Graham persuaded Henry Luce to shelve it permanently.[91] Finally, the evangelist made a statement on October 30 that he had concluded his "main responsibility is in the spiritual realm and that I shouldn't become involved in partisan politics."[92]

In the end, then, the religious structures of 1950s politics shattered under the weight of the complicated 1960 election, profoundly altering the depth and significance of the relationships Nixon enjoyed with Cronin and Graham. Despite this disastrous end, however, these examples illuminate the depth and breadth of the relationships enjoyed by leading members of the nation's religious establishment with the political establishment of the 1950s. Eisenhower biographer Piers Brendon has described the 1950s as "a decade of Dial-a-Prayer,"[93] and the pervasiveness of religious culture in the 1950s demonstrably extended to the highest levels of power.

Finally, and perhaps most significantly, this examination of the relationships Cronin and Graham enjoyed with Nixon illuminates their central concern: the safety and security of the United States in an era of Cold War. This concern trumped any doubts Cronin or Graham might have had about the vice president's religious affiliation or the strength of his religious credentials. Nixon was their anti-Communist knight in shining armor. These men were on the front lines of the struggle against atheistic Communism, and in Nixon, they believed, they had an ally. The "fighting Quaker" would do battle for their cause.

Laura J. Gifford

ENDNOTES

1. "History of 'In God We Trust,'" U.S. Department of the Treasury www.treasury. gov/education/fact-sheets/currency/in-god-we-trust.html, accessed 3 November 2003. Coins first featured the motto during the Civil War.

2. Joel A. Carpenter, *Revive Us Again: The Reawakening of American Fundamentalism* (New York: Oxford University Press, 1997), 213; Stephen J. Whitfield, *The Culture of the Cold War*, 2nd ed. (Baltimore: Johns Hopkins University Press, 1996), 83.

3. Christopher Owen Lynch, *Selling Catholicism: Bishop Sheen and the Power of Television* (Lexington: The University Press of Kentucky, 1998), 7.

4. Ibid., 27.

5. William Martin, *A Prophet With Honor: The Billy Graham Story* (New York: William Morrow and Company, 1991), 152.

6. Norman Vincent Peale, *The Power of Positive Thinking* (New York: Fawcett Crest, 1963; orig. published 1952), xi.

7. Fulton Sheen's 1980 autobiography indicates that he never believed his call to Christian service was directed toward sociological or political activity. In fact, he indicates a belief that the priestly vocation is opposed to this sort of activity: "If I feel my call is sociological dedication, there is no reason why I should enter a theological seminary. If I am convinced that a vocation is to be identified with the world, then I have completely forgotten Him Who warned: 'I have taken you out of the world.'" (Fulton J. Sheen, *Treasure in Clay: The Autobiography of Fulton J. Sheen* [Garden City, N.Y.: Doubleday and Company, Inc., 1980], p. 32). While he mentions his advocacy of social programs like inner-city renewal throughout his book, Sheen pays little attention to politics. Former New York Governor Al Smith is mentioned several times, but primarily in the context of personal friendship.

8. New York *Times* (5 January 1994).

9. Herbert S. Parmet, *Richard Nixon and His America* (Boston: Little, Brown and Co., 1990), 166.

10. Ronald W. Schatz, *The Electrical Workers: A History of Labor at General Electric and Westinghouse, 1923-1960* (Urbana: University of Illinois Press, 1983), 97.

11. Judith Stepan-Morris and Maurice Zeitlin, *Left Out: Reds and America's Industrial Unions* (Cambridge: Cambridge University Press, 2003); Schatz, 97.

12. Ibid., 1.

13. Irwin Gellman, *The Contender: Richard Nixon, The Congress Years, 1946-1952* (New York: The Free Press, 1999), 99; Thomas W. Spalding, *The Premiere See: A History of the Archdiocese of Baltimore, 1789-1989* (Baltimore: The Johns Hopkins University Press, 1989), 376; Athan G. Theoharis and John Stuart Cox, *The Boss: J. Edgar Hoover and the Great American Inquisition* (Philadelphia: Temple University Press, 1988), 217.

14. Spalding, *The Premiere See*, 377.

15. Theoharis and Cox, *The Boss*, 218.

16. John F. Cronin to J. Edgar Hoover, 9 February 1946, FBI File: John Francis Cronin, File 94-35404, Gloria Gae Gellman Collection, Nixon Library.

17. Handwritten note appended to 11 March 1946 memo, D. M. Ladd to Hoover, Cronin FBI File, Nixon Library.

18. Handwritten note appended to 27 June 1946 memo, Cronin FBI File, Nixon Library.

19. D. M. Ladd to A. H. Belmont, 13 November 1950, Cronin FBI File, Nixon Library.

20. Parmet, *Richard Nixon and His America*, 166.

21. John D. Donovan, "Crusader in the Cold War: A Biography of Fr. John F. Cronin, S.S. (1908-1994)," unpublished Ph.D. dissertation (Marquette University, 2000), 7-8.

22. John F. Cronin, *Economics and Society* (New York: American Book Company, 1939), viii.

23. Gellman, *The Contender*, 100.

24. Parmet, *Richard Nixon and His America*, 174.

25. Ibid., 167.

26. Garry Wills, *Nixon Agonistes: The Crisis of the Self-Made Man* (Boston: Houghton Mifflin Co., 1969), 27-8. See also Sharlene Shoemaker, "The Other Priest Who Wrote Speeches For Nixon," *National Catholic Reporter* (September 27, 1974)—Cronin files, University of Notre Dame. Cronin stated in the interview that "when Nixon faced Hiss in that famous interview he was playing with a stacked deck." Earl Mazo and Stephen Hess in *Nixon: A Political Portrait* (New York: Harper and Row, 1968) also refer to Nixon's foreknowledge, through Cronin, of the Hiss affair.

27. Theoharis and Cox, *The Boss*, 38; Kenneth O'Reilly, *Hoover and the Un-Americans: The FBI, HUAC, and the Red Menace* (Philadelphia: Temple University Press, 1983), 106-107; Spalding, *The Premiere See*, 377.

28. Gellman, *The Contender*, 498 fn88. See also Jonathan Aitken, *Nixon: A Life* (London: Weidenfeld and Nicolson, 1993).

29. Gellman, *The Contender*, 222; Parmet, *Richard Nixon and His America*, 167-8.

30. Donovan, "Crusader in the Cold War", 85-6.

31. Cronin to RN, January 1959, Series 320—General Correspondence, Cronin, Rev. John F., Box 191, NARA Laguna Niguel.

32. *National Catholic Reporter* (September 27, 1974).

33. Cronin to RN, October 20, 1950, PPS 3.546, Nixon Library.

34. Cronin to Dorothy Cox, September 5, 1952, PPS 10.428.1-2, Nixon Library.

35. Cronin draft, *Sign* magazine editorial, January 1953, Series 320—General Corr., Cronin, Rev. John F., Box 191, NARA Laguna Niguel.

36. Donovan, "Crusader in the Cold War", 43-4.

37. Cronin to RN, April 26, 1953, Series 320—General Corr., Cronin, Rev. John F., Box 192, NARA Laguna Niguel.

38. Judging from the dates in question and a Cronin reference in the above-cited letter to Nixon's "duties as host," I would conclude these letters refer to the same event. Cronin to Pat Nixon, April 27, 1953, PPS 267.85, Nixon Library.

39. Cronin to RN, October 20, 1955, Series 320—General Corr., Cronin, Box 191, NARA Laguna Niguel.

40. May 22, 1956 Lunch Meeting Notes, Series 320—General Corr., Cronin, Box 191, NARA Laguna Niguel.

41. RMW to staff, September 13, 1956, Series 320—General Corr., Cronin, Box 191, NARA Laguna Niguel.

42. Richard Nixon, *RN: The Memoirs of Richard Nixon* (New York: Grosset and Dunlap, 1978), 176.

43. Wills, *Nixon Agonistes*, 28.

44. Speech draft labeled "submitted by Jim Shepley," 1956, Series 320—General Corr., Shepley, James, Box 690, NARA Laguna Niguel; Gabriel Hauge to RN, 28 September 1960, Series 45—1960 Campaign Files, Box 1, NARA Laguna Niguel.

45. Donovan, "Crusader in the Cold War", iii.

46. Ibid., 118.

47. Cronin to RN, February 17, 1957, Series 320—General Corr., Cronin, Box 191, NARA Laguna Niguel.

48. Cronin to RN, March 22, 1957, Series 320—General Corr., Cronin, Box 191, NARA Laguna Niguel.

49. Walter H. Uphoff, *Kohler on Strike: Thirty Years of Conflict* (Boston: Beacon Press, 1966), 298.

50. Various, Cronin to RN, Series 320—General Corr., Cronin, Box 191, NARA Laguna Niguel.

51. JFC to RN, October 17, 1958, Series 320—General Corr., Cronin, Box 192, NARA Laguna Niguel.

52. Incidentally, this book was pilloried by conservatives who viewed the priest as having gone soft on the question of Communism. The ever-eloquent William F. Buckley, for example, penned a column in response to the volume: ". . . the principal error Father Cronin's pamphlet makes is to assume that we can beat the Communists by burnishing our own souls. Be honest, more tolerant, encourage national unity and racial integration, be charitable toward those with whom you disagree and—you will go to heaven, to be sure, but your passage there might well by expedited by a Soviet bullet" (undated WFB clipping, Series 320—General Corr., Cronin, Box 192, NARA Laguna Niguel).

53. New York *Times* (28 July 1960); Cronin to Bob Finch, Series 320—General Corr., Cronin, Box 191, NARA Laguna Niguel.

54. Various, Series 320—General Corr., Cronin, Box 192, NARA Laguna Niguel.

55. Donovan, "Crusader in the Cold War", 158. Nixon told a group of Protestant journalists that if underdeveloped nations sought birth control information from the United States, the United States should give it to them. These remarks, in Cronin's mind, marked a deliberate, public dissociation from views outlined by the Catholic bishops' conference the previous November.

56. Ibid., 160.

57. New York *Times* (28 July 1960).

58. JFC to RN, July 29, 1960, Series 320—General Corr., Cronin, Box 192, NARA Laguna Niguel.

59. JFC to RN, November 10, 1960; JFC to RN, December 28, 1960, Series 320—General Corr., Box 192, Laguna Niguel.

60. Billy Graham to RN, October 8, 1955, Series 320—General Corr., Graham, Dr. Billy, Box 299, NARA Laguna Niguel.

61. BG to RN, November 10, 1956, Series 320—General Corr., Graham, Dr. Billy, Box 299, NARA Laguna Niguel.

62. BG to RN, February 19, 1957, Series 320—General Corr., Graham, Box 299, NARA Laguna Niguel.

63. RN to BG, August 12, 1958, PPS 320.103.147, Nixon Library.

64. BG to RN, October 8, 1955, Series 320—General Corr., Graham, Box 299, NARA Laguna Niguel.

65. RN to BG, November 7, 1955; BG to RN, January 7, 1956, Series 320—General Corr., Graham, Box 299, NARA Laguna Niguel.

66. Unsigned memo on Office of the Vice President stationery, January 24, 1956, Series 320—General Corr., Graham, Box 299, NARA Laguna Niguel.

67. L. Diers to RN, July 25, 1957, Series 320—General Corr., Graham, Box 299, NARA Laguna Niguel.

68. Robert F. Cushman to L. Diers, September 10, 1957, Series 320—General Corr., Graham, Box 299, NARA Laguna Niguel.

69. Dispensational theology is a strain of evangelical Protestant thinking wherein "dispensations are ages in divine history in which God's plan of salvation for humanity is marked by special characteristics. . . . In each of these ages, God dealt with people according to a different method. Each dispensation was meant to provide a way of salvation for humanity, and each ended in judgement, as humans failed the test. . . . These various ages were pointing toward a final golden age, when a messianic kingdom would come to earth" (Carpenter, *Revive Us Again*, 248-9). Joel Carpenter's excellent appendix to *Revive Us Again* points out that as this doctrine pointed toward a final Apocalypse at the end of the last dispensation, it stimulated a particular reaction among dispensational believers. Rather than working for the kingdom of God on earth, the church's main mission was "rescuing souls from the wrath to come" (249). The notes of the Scofield Reference Bible, published in 1909, provide a good example of dispensational theology. William Martin described Graham as a sometime dispensationalist in *A Prophet With Honor*.

70. BG to RN, November 10, 1956, Series 320—General Corr., Graham, Box 299, NARA Laguna Niguel.

71. BG to RN, November 17, 1959, Series 320—General Corr., Graham, Box 299, NARA Laguna Niguel.

72. RN to BG, August 29, 1960, Series 320—General Corr., Graham, Box 299, NARA Laguna Niguel.

73. Adelaide Benner to RN, July 22, 1957, Series 207—Appearance Files, Box 67, Folder 18, NARA Laguna Niguel.

74. Dorothy W. Redfern to RN, July 21, 1957; Robert H. Scott to RN, July 18, 1957, Series 207—Appearance Files, Box 67, Folder 18, NARA Laguna Niguel.

75. Ella Kern Rhoads to RN, July 17, 1957, Series 207—Appearance Files, Box 67, Folder 18, NARA Laguna Niguel.

76. Mrs. M. W. Rowland to RN, August 1, 1957, Series 207—Appearance Files, Box 67, Folder 18, NARA Laguna Niguel.

77. Undated memo, Series 320—General Corr., Graham, Box 299, NARA Laguna Niguel.

78. BG to RN, August 27, 1958, Series 320—General Corr., Graham, Box 299, NARA Laguna Niguel.

79. Chicago Daily Tribune (21 May 1960).

80. LWH to RN, May 23, 1960, Series 320—General Corr., Graham, Box 299, NARA Laguna Niguel.

81. BG to RN, May 27, 1960; BG to RN, June 21, 1960; BG telegram to RN, July 22, 1960, Series 320—General Corr., Graham, Box 299, NARA Laguna Niguel.

82. BG to RN, August 22, 1960, Series 320—General Corr., Graham, Box 299, NARA Laguna Niguel.

83. Carol V. R. George, *God's Salesman: Norman Vincent Peale and the Power of Positive Thinking* (New York: Oxford University Press, 1993), 200-1. Graham did not attend the Washington, D.C. meeting, and some of Peale's friends later felt that Graham had abandoned Peale in a situation the evangelist himself had created.

84. New York *Times* (8 September 1960).

85. New York *Times* (16 September 1960).

86. Ibid.

87. Ibid.

88. RN to Peale, January 18, 1961, Series 320—General Corr., Peale, Box 583, NARA Laguna Niguel.

89. Peale to RN, January 29, 1961, Series 320—General Corr., Peale, Box 583, NARA Laguna Niguel.

90. BG to RN, September 24, 1960, Series 320—General Corr., Graham, Box 299, NARA Laguna Niguel.

91. BG to RN, June 12, 1961, Series 320—General Corr., Graham, Box 299, NARA Laguna Niguel.

92. AP wire, October 30, 1960, Series 320—General Corr., Graham, Box 299, NARA Laguna Niguel.

93. Piers Brendon, *Ike: His Life and Times* (New York: Harper and Row, 1986), 414.

CHAPTER 14

HISTORICAL ANALOGY AND THE FAÇADE OF RUSSIAN CONSTITUTIONALISM

Christian M. Lucky

The publication of this *Festschrift* coincides with the fifteenth anniversary of the collapse of the Berlin Wall. The end of communism was greeted as a heralding event when Eurasia, at long last, could consider the future. No sooner were the cadres of policy-makers, bankers and diplomats deployed to post-communist Eurasia to build the future, when Slobodon Milosevic reminded the world that 1989 marked not only the two hundredth anniversary of the storming of the Bastille but also the six hundredth anniversary of the Battle of Kosovo. From Dushanbe to Dubrovnik, a vanguard of restitution-seekers followed Milosevic's example and put the future behind them so that they could get on with the business of the past.

Within the policy-making community, as nation building stalled and disappointments mounted, psychological analogies used to sell reform policies ("shock therapy" was a favorite) gave way increasingly to historical analogies to serve as the foundation for decisions of moment.[1] The opacity of many of the societies exiting from communism fueled the tendency of observers to look to a past they thought they knew, in particular, the histories of England, France, and the United States, in order to make sense of a present that was increasingly indiscernible.[2]

One nagging issue of post communism that was frequently the

subject of weak historical analogy was the unexamined assumption that constitutional and economic reform progressed in historical stages as demonstrated by the experience of countries such as the United States. Robber-baron capitalism was deemed one such stage. Spoliation in Russia was not to be taken as a sign of the failure of reform, but rather an indication that reform was underway. To keep a brave face, neo-liberalism morphed at times into neo-Whigism. Surprisingly, the lure of the progress of history not only held the Anglo-Americans captive, but also many policy-makers from Germany, France and even Russia itself.[3]

In tribute to Professor Nordquist's commitment to the study and teaching of history and as penance for benefiting from his excellent teaching of history only to join a community that has so woefully disregarded history, I will take the occasion of this *Festschrift* to do my small part partially to remedy this common failure of the reform policy community by attempting to explain why and in what ways the historical analogy between Russia and the United States on the point of spoliation is mis-informative. When we look more closely into the comparison of America in the 1790s to Russia in the 1990s, we not only start to doubt some common predictions regarding spoliation in Russia, but we also gain a clearer picture of the links between varieties of economic development and constitutionalism.

SPOLIATION, THEN AND NOW

Perhaps the most notorious example of public theft in early America is the insiderism and graft that gave rise to the Supreme Court case *Fletcher v. Peck*.[4] In 1795, the Georgia state legislature privatized thirty-five million acres of Georgia's western territories, the "Yazoo" lands (located in present-day Mississippi), selling it to a band of well-connected speculators for $500,000, that is, for less than two cents an acre.[5] Among the original purchasers were United States senators and congressmen, federal and state judges, one territorial governor, and Robert Morris, the principal financier of the American Revolution and a business associate of John Marshall. Traveling in Georgia with $25,000 in cash on the day the grant was enacted, Supreme Court

Justice James Wilson was also among the purchasers.[6] Within months, parcels of the freshly privatized land were resold at several times the purchase price for a total return of over $1.5 million. The secondary purchasers included congressmen, members of the presidential cabinet, a governor of Massachusetts, the postmaster general, and a US attorney. The original sale was precipitated by bribery. Georgian legislators who agreed to support the grant were allotted shares in one of the companies that owned an interest in the real estate or they were paid cash outright. James Madison, whose responsibility it was to investigate the sale for the Jefferson administration, reported to the president that every representative who voted for the sale, save one, held a private financial stake in the proceeds of the grant.[7] To demonstrate his liberality, one legislator later cited his willingness to accept $600 for his vote in favor of the sale, rather than the $1,000 fee that several of his colleagues had demanded.

The timing of the sale was crucial to the purchasers, and the decision to bid on the Yazoo territory was based on information to which only political insiders were privy. Western lands were crisscrossed by conflicting claims lodged by the governments of England, France, and Spain, as well as by several Native American tribes.[8] James Gunn, a US senator from Georgia and a large shareholder in one of the purchasing companies, knew of the Senate's intention in 1795 to ratify with Spain the Treaty of San Lorenzo, by which Spain would abandon its claims to Georgia's western territories.[9] This treaty greatly increased the appeal of the territory to potential purchasers. The time was ripe, bribes were paid, and the land was privatized to public officials.

As with other parcels of land in the American West, alternative approaches to developing Georgia's western territories had been the topic of extensive public deliberation.[10] Georgia eyed the Yazoo tract as a possible source of wealth. Developing the land for the public good was a recurrent topic of popular discussion. Some thought that the land should be given to war veterans; others argued that it be built up as a protective frontier. Some argued that the land should simply be given away because the benefits of immediate settlement far outweighed any ephemeral profits the state might generate by its sale. But the state legislature could not easily decide what to do with the parcel and had rejected several bids to the territory by private investors.

Given the public interest in the Yazoo territory, it is not surprising that many Georgians were infuriated when their legislators sold Yazoo to themselves and their cronies.[11] Public protests broke out. Copies of the act of land sale were burned, grand jury investigations were convened, and pamphlets circulated. The Yazoo land sale quickly emerged as the central issue in the 1795 election to the Georgia legislature. Opponents of the sale ousted a number of state representatives implicated in the scandal and, in February 1796, citing fraud, collusion, and corruption, the Georgia legislature repealed the sale.

Early America and contemporary Russia, particularly during Yeltsin's tenure but under Putin as well, were both periods marked by spoliation of public resources, particularly natural resources. At first blush, the similarities between the Yazoo land sale and the work of the Russian political clans appears striking. The circumstances giving rise to public theft in the two cases are similar. In both 1790s America and 1990s Russia, the state held boggling amounts of undeveloped natural wealth. While there is some disagreement about the purposes and speed of development, most organizations and institutions with political and economic influence—as well as most members of the larger society—supported some form of distribution and development and also believed that the distribution might serve some political purpose.

These circumstances gave rise in each case to "syndicates," or informal networks of insiders, of a similar composition in each case, vying for the state's resources: officials of regional governments, financiers, and developers. In the Russian case, the clans depended on the local authority of governors, the lobbies of one or two mining industries, and on the financing of private banks. In the Yazoo case, the band included local power holders (primarily the state legislators who approved the sale), lobbies of land companies (the Georgia Mississippi Land Company was one), and financiers (that intrepid venture capitalist, Robert Morris).

In the context of the transfer of large quantities of natural resources from the state to private (or semi-private) interest groups, the similarities between the Yazoo sale and contemporary Russia suggest

that syndicates specialized in the below-market purchase of public assets rely on a variety of strategies. In Russia, during the 1990s, such
syndicates performed several operations including lobbying, bribery,
raising capital, expatriating profits, control of physical assets (like
pipelines and diamond mines), and murder. One less frequently ex-
amined operation of these syndicates is the valuation of public assets.
Determining the true value of an under-priced asset at a particular
time is among the most important functions of such clans and shapes
the structure of these syndicates.

By itself, the ability to acquire or physically control a resource
is not sufficient to make it worthwhile to grab it, by corrupt means,
from state hands. Acquisition and control costs, as well as opportunity
costs, may often be poor investments if a clan is not able accurately to
judge which "resource bundles" are worth heisting. Information per-
tinent for valuation involves knowledge of secondary purchasers, the
policy intentions of the national government, the economic connections of local government officials closest to the resource, the bribing
price, the cost of controlling an asset against competitors, as well as
the prospects for the development of other assets related to the asset
being considered for "cherry picking." The value of an oil well is dependent upon the existence of a pipeline; the value of a diamond mine
on a railroad; the value of a canal on a port.

Clans operate in a competitive market. Generating a reliable
stream of income to pay bribes and private armies is crucial to maintaining a syndicate against the advances of other syndicates. Poor
choices—paying to grab assets that turn out to be worth less than
believed or turn out to be competitive with the interests of other
more powerful clans—can be lethal to members of a syndicate. One
stumble can end the career of a political insider, as illustrated by the
unceremonious arrest warrants issued for Vladimir Gusinksy and
Boris Berezovsky, among others. Indeed, after financing the American Revolution, Robert Morris himself spent many of his last days
in the "Prune Street" debtors prison due to failed speculation in real
estate.[12]

In order for a syndicate to learn of prospective grabs and to
value to-be-privatized public assets accurately, it must operate on both

national and local levels and in both the political and commercial sectors. The syndicate must be highly sensitive to the intentions and predilections of government officials at both national and local levels. Up-to-date information regarding intentions of government officials is crucial. In the Yazoo case, the knowledge crucial to valuation was the intention of the US Senate to sign a treaty with Spain and the willingness of particular legislators in Georgia to be bribed for their votes. In Russia, where a good portion of the economy remains heavily regulated and discretionary control of resources by government officials is rampant, knowledge of the facts that influence the valuation of a resource is vital. Locally situated participants are particularly adept at pricing the bribery of local officials, determining the control costs of an asset, and identifying a buyer for the resource who is situated to exploit the resource better than either the graft-takers or the original investors. Some thought the Yazoo lands were worthless. As it turned out, they were resold within one year for a six-hundred percent profit.

Syndicates typically access a widespread investing community and marshal large amounts of capital quickly. In the Yazoo case, the financiers came from all over the country, allowing the $500,000 purchase price to be raised more quickly than if all capital had to come from Georgia alone. Capital pours into the local industrial lobbies, which then have the local know-how to pay off the group of people who can make the sale happen. The national nature of the syndicate also allows for capital to be mobilized quickly, to defeat any other interests that are more closely situated to the resource—whether geographically, historically, politically, or commercially (for instance, vertically or horizontally within a similar stream of production and sale). The industrial lobbies and companies provide the conduit between the national capital and the local bribes.

With inside information and deep pockets, public wealth was heisted at what appeared to be lightening speed to those outside the loop. This explains, in part, why observers on the ground in Russia were often stunned by the speed at which thefts occurred. By the time many observers, however alert, learned of the possibility of a heist, the corrupt transfer has already taken place. This also explains why the

Georgia legislature could brassily sell the land to themselves. By the time the citizens had figured out what was happening, the land had already been granted.

The private engrossment of state assets affects political life in similar ways in early America and in Russia. Grabs for control of state-held resources informed the political constellation within Russia as demonstrated by the arrest of oil tycoons Mikail Khordokovsky and Platon Lebedev after their attempted bid to take control of Roman Abramovich's oil-producing giant, Sibneft. We observe hints of this in the Yazoo sale as well. The chief antagonist of the purchasers and the leader of the movement that led to the repeal of the sale was a US Senator from Georgia, James Jackson. Jackson spent the decade following the repeal fighting to punish the purchasers; and out of this issue, he built a political machine which exerted considerable influence over, and at times, dominated, Georgia politics. Jackson may have been a political opportunist, and he also may have been angry that he had not been included in the grab. His former guardian, John Wereat, had offered $800,000 for the Yazoo parcel and was turned down by the legislature.

The problem of public corruption in privatizing economies can be even more acute than outlined thus far. In order to come closer to understanding the political dynamics of massive pilfering of public wealth, we should look to the reasons why the US federal government supported the land grab in the Yazoo and even compensated the purchasers for the hardships they suffered at the hands of angry Georgians. What is most striking about the Yazoo sale is less the theft itself, than the fact that three presidents, Congress, and the Supreme Court essentially condoned the sale and that the purchasers grew wealthy with no lasting damage to their public careers.

The Ambivalence of Building Markets

Influential members of the early American federal government, including such diverse figures as George Washington, Alexander Hamilton, John Marshall, John Adams, and James Madison, realized that the federal government could not raise enough taxes to build bridges, roads, and canals or pay war veterans. The government, on its own, could not raise armies to bring a final solution to the "Indian problem" or defeat the Spanish and French who were competitors for western land. They also knew that they could not easily co-opt the state governments to undertake these tasks. They instead adopted two policies designed to encourage private American citizens to do much of this work for them: settlement and charters.

Settlement was a crucial component of American state-building, and immigration was promoted. At the turn of the century, most of the western territories were in the process of being subdivided and sold or granted to settlers. The hope was that settlement would create a human wall between the wild west and the populated coast, increase the American claims to the territory, and at the same time, benefit (and mollify) the poorer members of society. By selling to private interests the lands that the states and federal government had gained in the settlement of the Revolutionary War, the states and the federal government could raise revenue to pay their war debts, especially to their veterans.

Scrub farmers, immigrants, and laborers made great settlers, but they would not build roads, canals, and ports, at least not in the east, nor would they found banks and insurance companies. The states concluded that private enterprise needed to be encouraged to take these risks. The joint stock company was one of the primary vehicles by which state governments attempted to promote investment and economic growth generally and to target specific improvements. The joint stock company was born of a charter between a state government and a company and entitled the company to a license (usually exclusive) to undertake some activity. The charter would place certain restrictions on that activity, for instance, capping the amount of toll that could be collected on a bridge, road, or canal. Banks and insurance companies were also restricted by ad hoc regulation of rates and board memberships (some agrarians, some merchants).

For its part, the state agreed to prevent infringement of the charter by other private interests; and it also agreed to be bound by the terms of the charter. So in the case of a toll road, the state would prevent any other interests from building a road that would reduce the value of the chartered toll road, and the state also agreed not to change arbitrarily the amount of agreed toll that the joint stock company could gather. Many states even took further measures to encourage investment and improvements by establishing state development funds that purchased shares in the stock of chartered companies in order to promote their creation and, sometimes, to bail out troubled companies.

Exclusive charters were legal mechanisms to promote investment by increasing chances for returns. But charters required that the state make selections among various bidders. If a company failed, the hoped for improvement was not made, and the state had to solicit others to do the task. Some improvements languished for decades. Also, many companies failed because the states and private parties had an extremely difficult time determining the costs of an improvement and predicting profits. The value of one improvement depended on the likelihood that another improvement would be completed.

In order to prioritize development projects rationally and select among various bidders, states would often have to find well-situated and knowledgeable firms to manage the development of some undertaking. The people with the knowledge to advise the state or make government decisions about improvements often had acquired the knowledge based on their own private investments. For instance, in 1812, John Marshall was appointed chairman of a commission to survey the upper James and trans-Allegheny Rivers, in order to determine whether the James River could be connected to the Ohio River. Marshall was selected because he was very familiar with the proposed improvement, and his company, the James River Company, had been considering undertaking the project for several years. Marshall was selected a commissioner for the project, not in spite of the fact that he had private interests in it, but because he did so. The concept of conflict of interest does not seem to have inhibited such arrangements.

Throughout this period, the federal government competed with the states for control of the western lands and, for the most part, successfully pressured the states to make cessions to the federal government. The federal government often traded its services to the states in return for land, by agreeing to help the states solve their nagging problems with Native American tribes. Cession agreements often included federal compensation for any private claims to the territory.

With this mix of cessions and sell-offs, a policy of compensating private interests, and the general pro-development atmosphere, it is not surprising that the Yazooists saw the federal acquisition and development policy as a possible opportunity to receive generous compensation for the state's having reneged on its deal with them. After all, they were politically well-situated citizens and willing investors who had made a large purchase that had been overturned by a state government. If states were allowed to cancel development projects, investment would be discouraged. The Georgia State Repeal Act offered refunds to purchasers, but most declined because they did not wish to renounce their claims to the territory, as was required by the act before refunds were issued. The Yazooists preferred to turn to the national Congress to press for a more profitable compensation.

The national government had been attempting to persuade the Georgia legislature to cede the Yazoo lands for several years. The cession would certainly include a provision to set aside a portion of the territory to settle private claims. Knowing they would not receive from the state of Georgia the compensation they wanted, the purchasers supported the cession and were well-positioned to pressure the national Congress to incorporate their claims into the acquisition of Georgia's western territory.

In 1798, Congress enacted legislation requesting the president to negotiate with Georgia for the cession of the Yazoo lands to the national government. During his administration, Jefferson appointed James Madison to head a commission to negotiate the sale, and an agreement was reached in 1802. According to the agreement, Georgia would cede the lands to the national government for $1.25 million and the US would set aside one-tenth of the territory for the purpose of satisfying any private claims to the territory. In a follow-up to the sale, Madison issued a report to Jefferson stating that the claims of the Yazooists could not be supported, but that the interest of national tranquility suggested that a reasonable compromise be reached with the private claimants. In 1805, Congress enacted a law recommending that a settlement be reached with the Yazoo claimants.[13] In the end, the Yazooists had engineered a corrupt sale of Georgia state land and then successfully persuaded Congress and the presidential administration to reimburse them with American tax dollars for the financial loss they suffered when the citizens of Georgia attempted to repeal the insider deal.

The ambivalence of Madison's report suggests the tension that may at times exist between economic development and liberal-democratic reform. Privatization in transition economies may be necessary but it gives rise to vast opportunities for corruption. For reasons both political and economic, self-dealers may often be the best available allies for economic development in transition societies. And economic development may serve some further important purpose, such as state-building or market reform. The ambivalence creates a good deal of policy confusion in understanding reforms throughout post-communist Europe. At the same time, left unreformed, insiderism can lead to nonaccountability and poor management. The desire for profit alone cannot build a market. This often means that governments have to participate in building them. To do so, governments must, among other things, select partners, thereby creating insiders who are able to steal or, at a minimum, self-deal. For observers and participants alike, it is difficult to identify where cronyism ends and strategically clever economy-building begins.

Investment Economies vs. Extraction Economies

Even though the US Congress had enacted a law that allowed for their reimbursement, the Yazooists still had to push Congress actually to get paid, and they had trouble mustering the votes to push through a payment bill. Considered to be among the best lawyers in early America, Alexander Hamilton was sympathetic to the claims of the Yazooists, but found their arguments legally deficient. Hamilton published a pamphlet in which he argued that the sale of the Yazoo lands by the Georgia legislature should be understood as a contract. The subsequent repeal by the Georgia legislature, according to his view, violated Article I, section 10 of the federal Constitution: "No State shall . . . pass any . . . Law impairing the Obligation of Contracts." Whatever the motives of the members of the Georgia legislature when selling the Yazoo tract, Hamilton argued, Georgia had violated the contracts clause of the US Constitution when it repealed the sale.[14]

Hamilton's arguments prompted the Yazooists to consider bringing a complaint to the US Supreme Court. Up until then, they had largely ignored the possibility of petitioning the Court due to its apparent feebleness. Jefferson's attack on the Federalist- dominated judiciary had scared many judges. While Justice William Chase was on trial, Chief Justice Marshall had even testified before Congress that he would be willing to consider a legislative override of Supreme Court opinions if Congress would call off its attack on the judiciary. The Court did not seem well-positioned to help the Yazooists.

But the Yazooists finally decided that a Supreme Court ruling in their favor would add some weight to their arguments in Congress. And the Yazooists knew that they had a good chance of winning at the Court. While a congressman, John Marshall—who had once lost a good deal of money as a result of debtor relief laws—voted in favor of compensation to the Yazoo claimants.

Marshall was also one of the architects of the "Federalist Junto" in Virginia, which effectively bid on many development projects and publicly argued for the state to favor the interests of developers. Given his private sympathies and public pronouncements, there was little doubt that Marshall would rule in their favor. In June 1803, Robert Fletcher and John Peck colluded to bring a case in which Fletcher sued Peck for a covenant broken on the grounds that Peck had sold him a parcel of land in western Georgia territory that he did not rightfully own. The contract of sale was drafted in order to emphasize the issue of whether the Georgia state legislature had had the right to repeal the sale. A federal jury in Massachusetts ruled against Fletcher and, in so doing, implied that Peck's claim to the territory was valid and the repeal invalid.

Fletcher appealed the case to the Supreme Court. In 1809, after many delays, *Fletcher v. Peck* was argued before the Court. John Quincy Adams represented Peck and argued the Yazooist case. Luther Martin, one of the most prominent appellate attorneys then appearing before the Supreme Court, argued the repeal position. Martin had defended Samuel Chase during his impeachment trial and had also represented Aaron Burr at his trial for treason. Martin argued that the Georgia Repeal Act was valid, but he never addressed the most critical point of the case, whether the corrupt sale of the territory was invalid in the first place.

The Court ruled in favor of Peck and the Yazooists. The core of Marshall's opinion consisted essentially of a recitation of Hamilton's argument: grants were contracts; and Article 1, section 10, prohibited states from interfering with contracts. Since the language of the Constitution did not state otherwise, the restriction applied to contracts between private parties and the states themselves. His cursory dismissal of the idea that the Yazoo sale was invalid because it was motivated by bribery suggests that he may have accepted as inevitable the fondness of public officials for instant enrichment in the process of nation-building.

In the wake of the opinion, in 1814, Congress enacted a law compensating the secondary purchasers the full amount that they had paid for parcels in the Georgia western territory. The original purchasers had paid only $100,000 of the original purchase price of $500,000. The remainder was mortgaged. With the repeal, payment on the mortgage to the state ceased. The original purchasers resold the land at several times the original purchase price and at many more times what was actually paid. The secondary purchasers were compensated by the federal government. In addition, the original purchasers continued to have successful public lives in Georgia and to hold political office.

Marshall's interpretation of the contract clause in the Fletcher opinion is widely believed to have set the terms for the relationship between government and commerce that allowed for and promoted economic growth in early America. Contracts were to be enforced, even if the sales in question were tainted by insider dealing. At the same time, Hamilton and Marshall's abhorrence of meddling with first-order distributions of state wealth appears somewhat self-serving. Settlements, charters, and investment companies allowed well-placed individuals to benefit from the flow of public wealth into private hands; the reliance principal (*pacta sunt servanda*) locked in those gains, even ill-gotten ones.

Does this suggest that we can expect some such reliance interest to develop in Russia as well? Are Vladimir Putin's rise and the assertion of the power of the Kremlin signs that such a reliance interest is developing in Russia? Will the current breed of privatization-millionaires, now humbled by Vladimir Putin, use their influence to help stabilize the legal environment, in order to lock their gains in place?

Once they had grabbed what they could, legal certainty served some members of the political elites in early America very well. But the specifics of their self-preserving behavior are important to consider. The fundamental wealth-producing strategy of the political elite in early America was the development of land and commerce, in the context of a large, open, and unified market. One of the central complaints against the Articles of Confederation was the impossibility of a nation-wide market developing under them. It was widely understood that investments would appear attractive to entrepreneurs only if property claims were secure. In the context of market development in an investment economy, one entrepreneur often has a substantial interest in the well-being of other entrepreneurs, even those who live and work very far away. For instance, the canal operator in Virginia has a personal interest that harvests in Ohio are not confiscated. The income of an individual entrepreneur is very closely tied to the economic and physical well-being of others, as reflected in national income, inflation, and unemployment. Entrepreneurs also have an interest in the well-being and disposable income of their consumers. In the case of commodities, such as manufactured goods and agricultural products, entrepreneurs in early America could rarely rely on a single customer. Therefore, the more consumers, the better for business. The elites in early America often explain that their wealth-building strategy of producing for domestic consumption broadened their interest in the well-being of others.

Security is also important. The canal operator in Virginia does not care whether the Ohio harvest is confiscated by the government or by bandits. Either way, business is disrupted and profits are likely to be lost. Reliable law enforcement is important for all property holders. A competent police power, capable of securing ownership throughout the system, is crucial to an investment economy.

But what if the best wealth-maximizing strategy for America's political insiders had not been investment and production for domestic markets? What if there were a seemingly endless stream of property to be distributed by the state in never-ending iterations? And what if the privatized property offered profits only by its direct sale abroad and not by continued investment into it? Natural resource development in contemporary Russia resembles a never-ending land grab.

As in the Yazoo case, the distribution of former state assets may largely hinge on who is situated at the crossroads of politics and property. The allocative principal may be essentially lawless and follows political connections. It is similar to the Yazoo sale in many respects, but an economic motive for a rise of rules appears lacking. So, unlike the Yazoo case, there is little reason for the Russian clans, whether they be aligned with the billionaires or with the Kremlin or both to abandon insiderism, and support the development of the rule of law.

Unlike the politics of investment, where political elites have an interest in the success of others, including ordinary consumers, the clans in Russia who control natural resources have scant interest in the well-being of others. Oil, diamonds, and gas are sold on the international market. Average national income and living standards, unemployment, mortality and morbidity, and even inflation or the current account deficit, have little impact on the elites who control the resources. Similarly, the absence of confiscatory policies or the efficient resolution of disputes for a wide number of people is unimportant to the most influential clans. Well-paid private security forces are a more efficient and reliable mechanism to secure natural resource claims than are the courts. There is no strong reason for the clans in Russia to take an especial interest in property and contract rights or in the physical well-being of ordinary Russians with which they have no immediate involvement. Economies of extraction give rise to two subsidiary economies: extortion and expatriation of profits. If large sectors of the elite have little interest in the physical or commercial well-being of their compatriots, they will invest very little time and energy trying to protect the latter from extortionists. The clans do not care if shopkeepers make a profit because the spoils of the clans are not dependent on the shopkeeper staying in business. Behind the façade of Russian constitutionalism lies the politics of extraction.

ENDNOTES

1. Throughout the region, constitution-drafters often used analogies between their present circumstance and the successes (sometimes illusory) of a past model. See, for example, Jon Elster, ed., *The Roundtable Talks and the Breakdown of Communism* (Chicago: University of Chicago Press, 1996).

2. See, for example, Thomas Carothers, *Aiding Democracy Abroad: The Learning Curve* (Washington: Carnegie Endowment for International Peace, 1999), 91, where Carothers observes, "USAID and most other federal agencies involved in democracy promotion derive their model of democracy, not surprisingly, from a somewhat idealized sense of the American experience."

3. For example, "As I pursued the trail of the mafiya through post-Communist society, I kept encountering officials who honestly felt that organized crime was a necessary evil in the transition to a market economy." Stephen Handelman, *Comrade criminal: Russia's new mafiya* (New Haven: Yale University Press, 1995), 336.

4. *Fletcher v. Peck*, 10 U.S. 87, 6 Cranch 123, 1810.

5. For an extended discussion of the scandal, see Peter Magrath, *Yazoo: Law and Politics in the New Republic* (Providence: Brown University Press, 1966).

6. Charles Haskins, "The Yazoo Land Companies", in *Papers of the American Historical Association*, 5 vols. (New York and London: G.P. Putnam's Sons, 1891), V, Part 4.

7. *American State Papers*, *Public Lands*, 8 vols. (Washington: Gales and Seaton, 1832-61), I, 134 and following.

8. Antonio de Arrenda, *Historical Proof of Spain's Title to Georgia* (Berkeley: University of California Press, 1925).

9. Magrath, *Yazoo: Law and Politics*, 6.

10. See, for example, *Speeches of Mr. Randolph, on the Greek question, on internal improvement, and on the tariff bill, delivered in the House of Representatives of the United States* (Washington: Gales & Seaton, 1824); Kenneth Coleman, *Colonial Georgia: A History* (New York: Scribner's, 1976); A.M. Sakoski, *The Great American Land Bubble* (New York and London: Harper & Bros., 1932).

11. William Stevens, *A History of Georgia*, 2 vols. (New York: D. Appleton and Co., 1847), II, 491.

12. Ellis Oberholzer, *Robert Morris: Patriot and Financier* (New York: Macmillan Co., 1903), 335.

13. Annals of Congress, 9th Congress (Washington, D.C.: Gales and Seaton, 1834-1856), March 28, 1806, col. 912.

14. Magrath, *Yazoo: Law and Politics*, Appendix D.

Chapter 15

Contributors

ROBERT P. ERICKSEN received his B.A. degree from PLU in 1967, an M.A. degree from the State University of New York-Stony Brook in 1969, and a Ph.D. from the London School of Economics and Political Science in 1980. He is currently professor of history at PLU, where he has taught since 1999. His books include *Theologians under Hitler: Gerhard Kittel, Paul Althaus, and Emanuel Hirsch* (1985) and the co-edited collection *Betrayal: German Churches and the Holocaust* (1999).

MICHAEL J. HALVORSON received a B.A. degree from PLU in 1985, and M.A. and Ph.D. degrees from the University of Washington in 1996 and 2001. Michael was employed at Microsoft Corporation from 1985 to 1994, and has written numerous books about computers and technology, as well as historical subjects. He has worked as a visiting lecturer at PLU and the University of Washington since 1998, and joins the PLU history department in 2005 as an assistant professor. His most recent book is the edited collection *Loharano (The Water Spring): Missionary Tales from Madagascar* (2003).

CHRISTOPHER R. BROWNING received a B.A. degree from Oberlin College in 1967, and M.A. and Ph.D. degrees from the University of Wisconsin-Madison in 1968 and 1975. He taught in the history department at PLU from 1974 to 1999, and currently holds the Frank Porter Graham Chair in History at the University of North Carolina, where he has taught since 1999. His books include *Ordinary Men* (1992) and *The Origins of the Final Solution: The Evolution of Nazi Jewish Policy, September 1939-March 1942* (2004).

PHILIP A. NORDQUIST received a B.A. degree from PLU in 1956, and M.A. and Ph.D. degrees from the University of Washington in 1960 and 1964. He has taught in the PLU history department since 1963, and is the author of PLU's centennial history *Educating for Service, Pacific Lutheran University, 1890-1990* (1990).

MEGAN BENTON received a B.A. degree from PLU in 1976 and a Ph.D. in book history from the University of California-Berkeley in 1997. From 1986 to 2003, Megan taught in the PLU English department and directed its Publishing & Printing Arts program. She is currently a faculty fellow in the humanities at PLU. Megan is the author of *Beauty and the Book: Fine Editions and Cultural Distinction in America* (2000) and coeditor of *Illuminating Letters: Typography and Literary Interpretation* (2001).

SAMUEL TORVEND received a B.A. degree from PLU in 1973 and a Ph.D. from St. Louis University in 1990. He is currently an associate professor of religion at PLU. His most recent book is *Daily Bread, Holy Meal: Opening The Gifts Of Holy Communion* (2004).

MARY ELIZABETH AILES received a B.A. degree from PLU in 1989, and M.A. and Ph.D. degrees from the University of Minnesota in 1992 and 1997. She is currently an associate professor of history at the University of Nebraska-Kearney. Her most recent book is *Military Migration and State Formation: The British Military Community in Seventeenth-Century Sweden* (2002).

MICHAEL R. LYNN received B.A. and B.S. degrees from PLU in 1989 and a Ph.D. degree in history from the University of Wisconsin-Madison in 1997. He is now an associate professor of history at Agnes Scott College in Decatur, Georgia. His current book project is tentatively titled *Shocked Monks and Savant Dogs: Popular Science in Enlightenment France.*

Neil Waters received a B.A. degree from PLU in 1967, an M.A. degree from Washington State University, and a Ph.D. from the University of Hawaii. He is currently the Kawashima Professor of Japanese Studies at Middlebury College in Vermont. His publications include *Japan's Local Pragmatists: the Transition from Bakumatsu to Meiji in the Kawasaki Region* (1983) and the edited collection *Beyond the Area Studies Wars* (2000).

MOLLY LOBERG received her B.A. degree from PLU in 1998 and is currently a doctoral candidate in history at Princeton University. Her dissertation research is focused on the city of Berlin between the World Wars and is tentatively titled "Berlin Streets: Commerce, Consumption, and Violence, 1918-1938." Molly was the recipient of the Alexander von Humboldt Foundation-German Chancellor Award in 2003-04.

GERALD A. FETZ double-majored in history and German at PLU and received a B.A. degree in 1966. In 1972, he received a Ph.D. degree in German literature from the University of Oregon. He is currently Dean of the College of Arts and Sciences and Professor of German Studies at the University of Montana in Missoula. His recent book projects include a study of Martin Walser (1997) and a forthcoming book on W.G. Sebald published by Camden House Press.

LAURA J. (RITCHIE) GIFFORD received a B.A. degree from PLU in 2000, an M.A. degree in history from the University of California, Los Angeles, in 2003, and is currently a doctoral candidate in history at UCLA. Laura's dissertation analyzes changing dynamics in American party politics after World War II and is tentatively titled "The Center Cannot Hold: The 1960 Election and the Rise of Modern Conservatism."

CHRISTIAN M. LUCKY received a B.A. degree from PLU in 1989 and a J.D. degree from the University of Chicago in 1994. From 1994 to 1996, he was a member of the Law Faculty of the Central European University. He is a partner in the law firm Davies Ward Phillips and Vineberg and is currently a senior policy analyst for the Open Society Institute–Soros Foundation, where he focuses on the recovery of stolen public assets and the reform of natural resource extraction industries.

A Lutheran Vocation

was designed by Robyn Ricks and Michael Halvorson.

It was composed in 12-point Adobe Garamond Pro type
using Adobe InDesign software.
Composed pages were sent to the printer as electronic prepress files.

Cover design: Robyn Ricks
Interior layout: Robyn Ricks

Supervising editors: Robert P. Ericksen and Michael J. Halvorson
Production editor: Laura Callen

Cover image permissions: Corbis, Inc.